Researching Change in Caribbean Education: Curriculum, Teaching and Administration

T. Bastick
A. Ezenne

Department of Educational Studies
University of the West Indies, Kingston, Jamaica

Researching Change in Caribbean Education: Curriculum, Teaching and Administration/
Tony Bastick and Austin Ezenne Editors; foreword by Zellynne Jennings.
p. cm.
Includes bibliographical references.
ISBN: 976-632-045-4
1. Education - Caribbean, English-speaking. T. Bastick, Tony; A. Ezenne, Austin
LB1028.25. C27 R47 2003 371.2

CONTENTS

Section 1

CURRICULUM

Section 2

TEACHING

Section 3

ADMINISTRATION

INTRODUCTION

Maxine Henry-Wilson, MP
Minister for Education, Youth and Culture, Jamaica

Historically, Caribbean parents have regarded education as an invaluable asset. Many of us who have now attained adulthood and who are second or third generation beneficiaries of the public education system recall the words of our parents "The book! 'The book! study your book. `That is what will carry you through."

In the contemporary Caribbean, policy makers, educators, and administrators sometimes opine that the value of education is lost on the current generation. This assertion for which, I am not sure there is any empirical evidence, confronts us with two (2) challenges - one is the issue of relevance; the other of methodologies for effective delivery. The stakeholders in the system will continue to pose to us the question asked in the essay in this edition titled - "Five Ways of Teaching and Learning in Haiti" by LeGrace Benson. "What do Haitians need to learn in school and College?" This is not a query relevant to Haiti only. It is a dilemma posed to every policy-maker, educator, administrator, student and the wider community.

New ways of teaching and learning using technology, with appropriate grading, collaborative learning, and functional teaching of language are all part of the mosaic of education today.

To teachers in the classroom, what you cannot do is give up. We have to equip ourselves with the most up-to-date methodologies and the latest thinking, because teaching is where "the rubber hits the road." The issues raised in these essays all speak to the diversity of challenges you face. The essays give you an insight into some directions, many of which require your ingenuity and adaptive capability to get them to work in your classroom and community settings. Over the years, you have proven that you are equal to every challenge. You have produced some of the best, capable of competing.

To the authors, you have identified many of the significant issues which will guide us at all levels, but which especially the policymakers need in order to make informed and rational policies.

To the editors, thanks for compiling such a coherent volume which in its limited number of pages has covered such a wide space of issues.

The potential for education is the richer for the collaborative effort reflected in this publication.

FOREWORD

Zellynne Jennings, PhD
Head, Department of Educational Studies.

Change is all around us and nowhere is the demand for change greater than in education. This book on *Researching Change in Caribbean Education* is timely because it touches on a number of issues and concerns that face us at all levels of our education systems in the Region and provides a backdrop against which we can reflect on the direction in which we should be going in education in the 21st century. There is no shortage of education policy statements, development plans and Regional reports which expound on this. I am reminded of four such reports.

The first is the Bourne Report (Caricom 1988)[1] which underscored that the development of a comparative advantage in global economic competition would require technological progress and "some amount of technological leapfrogging" (p40). That science and technology held the key to progress in the new millennium was also underscored by the second report which stressed the need for the education system in the Region to produce "large numbers of persons with a working understanding and functional skills in the areas of digital technologies, micro-computers and modern communications technology" (OECS Education Reform Group 1991: 38) [2]

But the extent to which these goals can be achieved depends on the effectiveness and efficiency of our education systems. Teachers of Science and Mathematics are becoming an endangered species in many Caribbean countries for a number of reasons including the inadequacy of provisions for science laboratories in secondary schools and the throughput of students who want to proceed to tertiary institutions for further studies in Science. Science is still perceived as a 'difficult' subject, just as is the case for Mathematics, and a combination of teaching methodology and negative attitudes perpetuates this perception. But we must not underestimate the importance of access to secondary education. As one of the authors in this book points out, the provision of equality of opportunity at this level, particularly for the marginalized in our societies, remains a persistent problem. Added to this is the aggressive recruitment of teachers from the Region by our more powerful neighbours from North America and Europe – the Chiefs of the global village. While to some this is a cause for great concern, to others this is a matter of responding to the market economy characteristic of living in a 'global village' and hence this provides an opportunity to capitalise on our human resources and educate for emigration. Education then becomes a service industry like Tourism.

Interestingly, John Figueroa,[3] a former professor of education at the University of the West Indies on the Mona campus, bemoaned the instrumentalism of education in the Caribbean in which" end products dominate over processes – and end products of a fairly limited kind: certificates, professions, white-collar jobs, the status of having been educated. The idea of radical change, the idea of the creative release of the human spirit through education – these are not current. Nor do they seem likely to be, for where change is coming it is coming in the direction of manpower planning –of trying to forecast how many 'hands"- of what kind – the private and public sectors will need, and how quickly and cheaply such " hands" may be supplied" (p.107-8). In this regard, has there been much change over the past three decades or so? Perhaps to the extent that our manpower planning is not just national or even at the regional level, but we plan with an eye for the global village One problem with the latter is the tendency for our indigenous values to be superceded by those of the Village Chiefs whose values become reified and we become unmindful of the fact that beside us are our neighbours whose values we need to appreciate and with whom we need to communicate.

And this brings me to the third report which was presented at a special session on Human Resource Development at the 18th Heads of Government Conference held in Jamaica in 1997. In the paper prepared by the Caribbean Community Secretariat, entitled "Towards creative and productive citizens for the twenty-first century", the characteristics of the ideal Caribbean person were highlighted. These characteristics included that of being a citizen –worker who, inter alia, was expected to demonstrate multiple literacy, including foreign language skills, and independent and critical thinking. It is the acquisition of foreign language skills that is our concern here because while Spanish may well rival English for pride of place in the immediate domain of the Village Chief on the North American mainland in the near future, in the Caribbean we have to be mindful of the fact that the lingua franca of many of our neighbours is French. Two chapters in this book, one on the French CAPE syllabus and the other on teaching French at the university level keeps this issue in the forefront. But we need also to be cognisant of the fact that if our young people are to be encouraged to take the learning of a second or third language seriously, it is not just a matter of providing them with opportunity to learn and study the language, they must also be persuaded of the value of such study to their personal futures. And this points to two problems that we have to address. One is that, in the case of French, more so than Spanish, our students are not being provided with sufficient opportunity to learn the language. With the exception perhaps of countries where the French Creole is the local dialect., French is offered less as an option in schools within the western part of the Caribbean. Secondly even where opportunities are provided, the priority given to areas such as science and technology in the schools conveys to the students the unimportance of studying a second language and this is exacerbated by the fact that often they cannot see what career opportunities such study opens up for them.[4] It goes back to the understanding - that education is not the panacea for all things. If it is not accompanied by employment generation for our young people, it becomes merely a service in which we offer them bread, but give them stone.

And finally the fourth report – Time for Action [5.] This report emphasised the need for tertiary institutions and the Universities themselves " to take a hard look at the standards and viability of their academic programmes, the efficiency of their delivery; and the costs of their operations" (p 248) and pointed to the need for increased access to these institutions through the use of distance education and linkages between tertiary institutions. One of the chapters in this book addresses collaborative learning in Caribbean higher education and uses data from observational studies of in-service teachers pursuing the Certificate in Education via the University of the West Indies Distance Teaching facility. This Certificate was initiated by the Department of Educational Studies in the mid-1980s and up to the present has serviced the Region with trained teachers in the areas of the Teaching of the Hearing Impaired, Science, Mathematics, Reading, Adult Education and Education Management and Supervision .Graduates of this programme have been able to proceed to the Bachelor of Education degree, with the professional specialisation in Educational Administration being offered by both modes of delivery – face to face and distance. In November 2002, the first batch of graduates of the B.Ed (Educational Administration) by distance graduated from the Mona campus. In January 2003, the B.Ed (Secondary) by distance commenced with its first batch out of a total of 3000 teachers in Jamaican secondary schools who have been targeted for training in this special project . This is going some way in meeting the need for 'substantial upgrading and enlargement of the teaching corps" (Time for Action p244) .Training is being offered in Science, Mathematics, English, History, Geography and Computer studies. Interestingly, only a small number of teachers have come forward for training in Spanish and French .

But this demand on tertiary institutions to increase access brings in its train other problems – mostly notably that of quality control and the maintenance of standards. One of the writers in this book addresses the issue of grade inflation and other problems associated with assessment practices at the University of the West Indies. This is an issue which must be taken seriously for a number of reasons. In collaborating with other tertiary institutions in programme offering the UWI has to be guarded against being perceived rather like the village Chief who imposes his values on the lesser mortals while at the same time ensuring the maintenance of a quality of product that will retain the universal acceptability that the UWI has preserved for over half a century. It is a challenge not unlike tip toeing on a tightrope strung across the Caribbean sea. To succeed is a major feat. To fall is to signal its demise. But such challenges are a part of our every day life in the University. We hope that our readers will appreaciate all that is of value and interest in our publication and that it will serve not only as food for thought but also as research which informs decision – making.

We hope that our readers find much of value and interest in our publication and that it will serve not only as food for thought but also as research which informs decision –making.

[1] Caricom (1988) *Caribbean Development to the year 2000:Challenges, Prospects and Policies*. London: Commonwealth Secretariat/ Caribbean Community Secretariat,Georgetw:Guyana.

[2] OECS Education Reform Working Group(1991).Foundation for the Future: OECS Education Reform Strategy.

[3] Figueroa, J.J. (1971*) Society,Schools and Progress in the West Indies.* New York: Pergamon Press

[4] See Jennings, Z. (2001) Teacher education in selected countries in the Commonwealth Caribbean: the ideal of policy versus the reality of practice. Comparative Education, Vol. 37,No.1 (107-134)

[5] *Time for Action: The Report of the West Indian Commission* : Black Rock, Barbados 1992.

CONTRIBUTING AUTHORS

Lindsey T. Allard	International Education Policy, Harvard Graduate School of Education, Cambridge, MA, USA.
Lillith Barnaby	Kingston College, Jamaica, West Indies.
Tony Bastick	University of the West Indies, Mona, Jamaica, West Indies.
LeGrace Benson	Professor Emerita, State University of New York, NY, USA.
Béatrice Boufoy - Bastick	University of the West Indies, Mona, Jamaica, West Indies.
Austin Ezenne	University of the West Indies, Mona, Jamaica, West Indies.
Aldrin E. Sweeney	University of Central Florida, FL, USA.
Glenda M. Prime	Morgan State, University, Baltimore, Maryland, MD, USA.
Olabisi Kuboni	University of the West Indies, St. Augustine, Trinidad, West Indies.
Jo-Anne L. Manswell-Butty	Center for Research on the Education of Students Placed At Risk, School of Education, Howard University, Washington, DC, USA.
Hugues Peters	University of the West Indies, Jamaica, West Indies.

EDITORIAL CONSULTANTS

The quality of the research contributions in this book is in large part due to our Editorial Consultants who are experts in the areas covered by the chapters. They have each given generously of their time, knowledge and experience, critically evaluating the scope, applicability and educational value of the contributions, offering encouragement and suggestions to ensure the highest standard of each chapter in this collection of Caribbean research papers.

Dr. Anne-Maria Bankay	Department of Educational Studies, University of the West Indies, Mona, Jamaica, West Indies.
Dr. Béatrice Boufoy-Bastick	Department of Modern Languages, University of the West Indies, Mona, Jamaica, West Indies.
Dr. Monica Brown	Director School of Education, University of the West Indies, Mona, Jamaica, West Indies.
Dr. Gloria Burke	Department of Educational Studies, University of the West Indies, Mona, Jamaica, West Indies.
Isabel Byron	Programme Specialist, UNESCO International Bureau of Education, Geneva, Switzerland.

Dr. Alexandra Cristea	Databases and Hypermedia group, Information Systems Department, Faculty of Computer Science and Mathematics, Eindhoven University of Technology, Eindhoven, Netherlands.
Dr. Michael Crossley	Director, Research Centre for International and Comparative Studies, University of Bristol, Graduate School of Education, Bristol, UK.
Dr. Leslie G. Desmangles	Professor of Religion and International Studies, Trinity College, Hartford, Connecticut, New York, NY, USA.
Ian Furlonge	Information Technology Education, Department of Educational Studies, UWI, Mona, Jamaica, West Indies.
Robert Anthony Geofroy	Community College of the Cayman Islands, Georgetown, Grand Cayman, West Indies.
Dr. June George	Department of Education, UWI, St. Augustine, Trinidad, West Indies.
Professor Sally Sieloff Magnan	Pickard-Bascom Professor of French, University of Wisconsin, Madison, WI, USA.
Dr. Dawn Kum-Walks	School of Education, Howard University, Washington, DC, USA.

Dr. Barbara Matalon	Institute of Education, University of the West Indies, Mona, Jamaica, West Indies.
Tom McArdle	Senior Director Planning and Project Development Division, HEART/NTA, Kingston, Jamaica, West Indies.
Dr. Donna Penn-Towns	Senior Research Associate, Center for Research on the Education of Students Placed at Risk (CRESPAR), Howard University, Washington, DC, USA.
Dr. Marcia Rainford	Department of Educational Studies, University of the West Indies, Mona, Jamaica, West Indies.
Dr. Jennifer Williams	Community College of the Cayman Islands, Grand Cayman, West Indies.
Dr. Drexel Woodson	Bureau of Applied Research in Anthropology (BARA), University of Arizona, Tucson, AZ, USA.

SECTION 1
CURRICULUM

SCIENCE EDUCATION IN THE CARIBBEAN: ANALYSIS OF CURRENT TRENDS

Aldrin E. Sweeney
University of Central Florida
USA

Chapter 1

As we enter the 21st century, Caribbean nation-states are faced with challenging and exciting times ahead. In particular, the region as a whole will be challenged "to significantly re-order its international economic arrangements in response to the monumental and continuing changes in the global marketplace" (Jules, Miller & Armstrong, 2000, p. 1). Such changes have been characterised by rapid advances in scientific knowledge and the increasingly ubiquitous use of information and communication technology (ICT) in business, industry, and education. The typically defined "developing countries" of the Caribbean[1] share with the more fully developed industrialised nations the need to educate and prepare their citizens to be competitive in the global economy, and over the past 20 years, have been engaged in a process of education reform (Jules, Miller & Armstrong, 2000, p. ix). Of particular significance for the region "... is an increasing demand for postsecondary education, particularly in the areas of science, technology and management. This is critical if the region is to steer its development and be equipped to address the challenges ahead" (Jules, Miller & Armstrong, 2000, p. xi).

A comprehensive synopsis of general education reform efforts in the Caribbean has been provided by Miller (2000a) and Jules, Miller & Armstrong (2000), and will not be treated in detail here. However, given the global contexts in which these education reform efforts are occurring (i.e. the centrality of science and technology in the development and maintenance of national economies; and the emergence of a science and technology based global economy), attention needs to be given to the nature and extent of science education in the Caribbean. The first section of this chapter therefore focuses on an analysis of science education research in the Caribbean[2], followed by sections which provide inexhaustive examples of science education policy and practice in the region. In these sections, emphasis is given to large scale national efforts occurring in three Caribbean countries, i.e. Barbados, Bermuda and Jamaica. The chapter concludes with a brief discussion, and provides recommendations for future directions in science education for the Caribbean region.

SCIENCE EDUCATION RESEARCH IN THE CARIBBEAN

Science education research in the Caribbean, while still relatively unknown and under-appreciated by many professional science educators outside of the region, has been occurring at a steady pace for at least the past 30 years. The work of Fraser-Abder (1988a; 1988b) serves as a comprehensive compendium of documented Caribbean science education research occurring during the period 1970-1987. During the early part of this period, it was clear that the role and purposes of science education in the Caribbean were of concern (e.g. Lambert, 1974; Lancaster & King, 1977; Mark, 1978). During the late 1970s-mid 1990s, several science education faculty at the University of the West Indies rose to prominent positions as internationally recognised Caribbean science education researchers, i.e. Workeley Brathwaite, Pamela Fraser-Abder, June George, Joyce Glasgow and Winston King. During this period, their published work focused on a number of issues pertinent to science education in the region, including *culture and cognitive development* (Fraser-Abder, 1982; 1985a; 1986; King 1978a); *science curriculum development* (Alexander & Glasgow, 1981; Fraser-Abder, 1985b; Fraser-Abder & Douglass, 1986; Glasgow, 1987; King, 1978b; 1978c); *science teacher education* (Brathwaite, 1978; Fraser-Abder, 1979; Fraser-Abder & Shrigley, 1980; Glasgow & Robinson, 1983); *the impact of science on social issues and concerns* (Lancaster & King, 1977; King, 1979; 1982; 1987; Brathwaite, 1985); *assessment* (King & Brathwaite, 1991); *scientific literacy* (Glasgow, 1986); *environmental education* (Glasgow, 1987; 1989; 1993); and *the relationships between Caribbean beliefs and conventional science* (George, 1988; George, 1995; George & Glasgow, 1988; George & Glasgow, 1989).

As noted by Abder-Fraser (1988a), Caribbean education researchers and policymakers in the 1970s and early 1980s justifiably could have been accused of force-fitting the results of educational research found in developed countries into Caribbean school settings (p. 1). During the latter part of the 1980s however, a trend could be seen in the science education research emerging from the region which sought to focus more specifically on the particularities of the Caribbean and the need for context specific research endeavours. George (1988), for example, argued that a failure to develop curriculum materials in which were identified context specific subject matter idiosyncratic to the Caribbean, might result in "students being hindered in their attempts to link school science with everyday experiences" (p. 816). In the same epistemological vein, Jegede (1995) proposed that prior knowledge and the sociocultural environment of the learner "are inseparable, with the latter creating and nurturing the former" (p. 100; cited in George & Glasgow, 1999, p. 3). Regarding these concerns, the recently published work of June George and Joyce Glasgow (e.g. George, 1995; 1999; 2001; George & Glasgow, 1999) has been of particular interest and significance.

Building on the basis of previous theoretical and empirical work in mainstream science education which investigated the influence of children's background knowledge and its interaction with formal science instruction (e.g. Driver & Erickson, 1983; Prout, 1985; Driver, Squires, Rushworth & Wood-Robinson, 1994), the thrust of George and Glasgow's collaborative work sought to provide an empirical basis upon which idiosyncratic Caribbean science-related beliefs might be analysed in the context of conventionally accepted scientific concepts and principles. Major science-related beliefs have been classified into the areas of *child rearing practices and injunctions*; *food and nutrition*; *pregnancy, birth and postnatal care*; *temperature changes*; *changes in the physical environment*; and *household practices* (see George & Glasgow, 1988; 1999; George, 2001 for a more detailed discussion of these beliefs and their relationships to concepts in the canonical life and physical sciences). Since the majority of teachers in the Caribbean share a similar cultural background with the children they teach, it is reasonable to assume that they (at least initially) also make sense of conventional science from the same kind of belief bases discussed in George and Glasgow's research (see George & Glasgow, 1999, pp. 13-23). This line of enquiry presents a number of important implications for the manner in which the whole enterprise of science teaching and learning is conducted in the Caribbean. Important implications exist for the formal processes of science teacher education (content and pedagogy), school science curriculum development and subsequent classroom instruction, and the types of assessments which are designed and administered. Although George and Glasgow's published research in this area drew on data from studies conducted in Jamaica and Trinidad & Tobago, respectively, there is broad applicability to the rest of the English-speaking Caribbean. It will be of interest to see how this line of science education research might successfully be applied to other Caribbean islands, e.g. the Dutch-, French- and Spanish-speaking islands whose traditional belief systems show broad similarities (and yet distinct differences, based on their own unique colonial and developmental histories) to the English-speaking islands.

Current developments in Caribbean science education research may be exemplified by the work of Kolawole Soyibo (e.g. Esiobu & Soyibo, 1995; Soyibo, 1995; Soyibo & Figueroa, 1998; Soyibo, 1999; Soyibo & Hudson, 2000) and Melody Williams (e.g. Williams, 1997a; 1997b; 2002). Soyibo's research has focused on clarifying the cognitive processes used by Jamaican science students in their science learning, and those exhibited by science teachers in terms of how they formulate appropriate assessment strategies in science. Other work has examined the structure and skill levels of laboratory activities used in science teaching, and the effectiveness of computer assisted instruction in science education. Notably, his work has been published widely outside of the Caribbean, which has provided a high level of international visibility for this line of research being conducted in a Caribbean context. Like Soyibo, Williams' research also has attempted to clarify issues relating to cognitive measures of science teacher knowledge and pedagogical effectiveness (e.g. use of concept mapping techniques) and has focused on the incorporation of technology/multimedia in science teacher preparation. As a matter of speculation, it may prove to be a highly informative and potentially rewarding undertaking for emerging science education research in the region to integrate George and Glasgow's work on Caribbean beliefs with the "cognitive processes" and technology/ multimedia based science education research being pioneered by Soyibo and Williams, respectively.

FUTURE DIRECTIONS

As Fraser-Abder (1988a; 1988b) pointed out over a decade ago, what appears to be absent -or at least, not very well developed- in Caribbean science education research efforts are cross-cultural studies involving not only various Caribbean islands, but other developed and developing countries. Most available published studies at the time reported the status of science education in specific Caribbean countries, and broader ranging empirical studies aimed at improving science education in the region as a whole were few. This still appears to be the case. While the examples of Caribbean science education research highlighted in this chapter all make major contributions to our understanding of science teaching and learning in the region, there also needs to be a body of work providing an empirical basis upon which useful cross-cultural comparative analyses and extrapolations may be made. A global assessment of science education/teaching in all the islands would be of interest in terms of possible coordination of efforts and long-range planning for future science education research efforts and resulting educational reforms in the region (see Abder-Fraser, 1988a, p. 15). Of particular concern is the relatively low extent of science education, as suggested by the number of students who successfully pass secondary level science examinations. A cursory review of Caribbean Examination Council (CXC) results in biology, chemistry, physics and integrated science over the past 10 years (1990-2000) indicates that pass rates have, for the most part, fallen below 50% in these subject areas. Current initiatives in science and technology education by two influential organisations, i.e. CARICOM (Caribbean Community and Common Market) and OERU (OECS Education Reform Unit), hold promise for the further development of focused science education research pertinent to the region (see CARICOM, 2002; OERU, 2002; OECS, 2002).

The relative lack of international visibility for science education research efforts occurring in the region undoubtedly is a factor which has discouraged such efforts. Prominent researchers in the region (e.g. George, Glasgow, King) have published in internationally visible science education journals (typically headquartered in the UK and USA), but currently, a mechanism no longer appears to be in place for discipline-specific publication within the region (the author's attempts to locate previous and current issues of the once active *Caribbean Journal of Science Education* were not successful). While the author is unaware of the reasons leading to the journal's demise, one can only speculate about the extent to which a journal outlet would serve as a means of more widely disseminating recent developments in the discipline to a regional and international audience.

SCIENCE EDUCATION POLICY IN THE CARIBBEAN

The generation of specific education policies usually is the most visible or publicised component of the "research-policy-practice" triad. However, the very phrasing of the term "research-policy-practice" implies a linear progression from initial research efforts (theoretically or empirically based), to policy formulation, and finally to implementation in teachers' actual pedagogical practices. For the academician interested in elucidating the relationships between research, policy and practice in formal education, several configurations of the three entities are possible, not all of which may be described accurately in a linear manner. It remains unclear -for the most part- whether the findings or implications of the research described above have had any direct or explicit influence on the development of current science education policies in the region. Lewin (2000a), for example, in his discussion of science education policy in developing countries writes that:

> A lot is known about how students learn science in different communities, what misconceptions they have, and what errors in reasoning and deductions they make. Much of this is not grounded in developing countries, but derived from research undertaken elsewhere. It is an issue for science education policy and planning to find ways of supporting research linked to development in different countries, which really does make a difference to the practice of science education. Progress on this has been disappointingly slow (p. 35).

Although the social and economic infrastructures to support productive research-policy relationships in the Caribbean still need to be developed adequately, national policies relating to education and training typically place emphasis on the importance of developing expertise in science and technology (see Lewin, 2000b). Clearly, this presents important implications for science teaching and learning in the Caribbean. In the following sections, brief descriptions of education policy initiatives from three Caribbean countries are presented, i.e. the *Reform of Secondary Education* (ROSE) project in Jamaica; the *Education Sector Enhancement Programme* (EduTech 2000) in Barbados; and Bermuda's development of its national *Science Performance Standards*. The initiatives themselves exemplify three "levels" or "types" of policy formulation as they relate to science education in the respective countries, i.e. a national education policy with a component addressing science teaching and learning (ROSE); a national technology-focused education policy with explicit applications to science teaching and learning (EduTech 2000); and policy specific to the teaching and learning of science in the form of national standards.

The *Reform of Secondary Education* (ROSE) project.

In 1993, the Government of Jamaica launched a major curriculum policy reform movement to address concerns of (i) the quality of curriculum offerings at the secondary level, (ii) access to these offerings, and (iii) inequities in the secondary school system. The *Reform of Secondary Education* (ROSE) project –jointly funded by the World Bank and the Government of Jamaica- targeted the five subject areas of the national curriculum, i.e. mathematics, English language, integrated science, social studies and resource & technology. The five year project (1993-1998) was designed to lead to improvements in secondary education for all students in grades 7-9; a subsequent phase of the project would address students in grades 10-11. The project aimed to improve access, productivity, quality and equity in lower secondary education. Previously there was no common curriculum for the six types of secondary school existing in Jamaica, each of which has different entry requirements and which vary greatly in terms of expectations of students and social status, resulting in a very inequitable system (UNESCO, 1999). More specifically with regard to teaching and learning and the formulation of educational policy, the ROSE project also sought to accomplish the following: introduction of multi-level teaching, collaborative learning, integration across subject areas, student-centred learning strategies and team planning among teachers; development of textbooks to support the new curriculum and recommended pedagogy; reform of the professional preparation of teachers of grades 7-9 to be consistent with the objectives of ROSE and to provide them with the necessary skills needed to execute the ROSE curriculum; introduction of new methods of assessment and evaluation at grades 7-9; and upgrading of school physical plants to provide the equipment needed to support the new curriculum and teaching strategies (Miller, 2000b, p. 144). Over the five-year period of the project, an intensive professional development programme for teachers of grades 7-9 was conducted in order to orient in-service teachers in both content and ROSE methodology. The professional development programme involved annual two-week summer workshops and periodic classroom visits during the year. With particular reference to the professional development offerings for science teachers, it was noticed that the science teachers were not using the recommended methodologies for the teaching of the science curriculum as intended. These methodologies included concept mapping, cooperative grouping and inquiry-based laboratory work. To assist science teachers in their understanding and utilisation of ROSE methodology, three self-instructional modules were developed and evaluated to address the incorrect use and inadequate understanding of the methodology (Williams, 1997a; 1997b; 2002). Beginning in January 2000, a four-year study entitled **M**ultimedia **A**nd **S**cience **T**eacher **E**ducation **R**esearch in **Jam**aica (*MASTER-Jam*) was launched to investigate the potential of multimedia case studies to promote reflective practice and enhance teacher learning. Although this is an independent research study which is not formally part of the ROSE programme, the aim of the study is to design, develop and evaluate an interactive multimedia case study on cooperative learning, one of the ROSE methodologies (Williams, 2002). Although the study is still in progress at time of writing, important policy implications are presented for the use of technology in the professional preparation and professional development not only of science teachers, but of all teachers involved in the ROSE project. This focus on the use of technology is evidenced in the education policy initiative of another Caribbean nation, Barbados, in its *Education Sector Enhancement Programme*.

The *Education Sector Enhancement Programme* (EduTech 2000).

As an education policy initiative, Barbados' *Education Sector Enhancement Programme* (more popularly known as *EduTech 2000*) perhaps stands as one of the most ambitious and comprehensive plans of its kind exemplified by a Caribbean nation. This US$ 213 million programme -financed by the Government of Barbados (45%), the Inter-American Development Bank (40%) and the Caribbean Development Bank (15%)- is a seven year project (beginning in December 1998) whose primary stated goal is to "effect an increase in the number of students contributing to the sustainable social and economic development of Barbados" (Barbados Ministry of Education, Youth Affairs and Culture, 1998; 1999; Cox, 2002). Of particular interest within the context of this chapter is one of the specific policy objectives of ensuring that "all children leave school with the basic skills and abilities that are required to participate productively in the skill- and information-intensive job market". Also of interest is the explicit reference in the policy documentation to *constructivism* as a guiding theoretical framework for how learning best occurs. As implied in the name, EduTech 2000 emphasises the use and application of information technology throughout the Barbadian education system. Specifically, the training of teachers and education officers in the use of information technology in education is one of the four main areas of focus of this programme (Miller, 2000a, p. 30). In a presentation made at a meeting of the British Foreign and Commonwealth Office (FCO) in April 2001, Barbadian Minister of Commerce, Consumer Affairs and Business Development, Ronald Toppin discussed several crucial procedural aspects of the EduTech 2000 initiative. Notable highlights of the presentation included the following excerpts:

> * <u>Procurement and installation of hardware and software</u>
>
> This component will see the introduction of technology into all of the island's primary and secondary schools. It will entail the provision of hardware, software and the necessary networking infrastructure. Somewhere between 8,000 and 10,000 computers will be provided under the project.
>
> * <u>Hardware</u>
>
> All primary schools will have at least one computer lab equipped with 30 networked computers and a teachers' media centre. Secondary schools will have computers in subject rooms. There will be five subject rooms with thirty computers each, two subject rooms with 20 computers each and one subject room with 10 computers, depending on the size of the school. *There will be a special computer lab for technical, vocational and science subjects. Libraries will be transformed into learning resource centres with facilities to access the Internet. This will facilitate information gathering and research regionally and internationally on any subject. All schools will have 4 to 6 computers in regular classrooms along with a multimedia centre for use by teachers.*
>
> * <u>Software</u>
>
> The focus for software will be as follows: Provide children with the requisite skills for computer use such as key boarding, word processing, accessing the Internet, etc; *use subject-based software packages which can facilitate the development of skills and knowledge in given subject areas*;

use interactive media and audio visual technologies in classrooms to assist with student learning.

* Expected benefits

The country's human resources will be carefully developed to match skills with available job opportunities; The education system will be better positioned to develop the nation's human resources such that it can serve as a catalyst for economic, social and political growth and generally help to improve the quality of life of all citizens.

(Toppin, 2001; author's italics)

Stephen Boyce (1999; 2000a; 2000b), a Barbadian based educational technology consultant and also a resident tutor for the EduTech 2000 teacher training programme, provides a cogent and articulate analysis indicating how the use of technology in education bears particular applicability to science teaching and learning. In a vividly portrayed prognostication into the technologically enhanced Barbadian classroom of the future, Boyce (2000b) envisions scenarios such as the following:

Technical drawing rooms will say goodbye to the T-square and compass and welcome AUTOCAD and industrial large-format printers. Mechanical engineering students with benefit from autotronics facilities, the greasy overalls will be replaced by lily-white lab coats. Science labs will have computers equipped with probes capable of recording physical and physiological data. Students will be able to plan, design and conduct exciting research and share their finding with peers and experts. Business students will create their own on-line businesses, trade stock and manage people in virtual offices (some of whom they may never see).

Boyce's scenarios are not mere flights of technological fantasy or instances of futuristic euphoria. In recent years, the power and versatility of the computer have been significantly enhanced with the coming of age of multimedia systems and telecommunications capabilities. The amount of software available for use by science students is growing almost exponentially and the Internet/WWW increases its accessibility (see Ebenezer & Lau, 1999). In addition, recent advances in video, audio and photographic technologies have extended the process skills and sensory experiences associated with science learning (Chiappetta & Koballa, 2002, p. 199). For the traditional school science subjects of biology, chemistry and physics, many innovative possibilities for science teaching and learning currently exist with "computer based instructional systems". Microcomputer-based laboratories (MBLs), allow for the juxtaposition of traditional laboratory investigations with the use of the microcomputer, software and appropriate peripherals to gather, display and analyse data. Calculator-based laboratory (CBL) probeware can allow for data collection and analysis outside of the school laboratory in "'everyday" situations. Other computer technology may be used to simulate or otherwise "capture" real time or time lapse investigations of natural phenomena difficult to reproduce for classroom instruction (e.g. bacterial reproduction in biology; rust formation (oxidation) in chemistry; radionuclide decay in physics), which may be archived electronically for future use. Science teaching and learning (both at the school level and the science teacher preparation level) also may benefit from the use of technology in "concept mapping" (Williams, 2002) and associated developments in "knowledge representation" of scientific concepts (see Fisher, Wandersee & Moody, 2000). While comprehensive, publicly released assessments of EduTech 2000 policy implementation and concomitant student learning outcomes still appear to be forthcoming, currently available information (Cox, 2002) suggests that the project is achieving a creditable measure of success. The *Education Evaluation Centre* (EEC) at the University of the West Indies (Cave Hill, Barbados campus) has been contracted by the Barbados Ministry of Education, Youth Affairs and Culture to monitor and evaluate the programme throughout its duration and, to date, has already administered baseline tests and questionnaires in selected demonstration and control schools as part of the evaluation process (Cox, 2002).

Development of *Bermuda Science Performance Standards*

Beginning in 1997, Bermuda, in response to international global developments in education, undertook a sweeping reform of its entire public education system. In a radical overhaul of its primary (elementary) and secondary education system, primary schools were reduced from seven year to six year schools; three year middle schools were created from the final year of primary school and the first two years of the secondary school (analogous to the conversion from "junior high schools" to "middle schools" in the U.S.); a new senior school (high school) was built; and the four year senior school began with a full complement of students. Concerted efforts were made to support these significant changes, including the phasing in of a new set of national curricula for the government (i.e. public) schools. Phase 1 introduced the *Bermuda Middle School Curriculum* (1997), followed by the *Bermuda Senior School Curriculum* (1999) in Phase 2 and the *Bermuda Primary School Curriculum* (2001) in Phase 3. In terms of science teaching and learning, the curriculum documents, mandated for use in the public schools, consist of *Bermuda Science Education Goals, Scope and Sequence* and instructional modules that were designed using national science education standards from the United States, Britain and Canada. At time of writing, the Bermuda Education System is in the final phase of systemic change. In 2001, a draft version of the *Bermuda Science Performance Standards* (BSPS) was released by the Bermuda Ministry of Education and distributed to science educators and other stakeholders for review and critique. The BSPS are intended to provide a framework supporting the year-by-year science curriculum spanning preschool to senior school. The curriculum (content standards) provides details of *what* students should know and be able to do at a particular stage in their academic and social development. The curriculum is aligned with the BSPS to indicate *how* students may effectively demonstrate their mastery and understanding of scientific concepts and skills (Blades, 2002; Bermuda Science Performance Standards, 2001). Although almost all other Caribbean countries have science curricula designed to "fit" their own circumstances and educational priorities, the case of Bermuda deserves special note. The BSPS document is distinctive in that it is the first major national work of its kind developed in the Caribbean which provides specific performance descriptions, sample activities and also examples of student work which clearly delineate desired levels of competence and achievement in science[2]. As such, the BSPS may be regarded as an instrument designed to very specifically assess understanding of a variety of important science concepts and skills.

The BSPS are categorised into five strands, i.e. *physical science* (SC1); *life science* (SC2); *earth and space science* (SC3); *the history and nature of science* (SC4); and *the nature of scientific inquiry* (SC5). Each strand also is subcategorised into "Learning Phases", with each phase corresponding to developmental benchmark/ grade levels. For the four phases, Learning Phase A (the first) corresponds to the preschool-Primary 3 grades (kindergarten and lower elementary grades in the U.S.) while Learning Phase D (the last) corresponds to the Senior 1-Senior 4 grades (high school grades 9-12 in the U.S.). Based on classical Piagetian developmental theory, the phases represent approximate cognitive levels for children and the performance standards are communicated as a hierarchy of knowledge as students progress from one phase to the next (Bermuda Science Performance Standards, 2001, p.1). Commendably, while the BSPS and its accompanying science curricula were based on science education standards developed in other countries, explicit mention is made in the Foreword of the *Bermuda Senior School Science Curriculum* (2000) document that the curriculum is "Bermudianized" (p. iii), i.e. tailored to the specific social, cultural and physical contexts within which instruction will occur. In common with the other two national policy initiatives here described, the BSPS also incorporates a strong focus on technology and competence in its use by science students. Currently, a technology infusion initiative (in collaboration with the Curry School of Education at the University of Virginia) is in process including training in the use of peripheral devices (probeware, robotic telescopes, digital microscopes etc.), identification of Internet/ WWW resources, introductory web development skills and the use of CD-ROM programmes to enhance instructional modules taught at the Senior 1 and Senior 2 levels (Blades, 2002). Interestingly, even though the technology infusion initiative involves instruction for science teachers in the use of technology, no teacher preparation institutions currently exist in Bermuda. Formal preparation in the use of the technology to enhance science instruction ideally occurs in the teacher preparation programme, and in other countries, is subsumed under pedagogical standards of "what science teachers should know and be able to do" (see the National Research Council's [1996] *National Science Education Standards*, for example). Given Bermuda's recent development of Science Performance Standards for students, perhaps it is now an opportune time to consider the development of an analogous set of Performance Standards for science teachers and the simultaneous development of an effective science teacher preparation programme to ensure the continuance of high quality science teaching and learning in the Bermuda Education System.

FUTURE DIRECTIONS

Issues relating to science, technology and science education will weigh heavily in future education policy directions in the Caribbean. In their *Caribbean Education Strategy Report*, Jules, Miller and Armstrong (2000) discuss a regional developmental objective of "an internationally competitive labor force and more effective and equitable education systems". As a proposed indicator indicating progress toward the realisation of this objective, the authors suggest that by the year 2020, the Caribbean region should be able to demonstrate "*a 30% increase in persons with qualifications in science and technology at the postsecondary level*" (p. xviii; author's italics). As another indicator, they also suggest that "by 2005, a *Virtual Caribbean Institute for Educational Research and Planning* will be in operation" (p. xix). As they point out, the year 2005 is significant since it is at this juncture when the North America Free Trade Area (NAFTA) will take effect in the region, and new trade agreements with the European Union will be phased in. This event will have significant implications for the future economic progress of Caribbean countries, affecting a wide range of regional concerns (all involving some level of scientific and technological literacy) such as agriculture, tourism, textile industries, the use/abuse of available natural resources, communications, and entrepreneurism, to name a few.

Clearly, education in scientific and technological matters must be a focus of formal teaching and learning in the Caribbean, and must play a central role in education policy. Lewin (2000a) suggests several ways in which information and communication technologies can contribute to education policy in developing countries, which include access to high quality learning material available from remote sites; facilitating novel learning materials; permitting open connectivity between learners and between learners and teachers independent of location; and managing learning and monitoring progress (p. 32). Others have investigated the feasibility of developing Internet-based education models (i.e. comparatively low cost virtual classrooms) in the Caribbean, especially where geographical access to physical facilities might hinder the process of formal education (see, for example, Osin, 1998; Grant, France & Hsu, 2000).

Consideration of the *ROSE*, *EduTech 2000* and *Science Performance Standards* policy initiatives described above suggests a number of exciting possibilities for the productive overlap of science education research and policy in the Caribbean. For example, efforts occurring in the teacher education component of Barbados' *Education Sector Enhancement Programme* and the ROSE-affiliated *Multimedia*

And Science Teacher Education Research project in Jamaica provide the potential for mutually beneficial collaborative work. To speculate further, integration of these efforts under the aegis of national science standards (such as those being developed in Bermuda), or perhaps even regional science standards, might provide the beginnings of the infrastructure which is needed for sustainable growth in science and technology education across the entire Caribbean region.

SCIENCE EDUCATION PRACTICE IN THE CARIBBEAN

Science education practice (i.e. those pedagogical actions which are actually performed in a formal or informal instructional setting by an individual science teacher or teachers, and which may be shown to have demonstrable positive effects on students' learning and understanding of science) is more difficult to document and discuss within the context of this chapter since many useful examples of science education practice will be at the individual school level across a range of Caribbean countries. For the purposes of this chapter, examples of science education practice in two Caribbean countries (Jamaica and Bermuda, respectively) will be highlighted. These examples indicate documented, relatively large scale efforts which may serve as useful models for adoption and modification by other Caribbean countries.

Science Matters in Life Everyday (SMILE)

Jules, Miller and Armstrong (2000), in discussing their Caribbean Education Strategy up until the year 2020 note that "the region as a whole lags far behind in science and technology and a more concerted effort is needed to bridge that gulf" (p. 27; author's italics). The Science Learning Centre in Jamaica is cited as an example of a "useful Caribbean initiative" which addresses the teaching and learning of science at the early childhood stage of development. In 1990, the Insurance Company of the West Indies Group Foundation (ICWI), in collaboration with the University of the West Indies (Mona campus) established a Science Learning Centre to promote the interactive learning of science. The mission statement of the organisation is "to act as demonstration centre to provide learning opportunities which will impact on the reform of science education at the early childhood and primary school level and in the wider community" (ICWI, 1999; ICWI, 2000a; ICWI, 2000b). As a demonstration resource and through its various community based activities (e.g. science clubs, workshops, school visits, provision of audio-visual aids and publications), it has had an impact on more than 200,000 students and 4,000 teachers (Jules, Miller & Armstrong, 2000, p. 28). The focus on early childhood science education began in 1997, and with the assistance of the Japanese Government Grass Roots Assistance Program and UNICEF, the Science Matters in Life Everyday (SMILE) early childhood programme was initiated in 1998. As indicated in the name of the programme, SMILE focuses on science in everyday life and has been developed for young children 4-6 years of age and their teachers. A range of science concepts and topics are taught by way of interactive activities and include: water; air; colours; shapes, sizes and textures; temperature; states of matter; sounds; grouping, classifying and estimating; and environmental awareness (ICWI, 2000). The programme produces low cost, hands on science activities for pre-school children, trains early childhood educators in the use of interactive materials and methodologies, and disseminates information on appropriate science and early childhood educational teaching and learning materials. The Center has a database of more than 300 indigenous activity materials as well as culturally appropriate international materials, science education videos, activity kits and guides and manuals. It is anticipated that an early introduction to the exciting world of science through low cost materials and training of teachers would stimulate continued interest in both the teaching and learning of science (Jules, Miller & Armstrong, 2000, p. 28).

Bermuda Schools' Science Enrichment Program

In collaboration with the Bermuda Ministry of Education, the Bermuda Biological Station for Research (BBSR) has developed the *Bermuda Schools' Science Enrichment Program* (see BBSR, 2002). In accordance with its mission statement (i.e. "*to conduct research and science education of the highest quality from the special perspective of a mid-ocean island and to provide well-equipped facilities and responsive staff support to visiting scientists, faculty and students from around the world*"), the program provide hands-on science experiences for Bermuda's school children and free professional development resources for Bermuda's science teachers. Through an assortment of widely funded initiatives, the Bermuda Schools' Science Enrichment Program encourages young Bermudians in the primary and middle grades to develop an interest in science, and encourages older students (high school and undergraduate levels) to enter the scientific field through experiences in authentic scientific research. The program plays a pivotal role in Bermuda's national science education reform efforts, and emphasises the value of "science in the community". As part of the year round enrichment program, hundreds of students are taken to nature reserves, marine science laboratories and science classrooms at these facilities. One facility sponsors a plankton tow to interested class groups. Many professional scientists donate their time as part of program to visit schools and speak with students. During these experiences, students begin to gain a better appreciation of the "real life" nature of science, how scientists work and recognise that science is indeed a human endeavour (Blades, 2002).

Bermuda is fortunate to have many other local facilities and community resources which are utilised to enhance the teaching and learning of science. At the preschool/primary and middle school levels for example, integrated projects by preschools and primary school students have been shown at the annual Bermuda Agricultural Exhibition and at school sites, and local organisations collaborate with the Bermuda Ministry of Education to support the Bermuda Government School curriculum with guided field trips, classes, teacher workshops, curriculum theme 'boxes" or packets for loan (Blades, 2002).

FUTURE DIRECTIONS

The programmes described above both demonstrate the philosophy that the teaching and learning of science does not happen only within the four walls of a classroom. As has been well documented by researchers interested in informal science education, the stimulation of children's curiosity and interest in science and technological matters occurs to an appreciable extent in informal (or nonformal) learning environments (see, for example, Falk & Dierking, 1992; Rennie & McClafferty, 1995). As both programmes indicate, science teaching and learning is best accomplished through concrete, hands-on, "everyday" experiences to which students can relate, and which typically play some role in their daily activities. Of particular importance is the attention to well designed science education practice targeted toward the primary or elementary grades. Typically interest (and hence academic achievement) in science declines for a substantial proportion of students during the upper elementary/lower middle school grades (see, for example, Neathery, 1997), and especially so for females. Such efforts will be of primary importance in the foreseeable future to the extent of scientific literacy among the wider Caribbean citizenry.

"Informal science education" currently is experiencing a great deal of professional interest among those whose work addresses the teaching and learning of science. Informal learning environments usually are characterised as institutions which promote learning that is voluntary, self-directed, life-long and motivated mainly by intrinsic interests such as curiosity, exploration, manipulation, task completion and social interaction. Representative examples of informal science learning environments include science and natural history museums; interactive science and technology centers; aquaria; nature centers; botanical gardens; arboreta; zoological parks; science clubs; and other community-centered activities. Informal science learning environments not only reinforce formal content instruction provided by schools in terms of encouraging and motivating children through direct hands-on experiences, but also may serve as laboratories and dissemination centers for teacher "accomplished practices" and as science "connections" which offer programmes, services and exhibits in direct support of the formal school science curriculum. Informal science learning environments also have influential and rapidly developing roles in science teacher education, in stimulating parents and other adults to support children's scientific interests at home, and in improving the scientific literacy of adults so that they are able to increase their appreciation and understanding of science and its respective technological applications (Druger, 1988; Boyd, 1990; Semper, 1990; Falk & Dierking, 1992; Rennie & McClafferty, 1995). Both the *Science Matters in Life Everyday* programme in Jamaica and the *Bermuda Schools' Science Enrichment Program* show significant potential for leadership in developing this aspect of science education practice in the Caribbean region.

DISCUSSION AND CONCLUDING COMMENTS

The ongoing development of science education research, policy and practice in the Caribbean will continue to receive a great deal of attention in the years ahead. As the region prepares itself to be even more competitive in the science and technology-oriented world of the 21st century, the quality and extent of science education in each country may well serve as one of the most important indicators of the region's progress as a whole.

As discussed above, published science education research emerging from the region has generated a great deal of information regarding science teaching and learning in a Caribbean context. However, better articulation and integration of science education research needs to be established across the region, with cross-case analyses and comparative studies performed in different Caribbean countries. Central to these endeavours will be the establishment (or re-establishment) of an appropriate vehicle for the dissemination of research findings, i.e. a dedicated publication outlet for the presentation of pedagogical implications, curricular innovations, etc. which are subject to review and critique by other science education researchers both within and external to the region. If the financial expense associated with printing and maintaining a traditional paper journal is prohibitive, perhaps a peer-reviewed electronic journal format ought to be considered (see Sweeney, 2001a; 2000). Also important for the development of science education research in the region will be the forging of closer links with national policy recommendations, which perhaps will require the undertaking of carefully designed experimental or quasi-experimental educational studies for replication and application to formal classroom teaching and learning.

In terms of science education policy in the region, the examples provided above indicate a range of noteworthy initiatives currently being undertaken in the respective countries. The initiatives hold much promise for the individual countries themselves, but more importantly, also hold promise for what may be learned by other countries in the region for possible adoption or adaptation to their own particular educational circumstances. The astute observer of educational policy initiatives and developments in the Caribbean (and other, so called "Third World" countries) will be aware that funding by external international financial organisations is a necessary fact of life for relatively vulnerable national economies such as found in the Caribbean. Although this is not an appropriate forum from which to pursue a lengthy discussion of the ramifications of *structural adjustment policies* on the economies of "developing countries" (see the work of other, more capable commentators such as Downes, 1992; Garrity & Picard, 1996), it nevertheless seems apposite to note that structural adjustment policies which directly or indirectly threaten the offering of universally accessible science education in the Caribbean should be treated with extreme caution. The region's future prosperity (economically as well as in regard to its human and environmental resources) means that the region cannot afford to do otherwise.

Universal accessibility to science education (or efforts toward such), coupled with an emphasis on public awareness of and involvement in science education are features of documented, nationally visible science education practice in the Caribbean. More examples like the *Science Learning Centre* and the *SMILE* programme in Jamaica, and Bermuda's *Schools Science Enrichment Program* are needed throughout the region in a concerted attempt to improve the scientific literacy of *all* sectors of the Caribbean population. A focus on informal science education at the early childhood and primary grade levels ought to accomplish much in terms of nurturing the scientific habits of mind and development of the technological skills needed for full adult participation in contributing to the sustainable social and economic development of the Caribbean.

Any discussion of science education research, policy and practice in the Caribbean would be incomplete without attention being given to the supporting mechanisms for the professional preparation of science teachers. High quality, effective science teacher education in the region is a major area of concern. Well prepared science teachers are *essential* to the successful attainment in the region of the much vaunted goals of developing critical thinking skills in students who are lifelong learners, proficient in the use of technology, and who are able to function productively in the "Information Age". In common with other developing countries (and also developed countries), the recruitment, retention, and facilitation of continuous professional growth of science teachers are concerns which must be adequately addressed by Caribbean countries (see Ware, 1992a; 1992b). As noted by Hall & Marrett (1996), Delannoy (2000), Miller (2000b) and Jennings (2001), the incorporation of technology into the formal process of teacher education generally (and science teacher education in particular) is rapidly becoming a central feature of teacher preparation in the region. For the development of science teacher preparation programmes in particular, the advances in distance education technology and use of sophisticated instructional software pioneered by the University of the West Indies may prove to be advantageous in recruiting and preparing much needed science teachers across the Caribbean (see, for example Hall & Marrett, 1996; Delannoy, 2000; Miller, 2000b; 2001; UWI/Commonwealth of Learning, 2001). Several resources may be utilised for enhancing the professional preparation of science teachers in the Caribbean. Since effective science teachers must exemplify mastery of their subject area specialties in addition to a thorough knowledge of learning theories and effective pedagogical practices, university faculty in the sciences (biology, chemistry, physics, etc.) also should play an integral role in the formal process of science teacher preparation, at both the elementary and secondary levels. Ongoing professional development for science teachers (preservice and inservice), and the maintenance of close links with university faculty mentors also may result in science teachers becoming more reflective, deliberate and intentional concerning their professional practice and its connections to student learning outcomes (Sweeney, 2001b; Sweeney & Tobin, 2000; Sweeney, Bula & Cornett, 2001).

The Caribbean is poised to transform the rhetorical advocacy of "scientific literacy for all" into a reality. When this is no longer spoken about in rhetorical terms (and when the initiatives described in this chapter are no longer initiatives, but instead are well established science education research activities, policies and practices across the Caribbean), the region will then be closer to achieving its considerable leadership potential, and well equipped to play its role in shaping the world of the 21st century.

ACKNOWLEDGEMENTS

The author wishes to acknowledge the kind assistance of Dr. Pamela Abder-Fraser, Ms. Joan Blades, Ms. Sylvia Cox, Ms. Gracelyn Cassell, Dr. Jack Holbrook, Dr. June George, Dr Joyce Glasgow, Dr. Winston King, Ms. Maki Mizuno, Ms. Dorothy Palmer and Ms. Melody Williams in locating important references and source materials cited in this chapter. Dr. Bastick's encouragement and patience have been instrumental in allowing this chapter to be written; many thanks. The author also wishes to acknowledge the insightful comments provided by three anonymous reviewers during the preparation of this chapter for publication.

NOTES

[1]The most inclusive definition describes the region (both in geographic and cultural terms), as that bounded to the north by Bermuda and the Bahamas; to the west by Belize located on the Central American mainland; to the East by that arch of islands extending to Barbados; and to the South by Guyana and Suriname on the South American mainland and the islands of Aruba, Curaçao and Bonaire (Miller, 2000a, p. 7). The Caribbean Region therefore represents a diversity of cultures, traditions, languages and ethnicities. For the purposes of this chapter, I have largely co-opted Jules & Panneflek's (2000) definition of the Caribbean (as used in their report) to include

Anguilla, Antigua & Barbuda, Aruba, The Bahamas, Barbados, Belize, Bermuda, The British Virgin Islands, The Cayman Islands, Dominica, Grenada, Guyana, Haiti, Jamaica, St. Kitts & Nevis, St. Lucia, Montserrat, The Netherlands Antilles, Trinidad & Tobago and *The Turks & Caicos Islands*.

[2]I have tried to be comprehensive in my review, discussion and analysis of contemporary science education research in the Caribbean; however, with limited space for discussion, any inadvertent errors of omission or oversight are my sole responsibility.

REFERENCES

Alexander, G. & Glasgow, J. (1981). UNICEF regional primary school project: Report on teacher training and curriculum development activities, 1978-1980. *Caribbean Journal of Education*, *8*(1), 75-101.

Barbados Ministry of Education, Youth Affairs and Culture. (1998). *EduTech 2000: An education policy framework for Barbados*. Bridgetown, Barbados: Author.

Barbados Ministry of Education, Youth Affairs and Culture. (1999). *EduTech 2000*. Bridgetown, Barbados: Author. Available online: http://www.edutech2000.gov.bb/edutech_2000.htm

Bermuda Biological Station for Research. (2002). *Bermuda Schools' Science Enrichment Program*. Available online: http://www.bbsr.edu/Education/Science_Enrichment/science_enrichment.html

Bermuda Science Performance Standards. (2001). Bermuda Ministry of Education, Hamilton, Bermuda.

Bermuda Senior School Science Curriculum. (2000). Bermuda Ministry of Education, Hamilton, Bermuda.

Blades, K. J. (2002). *Personal communication* (January, 2002). Science Curriculum Officer, Bermuda Ministry of Education, Hamilton, Bermuda.

Boyce, S. L. (1999). *Impact of technology on the teaching-learning process in the Caribbean: Experiences from Barbados and Jamaica.* Paper presented at The Caribbean and Technology-Enhanced Learning conference (sponsored by the Commonwealth of Learning), St. Michael, Barbados, November 24-27, 1999.

Boyce, S. L. (2000a). Impact of technology on the teaching-learning process in the Caribbean: Experiences from Barbados and Jamaica. *Technology in Education Online Journal, 1*(1). Available online: http://www.ccsedu.com/tcent/papers/paper01.htm

Boyce, S. L. (2000b). The classroom of the future: Imperatives for Barbados. *Technology in Education Online Journal, 1*(1). Available online: http://www.ccsedu.com/tcent/papers/paper02.htm

Boyd, W. L. (1990). Museums as centers of learning. *Teachers College Record*, 94, 761-770.

Brathwaite, W. E. (1978). *In-service strategies for improving teacher abilities in science education.* In Proceedings of the Regional Primary Science Conference, pp. 156-160. University of the West Indies, Cave Hill, Barbados: Caribbean Regional Science Project.

Brathwaite, W. E. (1985). Social relevance in science education: Problems and strategies in a Third World island economy. In G. B. Harrison's (Ed.), *World trends in science and technology education*, pp. 82-87. London, UK: Trent Polytechnic.

CARICOM. (2002). *Caribbean Community and Common Market.* Available online: http://www.caricom.org

Chiappetta, E. L. & Koballa, Jr., T. R. (2002). *Science instruction in the middle and secondary schools* (5th edition). Upper Saddle River, NJ: Prentice-Hall.

Cox, S. (2002). *Brief on the GOB/IDB/CDB Education Sector Enhancement Programme* (personal communication, March 2002). Ministry of Education, Youth Affairs and Culture, Bridgetown, Barbados.

Delannoy, F. (2000). Teacher training or lifelong professional development? Worldwide trends and challenges. *TechKnowLogia*, *2*(6), 10-13. Available online: http://ipdweb.np.edu.sg/lt/feb01/pdf/teck_teachertraining.pdf

Downes, A. S. (1992). *The impact of structural adjustment policies on the educational system in the Caribbean.* Paper presented at the Round Table Meeting on *The Impact of World Bank Policies and Interventions on Education in the Caribbean*, sponsored by the World Confederation of Organizations of the Teaching Profession: Castries, St. Lucia, September 28-30, 1992. Available online: http://www.iacd.oas.org/La%20Educa%20116/downes.htm

Driver, R. & Erickson, G. (1983). Theories-in-action: Some theoretical and empirical issues in the study of students' conceptual frameworks in science. *Studies in Science Education*, *10*, 37-60.

Driver, R., Squires, A., Rushworth, P. & Wood-Robinson, V. (1994). *Making sense of secondary science: Research into children's ideas.* London: Routledge.

Druger, M. (Ed.) (1988). *Science for the fun of it : A guide to informal science education.* Washington, DC: National Science Teachers Association.

Ebenezer, J. V. & Lau, E. (1999). *Science on the Internet: A resource for K-12 teachers.* Upper Saddle River, NJ: Prentice-Hall.

Esiobu, G. O. & Soyibo, K. (1995). Effects of concept and vee mappings under three learning modes on students' cognitive achievement in ecology and genetics. *Journal of Research in Science Teaching*, *32*(9), 971-995.

Falk, J. H. & Dierking, L. D. (1992). *The museum experience.* Washington, DC: Whalesback Books.

Fisher, K. M., Wandersee, J. H. & Moody, D. E. (2000). *Mapping biology knowledge.* Dordrecht, The Netherlands: Kluwer Academic Publishers.

Fraser-Abder, P. (1979). The teaching of elementary science. *Journal of Education in Science for Trinidad and Tobago*, *7*, 8-11.

Fraser-Abder, P. (1982). The effect of science teaching on the Trinidadian fifth grade child's concept of Piagetian physical causality. *Caribbean Journal of Education*, *9*, 167-187.

Fraser-Abder,P. (1985a). The status and implications of the cognitive developmental levels of elementary students in Trinidad and Tobago. *Journal of Education in Science for Trinidad and Tobago*, *12*, 1-6.

Fraser-Abder, P. (1985b). The development of primary science education in Trinidad and Tobago. *Caribbean Curriculum*, *1*, 55-67.

Fraser-Abder, P. (1986). Sub-cultural differences in cognitive development among elementary students in Trinidad and Tobago. *Caribbean Journal of Education*, *13*(1-2), 27-41.

Fraser-Abder, P. (1988a). *Summary of science education research in the Caribbean, 1970-1987.* Paper presented at the Annual Meeting of the National Association for Research in Science Teaching, Lake of the Ozarks, MO, April 10-13, 1988.

Fraser-Abder, P. (1988b). *Sourcebook of science education research in the Caribbean.* Washington, DC: UNESCO.

Fraser-Abder, P. & Douglass, R. (1986). A curriculum journey: Science - A Process Approach for Trinidad and Tobago (SAPATT). In Pamela

Fraser-Abder's (Ed.), *Science education research in Latin America and the Caribbean* (conference proceedings), pp. 100-114. St. Augustine, Trinidad: Faculty of Education, University of the West Indies.

Fraser-Abder, P. & Shrigley, R. L. (1980). A status study on the science attitudes of elementary school teachers in Trinidad and Tobago. *Science Education*, *64*, 637-644.

Garrity, M. & Picard, L. A. (Eds.). (1996). *Policy reform for sustainabledevelopment in the Caribbean*. Amsterdam, The Netherlands: IOS Press.

George, J. (1988). The role of native technology in science education in developing countries: A Caribbean perspective. *School Science Review*, *69*(249), 815-820.

George, J. (1995). Health education challenges in a rural context: A case study. *Studies in Science Education*, *25*, 239-262.

George, J. (1999). Worldview analysis of knowledge in a rural village: Implications for science education. *Science Education*, *83*(1), 77-95.

George, J. (2001). *Culture and science education: A look from the developing world*. Accessed online at: http://www.actionbioscience.org/education/george.html

George, J. & Glasgow, J. (1999). *The boundaries between Caribbean* beliefs and practices and conventional science: Implications for *science education in the Caribbean*. Monograph series No. 10 (Series Editor: Lynda Quamina-Aiyejina), Education for All (EFA) in the Caribbean: Assessment 2000. Kingston, Jamaica: UNESCO.

George, J. & Glasgow, J. (1988). Street science and conventional science in the West Indies. *Studies in Science Education*, *15*, 109-118.

George, J. & Glasgow, J. (1989). Some cultural implications of teaching towards common syllabi in science: A case study from the Caribbean. *School Science Review*, *71*(254), 115-123.

Glasgow, J. (1986). Factors affecting scientific literacy in Jamaican grade nine students. In Pamela Fraser-Abder's (Ed.), *Science education research in Latin America and the Caribbean* (conference proceedings), pp. 234-252. St. Augustine, Trinidad: Faculty of Education, University of the West Indies.

Glasgow, J. & Robinson, P. (1983). *Environmental education: Modules* for pre-service training of teachers and supervisors for primary *schools*. Paris, France: UNESCO.

Glasgow, J. (1987). Science syllabi with environmental emphasis in the Caribbean. *Caribbean Curriculum, 2(1)*, 1-15.

Glasgow, J. (1989). Environmental education: Global concern, Caribbean focus. *Caribbean Journal of Education, 16*, 1 & 2, 1-12.

Glasgow, J. (1993). Teachers and environmental education: A Caribbean approach. In Walter Leal Filho's (Ed.), *Environmental Education in the Commonwealth*, pp. 64-94. Vancouver, Canada: Commonwealth of Learning.

Grant, E. S., France, R. B. & Hsu, S. (2000). Towards an Internet-based education model for Caribbean countries. *Journal of Educational Media*, *25*(1), 21-30. Available online (earlier version): http://www.col.org/tel99/acrobat/grant.pdf

Hall, W. M. & Marrett, C. (1996). Quality teacher education via distance mode: A Caribbean experience. *Journal of Education for Teaching*, *22*(1), 85-94.

Insurance Companies of the West Indies Group Foundation. (1999). Science Matters in Life Everyday: A guide for teachers, parents and *caregivers* (Volume I, April 1999). Kingston, Jamaica: Insurance Companies of the West Indies Group Foundation Science Learning Centre.

Insurance Companies of the West Indies Group Foundation. (2000a). Science Matters in Life Everyday: A guide for teachers, parents and *caregivers* (Volume II, March 2000). Kingston, Jamaica: Insurance Companies of the West Indies Group Foundation Science Learning Centre.

Insurance Companies of the West Indies Group Foundation. (2000b). *Programmes: Early childhood hands-on science*, "Science Matters in Life Everyday" (SMILE). Available online: http://www.jsdnp.org.jm/icwi_slc/progr.htm

Isaacs, P. A. (1980). Piaget's theory and the Caribbean. *Caribbean Journal of Education*, *7*(2), 110-130.

Jegede, O. (1995). Collateral learning and the eco-cultural paradigm in science and mathematics education in Africa. *Studies in Science Education*, *25*, 97-137.

Jennings, Z. (2001). Teacher education in selected countries in the Commonwealth Caribbean: The ideal of policy versus the reality of practice. *Comparative Education*, *37*(1), 107-134.

Jules, D., Miller, E. & Armstrong, L. A. (2000). *Caribbean Education Strategy Report.* St. Lucia: The World Bank.

Jules, V. & Panneflek, A. (2000). *Education For All in the Caribbean: Assessment 2000* (Subregional synthesis report, Volume I, Summary). Kingston, Jamaica: UNESCO. Available online: http://www.unesco.org/ext/field/carneid/synthesis-1.pdf

King, W. K. (1978a). *The interpretation of Piagetian developmental psychology in terms of primary science: The need for research.* In Proceedings of the Regional Primary Science Conference, pp. 84-94. University of the West Indies, Cave Hill, Barbados: Caribbean Regional Science Project.

King, W. K. (1978b). The development of an integrated science programme for the Caribbean. *Bulletin of Eastern Caribbean Affairs*, *4* (March/April), 1-14; (May/June), 23-30.

King, W. K. (1978c). Why teach integrated science? *West Indian Science and Technology*, *3*, 15-17.

King, W. K. (1979). Science and society: Implications for science education. *Caribbean Journal of Science Education*, *1*, 4-7.

King, W. K. (1982). Caribbean science education: A decade in review. *Hong Kong Science Teachers Journal*, *10*(2), 166-177.

King, W. K. (1987). Social and cultural responsibilities of science in the school curriculum: Objectives and teaching methods. *Caribbean Curriculum, 2*(1), 16-33.

King, W. K. & Brathwaite, W. E. (1991). School-based assessment in science: A Caribbean perspective. *School Science Review, 72*(261), 127-31.

Lancaster, C. & King, W. (Eds.). (1977). *Science education for progress: A Caribbean perspective.* London, UK: International Council of Associations for Science Education.

Lambert, E. N. (1974). New directions in science education in the 70s. *Journal of Education in Science for Trinidad and Tobago, 2*, 26-38.

Lewin. K. M. (2000a). *Mapping science education policy in developing countries.* Washington, DC: World Bank. Available online: http://www1.worldbank.org/education/scied/documents/Lewin-Mapping.pdf

Lewin, K. M. (2000b). *Linking science education to labour markets: Issues and strategies.* Washington, DC: World Bank. Available online: http://www1.worldbank.org/education/scied/documents/Lewin-Labor.pdf

Mark, P. (1978). Science education and development in the Caribbean: Desired directions. *West Indian Science and Technology, 3*, 11-13.

Miller, E. (2000a). *Education For All in the Caribbean in the 1990s: Retrospect and prospect.* Kingston, Jamaica: UNESCO. Available online: http://www.unesco.org/ext/field/carneid/monograph.pdf

Miller, E. (2000b). *Models in distance teaching in teacher education in Jamaica.* Paper presented at the Distance Education in Small States international conference hosted by the University of the West Indies Distance Education Centre (UWIDEC), Ocho Rios, Jamaica, 27–28 July 2000. Available online: http://www.col.org/resources/publications/SmallStates00/

Miller, E. (2001). A Western Caribbean profile: Innovating with ICT on a shoe-string. *TechKnowLogia, 3*(2), 70-74.

National Research Council. (1996). *National science education standards.* Washington, DC: National Academy Press.

Neathery, M. F. (1997). Elementary and secondary students' perceptions toward science: Correlations with gender, ethnicity, ability, grade, and science achievement. *Electronic Journal of Science Education, 2*(1). Available online: http://unr.edu/homepage/jcannon/ejse/neathery.html

OECS. (2002). *Organisation of Eastern Caribbean States.* Available online: http://www.oecs.org

OERU. (2002). *OECS Education Reform Unit.* Available online: http://www.oeru.org

Osin, L. (1998). *Computers in education in developing countries: Why and how?* Education and Technology Series, Vol. 3, No. 1. Washington, DC: World Bank.

Prout, A. (1985). Science, health and everyday knowledge: A case study of the common cold. *European Journal of Science Education, 4*(7), 399-406.

Rennie, L. J. & McClafferty, T. (1995). Using visits to interactive science and technology centers, museums, aquaria and zoos to promote learning in science. *Journal of Science Teacher Education*, 6 (4), 175-185.

Richardson, V. (1996). The case for formal research and practical inquiry in teacher education. In Frank B. Murray's (Ed.), *The teacher educator's handbook: Building a knowledge base for the preparation of teachers* (pp. 715-737). San Francisco, CA: Jossey-Bass Publishers.

Semper, R. J. (1990, November). Science museums as environments forlearning. *Physics Today*, 2-8.

Soyibo, K. (1999). Gender differences in Caribbean students' performance on a test of errors in biological labelling. *Research in Science and Technological Education, 17*(1), 75-82

Soyibo, K. (1995). Using concept maps to analyze textbook presentations of respiration. *American Biology Teacher, 57*(6), 344-351.

Soyibo, K. & Figueroa, M. (1998). ROSE and NonROSE students' perceptions of five psychosocial dimensions of their science practical activities. *Research in Science Education, 28*(3), 377-385.

Soyibo, K. & Hudson, A. (2000). Effects of computer-assisted instruction (CAI) on 11th graders' attitudes to biology and CAI and understanding of reproduction in plants and animals. *Research in Science and Technological Education, 18*(2), 191-199.

Sweeney, A. E. (2000). Tenure and promotion: Should you publish in electronic journals? *Journal of Electronic Publishing.* Available online: http://www.press.umich.edu/jep/06-02/sweeney.html

Sweeney, A. E. (2001a). E-scholarship and educational publishing in the 21st century: Implications for the academic community. *Educational Media International, 38*(1), 25-38.

Sweeney, A. E. (2001b). Incorporating multicultural and Science-Technology-Society issues into science teacher education courses: Successes, challenges and possibilities. *Journal of Science Teacher Education, 12*(1), 1-28.

Sweeney, A. E., Bula, O. A. & Cornett, J. W. (2001). The role of personal practice theories in the professional development of a beginning high school chemistry teacher. *Journal of Research in Science Teaching, 38*(4), 408-441.

Sweeney, A. E & Tobin, K. G. (Eds.). (2000). *Language, discourse and* learning in science: Improving professional practice through action research. Tallahassee, FL: Eisenhower Consortium for Mathematics and Science Education at SERVE.

Toppin, R. (2001). *The use and application of Information Technology in education in Barbados.* Presentation given by the

Honourable Ronald Toppin (Minister of Commerce, Consumer Affairs and Business Development, Government of Barbados) at the Foreign and Commonwealth Office E-Government Seminar April 4-6, 2001, London, England. Available online: http://www.kheta.ge/london/materials/national/barbados.doc

United Nations Educational Social and Cultural Organization (UNESCO). (1999). *Survey on curriculum development needs at the upper primary and secondary education levels in the Caribbean Sub-region, May 1999* (Annex 3; Jamaica: Curricular reforms). Available online: http://www.ibe.unesco.org/Regional/CaribbeanSurvey/caribbee.htm#annex3

University of the West Indies/The Commonwealth of Learning. (2001). *Distance education in small states.* International conference hosted by the University of the West Indies Distance Education Centre (UWIDEC), Ocho Rios, Jamaica, 27–28 July 2000. Available online: http://www.col.org/resources/publications/SmallStates00/

Ware, S. (1992a). *The education of secondary science teachers in developing countries.* Washington, DC: World Bank.

Ware, S. (1992b). *Secondary school science in developing countries: Status and issues.* Washington, DC: World Bank.

Williams, M. A. (1997a). Integrating concept mapping into science curriculum and instructional practice: Teacher experiences, observations, and recommendations for future projects. *Journal of Interactive Learning Research, 8*(3/4), 457-485.

Williams, M. A. (1997b). *A formative evaluation of self-instructional modules comprising information on methodology and procedural specifications for the Jamaican Reform Of Secondary Education (ROSE) science curriculum.* Unpublished Master's thesis at the Faculty of Educational Science and Technology, University of Twente, Enschede, The Netherlands.

Williams, M. A. (2002). *Science education research and practice in Jamaica.* Personal communication (February, 2002), Faculty of Educational Science and Technology, University of Twente, Enschede, The Netherlands.

ADDITIONAL REFERENCES OF INTEREST

Braveboy-Wagner, J. A. & Gayle, D. J. (Eds.). (1997). *Caribbean public policy: Regional, cultural, and socioeconomic issues for the 21st century.* Boulder, CO: Westview Press.

de la Rosa, C. L. (2000). *Improving science literacy and conservation in developing countries.* Available online at: http://www.actionbioscience.org/newfrontiers/delarosa.html

Jules, D. (1994). Adult education policy in micro-states: The case of the Caribbean. *Adult Education Policy and Performance: An International Perspective, 13*(3-4), 415-432.

Macedo, B. (2000). A panorama of science education in the Latin America and Caribbean region. *UNESCO International Science, Technology & Environmental Education Newsletter*, Vol. 25, Issue 3/4, 10-12.

Ware, S. (Ed.). (1999). *Science and environment education: Views from developing countries.* Washington, DC: World Bank. Available online: http://www1.worldbank.org/education/scied/documents/Ware/Ware1999.pdf

A DECADE OF RESEARCH IN TECHNOLOGY EDUCATION: IMPLICATIONS FOR CARIBBEAN CURRICULUM

Glenda Prime
Morgan State University
USA

Chapter 2

PERHAPS THE most significant curriculum innovation of the last two decades has been the inclusion of technology education as a component of general education. This innovation has been widespread, having occurred in the so-called developed and developing countries of both the East and West. The Caribbean territories have not been behind in this effort. The initiative to introduce this subject into the primary and secondary schools of the Caribbean was spearheaded by the Caribbean Community (CARICOM), with funding from the Common-wealth Secretariat and the Caribbean Region Institutional Strengthening Project(CRISP). The principal executing agency was the University of the West Indies, St. Augustine, Trinidad. The result of this initiative has been the production of *A Curriculum Guide for Technology Education for Primary and*

Secondary Schools in the CARICOM, Unit Plans in Technology Education for Forms in Lower secondary Schools in the CARICOM, and *A Curriculum for Technology Education at the Primary Level.* These curriculum materials are now in various stages of piloting and implementation in the different CARICOM territories.

In the international arena, the struggle to forge an identity for this new curriculum area has been marked by healthy debate both from within the field and among stakeholders outside of it. Research has played a major role in this debate. The first objective of this chapter is to synthesize the research of the last decade, with a view to identifying the major trends and issues that have been the focus of inquiry during that period. It will thus be a reflective statement of the current state of our knowledge in technology education, and by implication, will point to those areas where our knowledge is weakest. In this effort I stand on the shoulders of Foster (1992), who analyzed the research topics of graduate students in industrial education and technology education, of Zuga (1994), who reviewed research in technology education for the period, 1987 to 1993, and of Petrina (1998a), who reviewed research published in the JTE. The review presented in the first part of this chapter, will depart from these earlier ones in at least two important respects, (a) it makes a deliberate attempt to highlight contrasting emphases in the research conducted on opposite sides of the Atlantic, and (b) it seeks to stimulate the use of theoretical insights from other areas of educational research in the search for solutions to problems in technology education. The new school subject has had a much longer history outside of the Caribbean than within it, having been brought into being in the national curriculum of the UK with the 1988 Technology Order. In the USA the 1984 name change of the American Industrial Arts Association to the International Technology Education Association (ITEA), might be considered to be the launch of technology education as a school subject. By far the majority of the research in this field has therefore been generated outside of the Caribbean. The second part of the paper is an examination of the technology education curriculum initiatives of the Caribbean Community (CARICOM) in the light of the major findings of the research, with a view to making some suggestions about how Caribbean technology education curricula could benefit from the experiences of other countries while avoiding the pitfalls.

In reviewing the research I chose to focus mainly, though not exclusively, on work published in the Journal of Technology Education, as representing an important forum for reporting technology education research in the US, and the Journal of Technology Studies, also published in the US, and on the International Journal of Technology and Design Education, as one of the foremost technology education journals in the UK. I am not unaware of the fact that all of these publications are open to international researchers, but the country of origin of research is usually disclosed.

The method employed might be described as a modified content analysis. All of the articles published in these three journals in the period 1990 to 2002, were listed and classified according to content, as indicated by topic. Subsequent reading of an article often resulted in its being put into more than one category. Additional research articles were also utilized whenever references to them indicated that they might be germane to the specific topic under review. The categories of articles that emerged were, *nature of technology, technology curriculum, outcomes and assessment of technology education, children's thinking in technology, technology teacher education, and gender and values issues in technology education.* These are therefore indicative of the major themes in the technology education research over the past decade or so.

NATURE OF TECHNOLOGY

Discourse on the nature of technology education has been vibrant though inconclusive. At the center of the discussion has been the issue of whether or not there is a core of knowledge, which defines technology as a discipline, and if so, what knowledge constitutes that core. It is interesting that most of the pre-occupation with this issue has been evident among researchers in the U.S. In the U.K. there has been far greater emphasis on the pedagogical aspects of technology education than on questions to do with the nature of technology. Of course, assumptions about the nature of technology are implicit in views about the way it should be taught, but it is in the US literature that explicit discussion about the nature of technology is most evident.

There has been from some participants in the discourse, a persistent call for clarity about the conceptual structure of technology. Recently, the call has been set forth in the curriculum document Technology for All Americans (International Technology Education Association, 1996), which suggests that such a structure could be developed around the elements of process, content and contexts. Prior to that, DeVore (1970), Dugger (1988), Lewis (1991), Lewis and Gagel (1992), and Waetjen (1993) had all emphasized the importance of a determination of the disciplinary structure of technology. Indeed such a determination was seen as indispensable to the acceptance of the subject as having a rightful place in the school curriculum, to defining its desirable outcomes, and to a delineation of its content (Waetjen, 1993). After more than a decade of research that structure remains elusive.

Now as we enter the twenty first century, there is a growing belief that our energies may have been misplaced. Lewis (1999) opines, "we may have overdone the quest for structure, forgetting the grander importance and purpose of schooling and the educative role of the subject. " (p. 57). He, along with Zuga (1997), and Petrina (1998b), suggests that the obsession with disciplinary structure was influenced by political concerns for status, acceptance and control. Overdone or not, the quest for structure has yielded some valuable insights into the nature of technology and hence technology education.

One of these insights is the content/process dichotomy in technology. Lewis (1999) describes content and process, as "two pre-eminent ways in which technology educators conceive of curriculum" (p. 56). The effects of viewing these as two dichotomous paths in the subject is seen in sharp contrast when one compares technology education as purveyed through the U.K National Curriculum, with technology education as practiced in the U.S. In the former case, there is a clear emphasis on process, specifically, "designing and making", and in the latter, the continued attempt to find a conceptual structure around which to build the curriculum, has resulted in a curriculum in which children appear to be learning about technology to a greater extent than actually doing technology. It is indisputable that technology is both content and process, but the nature of each of these elements, and the relationship of the one to the other, needs to be understood, if we are not to follow the same fruitless path along which science education traveled in the 1970's, and from which it has since retreated, the path of designing curricula which emphasize one to the neglect of the other.

In 1995, Herschbach provided useful insight into the nature of the content or knowledge dimension of technology. He suggested that while technological knowledge has its own abstract concepts, theories and rules, it is not "a type of formal knowledge similar to that associated with the recognized academic disciplines " (p. 35). The "distinct epistemological characteristics" that distinguish between technological knowledge and formal knowledge is that the theories, rules, concepts, and structure and dynamics of change are really "applications to real situations" (Herschbach, 1995). If this is so, then the concepts and theories which constitute technological knowledge are necessarily multidimensional, since they are ordered, generated and used through activity and only derive meaning in the context of their application to particular real situations. Perhaps, it is this characteristic of technological knowledge that has defied attempts to impose a structure equivalent to that of the academic disciplines.

In developing his position on the nature of technological knowledge, Herschbach (1995) uses Vincenti's (1984) categorization of knowledge into descriptive, prescriptive and tacit knowledge. Technological knowledge comprises all these, the content is primarily descriptive and while it draws on the formal knowledge of such disciplines as mathematics, physics or biology, it is not itself a discipline, since its theories derive from specific applications and there is no "clearly generalizable, representative structure characterizing all of technology." (Herschbach, 1995,p.35)

Petrina (1998) makes the same point when he argues for a view of the nature of technology as an interdisciplinary or cross-disciplinary subject. He suggests that the whole issue of whether an area of human thought and activity constitutes a discipline or not is far more of a political question than an epistemological one and that the prolonged attempt to establish technology as a monodiscipline is a political move designed to confer status.

The past decade of research on the nature of technology suggests that in our efforts to determine what should comprise the technology curriculum, it might be more fruitful to turn our focus to a determination of what should be the outcomes of technology education. Such an approach would require that those aspects of technology that are most disclosive of the descriptive and prescriptive knowledge that we want children to acquire, and those experiences that foster the development of tacit knowledge of technological processes are the ones which should comprise the curriculum. These will of necessity be context-dependent. In this line of research the work of Petrina (1998) might provide some useful pointers and might prove to be seminal.

On the "process" side of the discussion, McCormick (1996) reminds us that technology is "more of an activity that a discrete body of knowledge" (p. 24). There is widespread acknowledgment that designing and making are at the core of technology, but the role of these processes in technology curricula has been the subject of much debate. Lewis (1999) makes a strong case for a greater role for *making* in technology curricula, while cautioning against any attempts to routinize this activity as though a single technological method exists. The context-specific nature of designing and making suggests that such an approach would not be a true reflection of technological activity. While affirming the centrality of designing and making in technological activity, it should not be forgotten that the purpose of these is as the means of solving problems. Without this dimension, designing and making become craft. Indeed, Waetjen (1989) and the ITEA (1996) have both identified problem-solving ability as one of the defining characteristics of a person who is technologically literate. It is this aspect of the nature of technology that Williams (2000), is cognizant of when he makes the case for a much broader conceptualization of the procedural knowledge component of technology and suggests that both manipulative and cognitive processes are aspects of the procedural knowledge involved in designing and making. The emphasis on one, to the neglect of the other, would represent a distortion. Perhaps the most instructive outcome of the content/process discussion has been the recognition of the importance of *context* in defining technology. Such processes as evaluation, communication, modeling, generating ideas, and research and investigation cannot be claimed as unique to technology but in the context of tools and materials they become technological processes. It is the context that makes them technological or not.

Another useful outcome of the "nature of technology" research has been the discourse on the notion of technological literacy. In spite of an acknowledged lack of clarity about its meaning, and claims that it is primarily an attention getting slogan (Barnett, 1995), the term technological literacy continues to be used to describe the outcome of technology education. Although a substantial body of literature had been written on the subject, the ITEA, in 1996, still made the call for the operationalizing of the term. Its recent documents (ITEA, 2000; ITEA, 2002) implicitly attempt such an operationalization in the articulation of a set of standards for technological literacy. The 2002 revised draft Standards implicitly describe the technologically literate person as one who possesses knowledge of the characteristics, scope and core concepts of technology, understands its relationship to society and the environment, has acquired a measure of design and problem-solving capability as well as some specific abilities related to the major categories of technological applications. Prior to the publication of the Standards, Lewis and Gagel (1992) and Waetjen (1993) had suggested that clarity about the term would continue to be elusive until the disciplinary structure of technology has been articulated. Discussions about the nature of technological literacy have become less evident in the literature since 2000. This might be an indication that for the community of technology educators some level of consensus about the construct has been achieved. On the other hand, Petrina (1998) suggests that we abandon the notion of literacy and replace it with "technological sensibility, participation and sagacity" as the intended outcomes of technology education. This might be more than a semantic exchange. Petrina describes a person possessing these qualities as "an adult with a complex, political understanding of technology, participating in a democratic, peaceful, sustainable society." While this, in its entirety, is an unrealistic goal for technology education, it calls to attention the political and social dimensions of technology, which are not often explicitly captured in attempts to describe the technologically literate person and hence, may not be addressed at all in technology curricula.

An even less researched aspect of technological literacy, than its characteristics, is the question of how it is to be assessed or measured. Waetjen (1993) and Lewis (1999) have both pointed to the developmental nature of literacy and of the need for measures that take account of the fact that manifestations of technological literacy would vary from one stage of the child's development to another.

CHILDREN'S THINKING IN TECHNOLOGY

Whether because of, or in spite of, the absence of any extensive debate in the UK about the disciplinary structure of technology, technology education has become far more firmly entrenched in the school curriculum in the UK than it has in the United States. In the UK, Design and Technology is part of the educational entitlement of all children, and that fact, along with the centrality of process in the curriculum makes it understandable that there has been considerable research directed at an understanding of children's thinking and learning in technology. By contrast, Lewis' (1999) call, in the US, for classroom research that focuses on children's experiences while learning technology has largely been ignored.

How do children acquire technological concepts? How do they acquire technological skills? Under what conditions might such acquisition occur most effectively? How do children think as they engage in design activities? Most of the research addressing such questions comes out of the UK and Canada. Perhaps the most important revelation yielded by such research is the consistent finding that children's problem-solving strategies do not match the linear, stylized, sequential models so prevalent in curriculum materials (Gustafson et al., 2000; Johnsey, 1997; Ridgeway & Passey, 1992; Roswell & Gustafson, 1998). Work by Davies (1996) suggests that even professional designers do not work according to these models and that indeed there is a similarity between children's instinctive design activities and those of professionals. This study also highlighted the importance of talk in children's design activities. Davies (1996) suggests that children use talk to order their thoughts and to relate their thoughts to external reality. It seems too that the processes of manipulating and modeling serve not only to externalize ideas but also to generate them, "as if the hand rather the brain were doing the thinking"(p.10). The implication of this for research is that there needs to be far greater emphasis on research which analyzes children's talk as they engage in technological activities as well as on research which places children at the focal point. The work of Twyford and Jarvinen (2000) is an example of such research. They employed qualitative methods to explore children's understanding of a technological concept after they had been engaged in a problem-solving task. The findings relate both to aspects of the nature of children's knowledge construction and to the conditions of such knowledge construction. These researchers suggest that technological knowledge occurs in social, interactive settings which are shared with members of the learning community, and that "children's understanding of technology can best be achieved by enabling them to work in the same spirit in which technologists work" (p.45). Such investigations hold the promise of helping us to understand those activities which are the very heart of technology education, that is the teaching and learning. One possible application of knowledge about children's intuitive thinking in technology is that if such thinking could be adequately characterized it could lead to the formulation of models for teaching in technology education. (Gustafson, Rowell & Guilbert, 2000).

Gustafson et al (1999) found evidence that children were not always successful in transferring ideas learned in one context to another. The conditions for such transfer need to be more fully explored, as does the role of knowledge and insight gained in informal settings. It appears that the same is true about the transfer of skills. Ridgeway and Passey (1992) report little evidence of skill transfer and suggest that some skills are better transferred than others and that factors such as contextualization, the nature of individual children's knowledge construction, and the amount of time spent learning the skill, might determine the success of transfer. In the previous section of this paper it was suggested that the context of children's problem solving was what gave meaning to the processes in which they engaged. Wolff-Michael (1996) suggests that the context of children's problem-solving tasks might be an important determinant of the learning outcomes that are realized. He stressed the importance of providing contexts which "bear similarity with out-of-school and workplace settings in terms of the social, material and open-ended aspects of the tasks to be completed" (p. 108). A final issue of great import for curriculum, is the development of criteria by which we can measure progression in children's technological thinking and competence. Work done by Anning (1994), involving detailed classroom observation is the kind of research required to further our understanding of the nature of progression in thinking. Solomon & Hall (1996) used cognitive psychology and the results of teacher action research to search for evidence of progression. They make a call for research that is "close to the ground" to advance our understanding in this area (p. 279). It is evident that this strand of research has been underserved but it is clearly pivotal to progress in technology education. The areas of curriculum development and teacher education must be the poorer for the neglect.

OUTCOMES AND ASSESSMENT IN TECHNOLOGY EDUCATION

An issue not unrelated to the nature of technology itself, is the question of what ought the outcomes of technology education to be, and how ought these outcomes to be assessed. Not surprisingly, the research on opposite sides of the Atlantic reflects differing emphases. The goal of technological literacy, accepted in the US, has proved to be much harder to define in terms that are operational enough to guide its assessment. The International Technology Education Association's *Standards for Technological Literacy* (2000) defines technology as the "ability to use, manage, assess, and understand technology." These standards attempt to identify the content for technology education but as yet the ITEA has not been able to offer much guidance with respect to assessment. Prime (1998), in discussing the assessment of technological literacy has suggested that conceptual fuzziness about the intended outcomes of the technology curriculum can often be masked by broadly described learning activities, but the design of assessment strategies requires utmost clarity about outcomes. Dyrenfurth et al (1991) described technological literacy as "multi-dimensional" and suggests that it includes practical, civic and cultural dimensions. These provide some broad areas for possible assessment but the imprecise nature of the concepts makes assessment difficult. There is therefore relatively little research in the US literature about assessment and less still that is empirical. A wide range of strategies has been advocated. These include portfolios, individual and group interviews, observation of performance, and paper- and- pencil tests. Some of these strategies are in keeping with current thinking about assessment, but in the absence of clarity about the outcomes which they are being used to assess, and with little empirical data about their use in technology education, their advocates have provided little guidance for those seeking to enact technology education curricula.

In the UK, on the other hand, where there has been a clear emphasis on process in the curriculum, "capability" rather than literacy has been accepted as the outcome of technology education. The notion of capability is easier to operationalise and a considerable amount of research has gone into defining, analyzing and assessing this quality. Anning (1994) sees capability as having four "generic" features that are common to any model of technology education These are: communicating ideas through drawing, acquiring technical skills, acquiring technical knowledge and evaluating (p.167). These four categories of learning outcomes could provide a basis for assessment. In a study of Canadian teachers' views of the nature of technological capability (Kozolanka & Olson, 1994), revealed that those teachers valued the affective outcomes of technology education as the most important aspect of capability. For them, capability was having the qualities that it would take to live and find employment. These include team-work, and social and intellectual habits like patience, perseverance and good work habits. These were secondary school teachers and the imminence of their students' entry into the world of work must have loomed large in their minds. Although some of these outcomes appear to go beyond what could reasonably be called either technological literacy or capability, nevertheless, the concerns of these teachers draw our attention to the less easily assessed outcomes of technology education, which are important whether the goal is conceived of as technological capability or literacy.

The Pupils' Attitudes to Technology (PATT) studies, originally developed in Europe but undertaken in several countries, have been the best-known attempts to measure the affective outcomes of technology education. These have generally suggested that girls have less positive attitudes to technology than do boys, although there have been some countries, including Trinidad and Tobago, where this has not been the case. Equally important has been the finding that school technology experience has not been a significant factor in determining children's attitudes to technology (Prime, 1990).

The notion of progression, alluded to earlier, has also received some attention in the UK literature. Both Anning (1994) and Solomon & Hall (1996) have begun the work of assessing technological capability from a developmental perspective, in which children's progress along dimensions of capability is being measured. As reported in the earlier discussion of technological literacy, Waetjen (1993) has pointed to the need to devise methods of assessment that take into account the developmental nature of technological literacy.

In sum, there appears to be consensus that technology outcomes include the development of a range of understandings, competencies and qualities with respect to technology. The competencies include practical capability, the ability to assess the impact of technology on societies, and the willingness to engage with the political and social dimensions of technology. It is in the relative weight assigned to these outcomes that curricular differences are apparent. It is possible that the interests of children in different cultural and economic contexts are best served by differing emphases on these curriculum goals. With respect to assessment of these outcomes, very few advances have been made. Current thinking about assessment has much to inform the field of technology education. The field of cognitive psychology has had a major influence on current approaches to assessment of learning. It is being recognized that, across the curriculum, it is when assessment targets cognitive skills, rather than discrete packets of knowledge, that it has its most beneficial effects on teaching and learning (Glaser, 1987). Further, current views on assessment suggest that assessment tasks ought to require holistic, integrated demonstrations of both declarative and procedural knowledge. (Royer et al, 1993). The work of Herschbach(1995) cited earlier in this chapter suggests that this might be particularly applicable to technology education. Kimbell (1994), reflecting on the assessment of technological capability emphasized the importance of holistic judgments, as opposed to those approaches which suggest an atomistic view of capability. Glaser & Silver (1996) have identified six dimensions of cognitive skills, which could provide some promising guidelines for the assessment of learning in technology using the holistic approach advocated by Kimbell. These are, knowledge organization and structure, mental models, automaticity, problem representation, procedural efficiency and meta-cognitive skills. While a discussion of the applicability of these to the goals of technology teaching is outside the scope of this chapter, it seems likely that the use of these dimensions might provide a useful framework for the design of assessment strategies that assess important outcomes of learning about technology.

THE TECHNOLOGY EDUCATION CURRICULUM

In this section I examine the trends and issues with respect to curriculum as I read them in the literature. My exploration of the research agrees with that of Zuga (1994) when she reported an overwhelming concern with curricular matters. The articles reviewed fell into three broad categories. There were those which addressed approaches to the content, organization and delivery of technology curricula, those which addressed indicators of quality in technology curricula and those which offered comparisons and descriptions of curricula from different countries. To be sure, the treatment of these issues reflected the ideological positions of the authors with respect to technology and curriculum, but seldom were these assumptions explicitly addressed. Indeed, it is apparent that what was generally lacking in the discourse was an effort to build a philosophical framework to guide curriculum. Aspects of such a framework include the justification for the curriculum, the particular curriculum orientation most applicable to technology curricula, and the epistemological considerations which should undergird the curriculum. The absence of such discussion within the field leaves the curriculum development and implementation processes open to being shaped by political ideology, by the historical antecedents of the technology curriculum, and by organizational factors such as availability of resources. It is true that such factors always influence the curriculum, but a clearly articulated philosophical base provides some measure of safeguard against the loss of focus that can occur when such factors exert too great an influence on the curriculum. An example of this is possibly the cause of the contentions surrounding the early attempts to introduce technology as general education in the UK, and the apparent lack of focus which prompted Lewis (1996) to critique the 1990 Technology Order as failing to "sharply define what was and what was not technology in the curriculum" (p. 227).

One explicit attempt to address the issue of a philosophical base for technology education was seen in a series of discussions carried in a special theme issue of the Journal of Technology Education (Vol. 6,no.2) that looked at technology from the perspective of the five curriculum orientations (Eisner & Vallance, 1974); the academic/ rationalist, the technical/utilitarian, intellectual processes, personal relevance and social reconstruction. The five articles in that series each outlined the basic tenets of one orientation and sought to determine its applicability to technology education (Erekson, 1992; Petrina, 1992; Johnson, 1992; Zuga, 1992; Herschbach, 1992) The importance of such discussion lies in the fact that orientations are more than just theoretical and have implications for all aspects of curriculum design. They provide a coherent rationale for decisions about selection of content, outcomes to be achieved and methods of delivery.

The concern to identify a unified conceptual structure for technology that was alluded to in an earlier section of this paper clearly arises from the academic-rationalist perspective, which dominates the field of curriculum. Recently it has been suggested that such a structure might not exist for technology, and indeed, technology curricula developed within the period under review do not exhibit such structure. It seems fair to say that the academic-rationalist perspective might not have much to offer the design of technology curricula. The technical/ utilitarian and the social reconstruction orientations are probably the ones that are most evident in existing technology curricula. The UK Design and Technology, with its emphasis on process is clearly technical/utilitarian, and the ITEA's emphasis on literacy seems to exemplify elements of the social reconstruction orientation. Zuga (1992) provides a useful exemplar of how this orientation could be used to guide the selection of content in technology. The personal relevance orientation based on the humanistic philosophy of education has been described by Petrina (1992) as absent from all technology curricula that have been described in the literature, yet this orientation seems to accord with many of the stated goals of technology education and indeed Layton (1992) and Barnett (1995) have suggested that a humanistic framework might provide a basis for forging connections between technology and the rest of the curriculum.

The historical roots of technology in the curriculum continue to exert a profound influence on the organization and delivery of technology education curricula. The change from industrial arts to technology education was intended to signify a shift in emphasis from the craft skills to problem-solving, and from vocational preparation to general education. Today, approximately two decades after the American Industrial Arts Association changed its name to the International Technology Education Association, technology educators are still grappling with the need to articulate the relationship between technology education and work and with the basis for justifying technology education as a part of general education. Medway (1992), commenting on the origin of the subject in the UK, says that it was both the needs of modern industry as well as the need to gain status that gave impetus to the change from industrial arts to technology education. "The new subject would be both intellectually stimulating and legitimate in the eyes of career-minded students and their parents" (Medway 1992, p. 4). The continuing influence of industrial arts is seen in the fact that the most frequently proposed content organizers for technology education curricula are the work- place related technologies of production, communication, transportation and the bio-related technologies, leading Sanders (2001) to ask whether technology education represents a new paradigm or old wine. In a bold break with current practice, Savage (2001) has suggested that in addition to these traditional content organizers technology education curricula of the future should employ value-laden issues like "evolution, communication, spirituality, intelligence, consumerism and life cycles" as the new curriculum organizers so as to emphasize the human dimensions of technology (p.4).

With respect to delivery of technology education curricula, there were many calls, particularly at the beginning of the decade of the nineties, for integration of the technology curriculum with mathematics and science (Gloeckner, 1991) but such calls have been criticized as lacking in conceptual warrant, since the transferability of mathematics and science knowledge to children's technological problem-solving has not been demonstrated. It has been suggested that the calls for integration were motivated by a desire to get the subject established through linking it with mathematics and science, two firmly entrenched areas of the curriculum (Foster, 1994). Studies which attempted to show the effectiveness of integrated modules failed to do so (Childress, 1996). Towards the latter part of the nineties, concern shifted away from integration towards an identification of the most effective curriculum emphases and methods of delivery. Foster & Wright (1996) surveyed a number of leaders in the field as to their opinions about the most effective models for the design of technology curricula. The results suggested that these experts thought that the approach should change as the learner progressed from the elementary through high school grades. At the elementary level the preferred approach is one which was designated as *constructive methodology.* This approach placed emphasis on "hands-on activities". At the middle school, the experts favored a *modular approach.* This was essentially an organizational approach which suggested that the curriculum be delivered through self-contained units. At the level of the high school, mathematics/science/technology integration was thought to be most appropriate. It should be noted that these views are by no means typical of the views of technology educators. At all levels *design and problem solving* was rated highly. Continuing his contribution to the, discourse on approaches to curriculum, Foster (1997) classified existing approaches to elementary school technology into those which were organized around *process*, those which emphasized *content,* and those which saw technology not as having an independent place in the curriculum, but as a means of helping pupils to achieve the goals of other curriculum areas. The issue of whether or not technology education should be a separate subject or should be integrated with other curriculum areas has continued to receive much attention in the literature. It would appear that for the most part the subject is seen as having a place in the curriculum in its own right, although in very recent times, the pendulum has begun to swing in the direction of integration (LaPorte, 2002).

The kinds of learning experiences which are likely to result in the attainment of the desired outcomes are those in which learners are engaged in the solution of "ill-defined, multifaceted real-world problems" (Lavonen, Meisalo & Lattu, 2001 p.21), as opposed to those in which students replicate artifacts in teacher-dominated classrooms. Learning environments in which teachers and learners share risk-taking, (Davies, 2000) are thought to foster the creative problem-solving which is the core content of technology education.

Quality in technology education was another curriculum issue that came into prominence in the later years of the decade. Hill & Smith (1998), working in a Canadian context and Clarke & Wenig, (1999), describing a US case study, attempted to identify some quality indicators for technology education. In the former case, the findings represented the perspectives of one classroom teacher and his students. It is interesting that in this study it was the social dimensions of learning technology that featured most prominently in participants' assessment of what was good about their technology classes. In the second study, indicators of quality were gleaned from a survey of experts. Here the indicators related to philosophy and mission, instructional quality, and teacher professional development, among others.

An instructive component of the discourse about curriculum in technology education was the descriptions and comparisons of curricula across countries. Lewis (1996), writing about the value of country case studies, suggested that such analyses "can lead to insight that enlarges our vision of the possibilities of the subject" (p. 221). A description of technology education in South Africa, by Ankiewicz (1995), does just that. Here the subject, still in its developmental stages, is seen as having a role to play in the social and economic transformation of the country. Technology is seen as part of the broad general education needed to develop citizens who possess the "higher cognitive skills, creative thinking and problem-solving" abilities, which in one view, is the way to redress "a critical shortage of technological expertise" (p. 248). Ankiewicz sees the importance of making the "technological process" central in technology education to ensure that the process is" transformative" (p. 253). He advocates a pedagogy that is " participatory, critical, values-oriented, multi-cultural, student-centered, experiential, research-minded and interdisiciplinary"(p.253). The subject is seen as having a role to play in the removal of social, economic, and gender inequalities that were the legacy of the previous social order. It is to be taught as a separate subject and is compulsory for the first nine years of schooling. Lewis' (1996) comparison of technology curriculum in the US and the UK served to highlight some of the contrasting aspects of the two approaches, in particular, the content/process distinction and the concomitant literacy/capability issue. Gradwell (1996) traced the historical roots of technology education in England, France, and the United States and suggests that the differences in emphases that are evident in these countries' contemporary technology curricula can be accounted for by their differing histories. Caribbean territories, like many other of developing countries are in the process of introducing technology education as a component of general education and it is evident that in such contexts the subject is seen as having a major role to play in economic transformation through its perceived potential for producing the kind of workforce deemed to be best suited to effecting such a transformation. It is interesting that even though this is the case, it is the generalized life competencies rather than work related skills that are the valued outcomes of technology education. Such skills as,

> leadership, initiative, ability to think and adapt to change, flexibility, ability to transfer skills from one context to another, to work in teams, to be technically competent and proficient, to be able to solve problems and to apply knowledge, skills and competencies in any context (Ogunmola, 2001).

Further, the vision for technology, articulated by Ogunmola, is that it should not merely be an add-on to the curriculum but that it should be a "major contributor to a re-defined curriculum of general education in which practical capability moves to center stage and which is interdisciplinary and has no sovereign subject" (Ogunmola, 2001). It is clear that the field could benefit greatly from studies of curricula from other countries beside the US and the UK, particularly the so-called developing countries, in which technology curricula are enacted in social and economic contexts that are very different from those of the developed countries. These were however very sparsely represented in the literature.

The fore-going review of the curriculum landscape of technology education brings into focus some areas in which we need to clarify our thinking. The first of these has to do with the question of the justification for the place of technology in the curriculum. Academicians in the field need to base their advocacy on a firm footing if policy-makers and other stakeholders, especially teachers, are to be convinced to commit their resources to this subject. The "technology as a discipline" argument, essentially an academic/rationalist one, is hardly sustainable in the light of the fact that there appears to be no unified conceptual structure that defines all technology. All of the curriculum studies reviewed allude to the national economic benefits and to the personal relevance outcomes to be derived from adoption of technology education. These benefits ought to be clearly spelled out and their implications for the curriculum need to be identified. The way in which they are articulated must be a response to local social and economic conditions. The result of this might be that in both form and content technology education curricula look very different from one context to another but that need not be cause for concern. Indeed if we take the stance that it is the nature of technology that it is diverse, then the differences, will not be considered as tensions, but rather, as evidence of its rich potential to foster human development. Such differences as content versus process, and vocational versus general education and practice versus theory become questions of balance when we recognize that practical capability, the ability to function in the real world, is actually the result of a mix of all these. Perhaps our quest for unity of content in the field has been misguided.

Another curriculum issue has to do with the teaching strategies that are most effective in the teaching of technology. Except for a small number of studies, particularly those done in the UK, we have not addressed this aspect of curriculum. Currently held views from the field of cognitive psychology, particularly, situated cognition, might be instructive in this regard, since it directly addresses the relationship between practice and theory. The links between technology and other areas of the curriculum, especially, but not exclusively, science and mathematics, are obvious, but we do not know much about how to help children to transform knowledge acquired in these areas into a form in which it can be used in their technological activities.

TECHNOLOGY TEACHER EDUCATION

It is almost ironic that while scholars in the field have been engaged in debating the nature of technology, redefining the curriculum and advocating for technological literacy for all, they have given scant attention to recruiting and preparing teachers to enact the technology curriculum. Relatively little of the research of the nineties and beyond has had teacher education for technology as its focus. Volk(1997), surveying the trends in enrollment in technology teacher education programs made a bleak prediction about the possible demise of technology as a school subject unless the downward trend in the numbers of new teacher recruits is reversed. At least a part of the reason for the small number of teacher recruits in technology education has to do with the political concerns of status and equity. It is often the case that technology is not accorded the same status as the academic subjects. Hansen (1996) has suggested that political issues such as status ought to be an explicit area to be addressed in technology teacher preparation. Clearly, efforts must be made to increase the number of students who seek careers in teaching technology.

Wright & Custer (1998) surveyed approximately five hundred technology teacher education students about the factors which influenced their decisions to become technology education teachers. The findings of that study might have implications for teacher education recruitment practices. By far the most influential factors influencing those students in their decision to become technology teachers was their personal interests and hobbies. The second and third factors were their positive school experiences in industrial arts or technology education, and the positive role models played by industrial arts or technology teachers. These last two factors are dependent on the presence of knowledgeable and effective teachers. The dilemma is that given the general shortage of technology education teachers, relatively few high school students are having the kinds of experiences that might influence them into technology teaching.

Far more difficult than recruiting adequate numbers of technology education teachers is the problem of preparing them to do the job effectively. Research that helps to define what it is that technology teachers need to know and be able to do is scarce. What experiences prepare teachers to transform their own knowledge for the purpose of teaching? How do teachers' own experiences with technology and the conditions of their own learning of technological concepts influence how they teach? According to Feiman-Nemser (1990) the research on technology teacher education is lacking a conceptual framework to provide answers to these questions and to guide practice. Hansen (1993) proposed a model for technology teacher preparation that combines reflection and action. The four elements of the model are; technological foundations, included in which are the history of technology, the sociology of work and the sociology of technology education; pedagogical knowledge, that knowledge of the subject matter that allows the teacher to determine the core ideas of the subject that can be taught through experiences with a specific topic; curriculum theory; and, knowledge of the profession.

The absence of a long tradition within the field also impacts on the technology teaching profession in a number of ways. The number of technology teacher training programs is relatively small so that if the subject gains the kind of widespread implementation that its proponents advocate, alternative routes of teacher preparation will have to be found. Teachers from other disciplines like science will undoubtedly join the technology teaching force, many will be former industrial arts teachers and in the US many have already come from industry. This circumstance poses peculiar challenges for teacher preparation programs. Each discipline has its distinct culture and in the absence of deliberate strategies to enculturate teachers into technology, teachers coming from other disciplines might be unable to overcome the pervasive influences of their own prior experiences in other disciplines or in the workplace. Of particular concern is the emphasis on discursive as opposed to practical knowledge that characterizes so much of school learning but which is antithetical to the nature of technology. Clearly, the field of technology teacher education needs to be the focus of continued research.

VALUES AND GENDER ISSUES

In this section of the paper I discuss two distinct but related issues in technology education. It is widely recognized within the field that technology is a value-laden enterprise.

> There is a sense in which, technology, both its products and its processes, represents the embodiment of the culture. We create the things we value, the things we think beautiful or useful. We devise tools, machines and systems to accomplish the ends we value......Our beliefs, our values, our philosophies, our experiences, in short our

> *culture* is made manifest in the artefacts and systems we create (Prime, 1993, p. 30).

Conway (1994) suggests that "the centrality of value judgments in technology has important educational implications" (p. 109). It is true, however that these implications have not received the attention that they deserve. Typically, technology courses have been concerned with techniques of designing and making things that serve human needs or generate wealth, but has not addressed the more fundamental questions about whether those things should be made at all. Barnett (1994) reminds us that,

> Traditionally, technology courses have concentrated on technique, on questions of *how*, but goals of technological literacy require serious consideration of purposes and outcomes – questions of *why* and *with what results.* (p. 53).

The World Council of Associations of Technology Education (WOCATE) endorses a view of technological literacy as requiring that people should be able to understand and control technology. The realization of this goal requires explicit attention to the values issues that are inherent in Barnett's questions of *why* and *with what results.* Layton (1992) affirms that there is a need to bring values up to " the light of day" in the teaching and learning of Design and Technology.

There are at least two compelling reasons why attention to values in technology education is imperative. The first is that real world technology is the result of value choices. Most often the values guiding technological choices are technical and economic values... does it work efficiently and will it make money? However, technological processes and products always reflect other value choices such as aesthetic, social and environmental considerations. School technology, while it cannot exactly mirror real world technology must address these issues or it will not reflect the true nature of technology. The second reason is that technology education must prepare students to control and not merely use technology. The ability to control technology is dependent on the ability to understand its impact on individuals and society, and to make value- based judgments about how technology would be allowed to influence society.

There is relatively little research to guide technology education practitioners in the design of learning experiences that would bring values issues "into the light of day" in technology curricula. The evaluation of their own technological products and those of others is an activity that lends itself to engagement with values issues, and should be given a prominent place in the technology education curriculum. Prime (1993) has proposed a typology of values that includes aesthetic, social, cultural, gender and environmental values as well as the more usual technical and economic ones and suggests that these could be used to frame questions that children could be encouraged to ask of their own technological solutions as well as of those in the real world. The Nuffield Foundation Design and Technology curriculum has proposed the concept of *winners and losers*. Every technology brings benefits to some while causing loss to others. Asking who wins and who loses with respect to technological products or systems is an effective means of engaging children with the values aspect of technology.

The concept of appropriate technology, articulated in the work of Budgett-Meakin (1992), draws attention to the need to deliberately examine the values that are hidden in every technology and to make choices to reject, employ, modify or design technologies on the basis of conscious value- based judgments. In the so-called developing countries, such as the Caribbean territories, who are often the users of technologies transferred from other cultures, this is vital, since as Ursula Franklin (1992) reminds us technology has the power to reproduce in users, the social and cultural conditions of the creators.

The issue of gender in technology is itself a value issue. Asking who wins and who losses in technology often reveals otherwise unrecognized differences in the way that men and women are affected by specific technologies. A widespread finding of the Pupils Attitudes to Technology (PATT) studies alluded to earlier, is that girls have less positive attitudes to technology than do boys. It is interesting that of the two countries, where this difference did not hold true, Trinidad and Tobago was one and Nigeria was the other (Prime, 1990). This highlights the strong cultural component that must be taken into account in considerations of gender. Another gender issue that might influence the involvement of girls and women in technology has to do with the gender relations in the school and workplace. In a profession that is as predominantly female as teaching is, it is remarkable that this gender balance is reversed in technology teaching. There is also the perception that women have fewer opportunities for promotion to the higher levels of technological professions. At a more fundamental level, some like Zuga (1999) have suggested that there is need for research that investigates "women's ways of knowing" and the relationship between those ways and the practice and teaching of technology.

CONCLUSIONS

This paper has reviewed some aspects of the research in technology education that has been published over the last decade. Following is an attempt to capture this review in a few succinct statements. They are offered by way of a summary, with the knowledge that much is inevitably lost in any attempt to distill complex ideas into short statements.

1. Technology cannot claim a unique disciplinary structure. Its knowledges are declarative, procedural and tacit and the subject draws on several disciplines. The term "technological literacy has yet to be defined operationally and is currently being used in a very general sense to connote all of the desirable outcomes of technology education.

2. Little progress has been made in the area of assessment of technology learning outcomes. Assessment should be holistic and contextualized and should include the conative aspects of technological competence.

3. The "design process," widely conceived of as a uniform sequence, either linear or cyclical, does not stand up to the reality of either children's or designers' practice.

4. In children's thinking, knowledge does not transfer automatically from other areas of the curriculum, even related ones like mathematics or science, to their technological problem-solving.

5. Country comparisons of technological curricula suggest that technology is valued most for its expected contribution to economic growth. This goal is seen as being best served by developing broad generalizable technical and non-technical competencies, as opposed to narrow occupational skills.

6. Approaches to the content and organization of technology education curricula should be responsive to local cultural contexts.

7. A conceptual framework for technology teacher education is needed that takes into account the varying experiential backgrounds from which technology teachers are likely to come.

8. Values are central to technology and should be explicitly addressed in technology education.

THE CARICOM TECHNOLOGY EDUCATION INITIATIVE

In this section of the paper, I attempt to look at the CARICOM technology education curriculum for primary and lower secondary schools in the light of the research discussed in the previous sections. It is true that most of this research was generated outside of the Caribbean and with a few exceptions in the so-called developed world, yet I believe that if studied with an understanding of the peculiar characteristics of the Caribbean in mind, it can inform our own curriculum development and implementation efforts in such a way that we benefit from the insights gained, and avoid the mistakes made in other countries. In an editorial article of the International Journal of Technology Education, Cajas (2000) pointed to the growing number of international researchers who were publishing research in technology education as evidence of the fact that technology education was a widespread phenomenon. He further observed that the "problems and issues were amazingly similar from one country to another and that lines of inquiry somehow take similar albeit independent courses" (p. 76).

It is the nature of curriculum that it is always in process. This is particularly the case for a subject like technology education which lacks an established tradition as a school subject. Indeed the architects of the CARICOM technology education curriculum emphasized that the unit plans which they developed for primary and lower secondary schools were intended to be modified in response to the needs and circumstances of the different territories. It is with this in view that I make the observations which follow, in hope of contributing to the development of a curriculum which would prepare citizens of the Caribbean to live confidently and creatively in a world that is increasingly dominated by technology. The UK example is instructive in this regard. The Technology Order which established technology education as a school subject in England and Wales was issued in 1988. The demands which the new subject made on teachers who were struggling to understand its requirements, proved to be so difficult that within a few years a new, considerably modified curriculum was issued. This is not by any means to suggest that this would be the case with the CARICOM curriculum but only to suggest that curriculum development often benefits from repeated iterations.

Prior to the CARICOM technology education initiative, several member countries had begun to move in the direction of curriculum development for technology education. In the early 1990's, for example, the Ministry of Education in Trinidad and Tobago established a multi-disciplinary committee, whose responsibility was to develop guidelines for the development of a technology studies curriculum. Subsequent national curriculum policy documents included technology studies as a component of the educational provision at the primary and secondary levels, but conceptually the subject bore the impress of its curriculum antecedent and was more vocational in its emphasis than current thinking about technology education suggests. For a variety of reasons technology studies never became firmly established in the curriculum. A mere handful of Caribbean researchers undertook work in this field so there is relatively little empirical work to inform or document the curriculum process for technology education in the Caribbean.

The first output of the CARICOM technology education initiative was the *Blueprint for the Introduction of Technology Education in the Curriculum of Primary and Secondary Schools in the CARICOM*, in 1998. The decision to initiate a curriculum in technology education in the CARICOM was born of the concerns of member states about the impact of the region's under-application of technology and the effect that that had on the pursuit of the region's development goals. The CARICOM secretariat therefore engaged the services of the Education Research Center, at Mona , Jamaica to undertake the development of a blueprint to guide technology education curriculum development. Following the second revision of the *Blueprint,* a curriculum development project was undertaken, with the School of Education, University of the West Indies as the executing agency. The work was undertaken in two curriculum- writing workshops, with Dr Edrick Gift as consultant and three facilitators. The participants in the workshop represented a number of CARICOM member states. The outputs of those workshops were four documents, *A Curriculum Guide for Technology Education for Primary and Secondary Schools in the CARICOM; Preparations for the Introduction of a Curriculum in Technology Education into the Primary lower Secondary Schools in the CARICOM :Report on Workshop II: A Curriculum for Technology Education at the Primary Level;* and *Unit Plans in Technology Education for forms in lower secondary schools in the CARICOM.*

IMPLEMENTATION ISSUES

To date, the process of development of this innovation can be described as a study in exemplary practice. At all stages of the process, from the articulation of the need for the innovation expressed in the *Blueprint for the Introduction of Technology Education in the Curriculum of Primary and Secondary Schools in the CARICOM,* to the development of the *Curriculum Guide for Technology Education for Primary and Secondary Schools in the CARICOM,* to the preparation of change agents, there was the widest possible involvement of the relevant stakeholders. This should ensure the level of ownership of the innovation needed for its success. In addition, the personnel involved in these activities were themselves high- ranking officials in the education systems of the member countries. This speaks to the degree of commitment to the innovation. The document titled *Preparation for the Introduction of a Curriculum in Technology Education into the Primary and secondary Schools in the CARICOM* which reports on the activities of the second of two curriculum workshops, provides detailed strategies for dissemination and implementation, which if followed would help to ensure the success of this vitally important and ambitious innovation.

THE CARICOM PHILOSOPHY

Gift (2001) identified five components of a curriculum philosophy about which workshop participants were familiarized during the curriculum development activity. These were described as the strongly held beliefs of stakeholders. They were: a view of the existing realities of the national, regional and international realities which form the context of the curriculum, consensus about the structure of the subject discipline, moral and ethical issues relevant to the subject, a notion of the good society which the curriculum would foster and an image of the human person whose good the curriculum would promote (p.14). I wish to make some observations about the first two of these as they relate to CARICOM technology education. With respect to the first, "the existing realities of the national, regional and international environments", the *Blueprint,* in outlining the need for a technology education curriculum, described the CARICOM member states as being characterized by "underdeveloped human resources, underemployment and unemployment, under-application of technology, lack of emphasis on research and development and a heavy dependence on foreign imports"(p.1) and implied that education, and specifically technology education should contribute to the alleviation of these conditions. Further, The 17th Meeting of CARICOM Heads of Government, held in Barbados in 1996, outlined a " vision for what technology education should accomplish for the region"(Gift, 2001, p. 13). The vision included technological development and employment generation, self-reliance for entrepreneurship, enhancement of the quality of the labor force and the procurement of a competitive edge for the free market system (p. 13).

It is clear that in the minds of the political directorate and perhaps the policy makers, the need for technology education was predicated on labour market needs. In its statement of philosophy, the *Blueprint* declares that technology education "should be designed to equip individuals with the knowledge, competencies, skills, values and attitudes required to meet the needs of industry, business and government in order for the region to compete in the world economy and to effectively cope with an emerging technological society" (p. 14). It does also identify the more humanistic goal of developing a "creative and adaptive individual"(p. 13), but even this is seen in the context of solving the development problems of the region. The overriding concern appears to be the manpower needs of the region. Concern for manpower needs and for economic development is not inappropriate. However when this becomes the raison d'etre for technology education in the school curriculum, there is a risk that the curriculum takes on a decidedly occupational focus and is likely to become little more than a renamed programme of vocational education. The question to be considered is whether or not a study of technology has a contribution to make to the development of children's thinking that is independent of occupational choice or labour market demands. Are manpower concerns the only justification for the inclusion of technology in the education of children?

In fact, a review of the unit plans for lower secondary schools does indeed suggest that the developers were strongly influenced by the manpower concerns expressed by the political directorate and held a view of technology education as education for learning about the world of work. Gone is the emphasis on narrowly defined occupational skills that characterized the Industrial Arts curriculum but in its place is a curriculum that is heavily knowledge oriented with relatively little emphasis on technological *capability* or technological thinking. The primary level curriculum is more activity oriented as befits a curriculum for primary aged learners but even here there does not appear to be enough emphasis on capability as developed through designing and making in accordance with a design brief. There is sufficient evidence in the research that even young children are capable of engaging in such tasks. What is even less evident in the implied learning experiences, is the evaluation of products which is a vital element of technological capability. This issue relates to the goals of technology education and to a determination of how technology education relates to work. In this dilemma the CARICOM curriculum developers are not alone. Sanders (2000) in a discussion of the status of technology education practice in the USA observes that in terms of content there is a strongly evident industrial arts/ vocational education legacy and suggests that the subject still needs to define itself. He further observes that there is need for a clear articulation of the relationship between technology education and vocational education.

Technology education is undeniably related to work, not in the sense of narrow occupational skills but in the sense of broad competencies that prepare citizens to understand and respond to technology both in the workplace and in life outside of the workplace. In the review of research on the nature of technology, discussed in an earlier section of this paper, technology was described as consisting of both content and process (Lewis, 1999). The process aspect is largely "designing and making". This is the aspect of technology which needs greater emphasis in the CARICOM curriculum. Herschbach's (1995) use of "descriptive, prescriptive and tacit" to describe technological knowledge also affirms the centrality of designing and making in technological activity, for it is through these processes that children acquire tacit knowledge of technological processes. It should be borne in mind that designing and making is the means of technological problem-solving and that problem-solving involves the educationally valuable component of evaluation of products against predetermined criteria. These activities are the very heart of technology. Cajas (2000) emphatically declares that "the essence, the very soul of technology education is *doing* ......*doing* (or practice) forms the core of the content in the field. It would seem that students being taught from the CARICOM curriculum would not experience much *doing* of technology.

It is interesting that the CARICOM curriculum does not explicitly espouse the goal of technological literacy as a desired outcome of the curriculum. It is true that some debate still surrounds the concept, but its usefulness lies in the fact that it safeguards the curriculum from undue emphasis on narrow vocational preparation. Most definitions of technological literacy include some element of capability, the essential element of which is problem-solving through designing and making. This, in my view, has not been sufficiently developed in the CARICOM technology education curriculum. One way around the problem might be in a re-conceptualization of the curriculum organization. The use of fields of technology as the curriculum organizer makes it easy to fall into the trap of undue emphasis on descriptive knowledge to the neglect of other aspects of technological knowledge. Perhaps the use of key technological *concepts*, as curriculum organizers, rather than fields of technological applications, might better serve the cause of literacy and allow for the development of technological competence. Such concepts as systems, feedback and control, trade-offs, cost-benefit considerations could possibly be used as curriculum organizers and activities could be designed which would provide learners with opportunities to explore the manifestations of these key concepts in the different fields of technology, to employ them in their own designs and to use those concepts as the basis for evaluating their own technological products and those of others. The New Zealand technology education offers a useful example of how a curriculum to achieve technological literacy could be development through three interwoven curricular strands; knowledge and understanding of key concepts, capability in designing and making and the relationship between technology and society (Compton and Jones,1998). The use of key concepts seems to lend it self better to the realization of these outcomes. In such an approach, the selection of content for the curriculum would be driven not by fields of technology, but rather by those aspects of technology which are disclosive of the key concepts which a person has to have acquired in order to function competently in life and in the workplace. The content could then be chosen in a manner that would still allow exposure to the fields of technology, which in some curricula include other categorizations than the four used in the CARICOM curriculum. An added benefit of this approach would be that it could allow a reduction in what appears to be a rather voluminous curriculum, without sacrificing technological capability. Further, key concepts could be introduced and revisited at increasing levels of complexity in a manner that is consistent with the learners' developmental stage.

It is the understanding of broad pervasive technological concepts rather than knowledge of specific fields of technology, that makes for a technologically literate person, who can function creatively and with confidence and adaptability in a changing technological scene. We should be careful not to emphasize *knowledge* to the neglect of *capability* lest we prepare citizens to be merely users rather than creators of technology. I believe that these considerations should inform subsequent iterations of the CARICOM technology education curriculum.

Without wishing to belabour the point, another issue needs to be raised with respect to the importance of designing and making in technology education curricula for the CARICOM region. The notion of appropriate technology is particularly relevant to developing countries like those of the CARICOM region. Appropriate technologies are those which are socially, culturally and environmentally benign to the societies where they are being used. The peculiar conditions of small and developing countries make it likely that technologies created in the developed world would at least in some ways, be inappropriate when transferred to developing ones. Such technologies may have a negative impact on the environment, or may be incongruent with the social and cultural norms of the recipient society. Indigenous technologies are more likely to reflect the values and norms of the people who design and use them and would thus be more appropriate. Design capability is thus indispensable to the education of citizens of small and developing countries, who need to develop the competence to advance the development of such countries in ways that are appropriate. Indeed, so critical is this concept in the development of technologically literate citizens that it should be considered a key concept and be extensively treated in the CARICOM curriculum.

It is clear that the curriculum developers are not unaware of the importance of designing and making in technology education. This is evident in the discussion of the principles which should guide the selection of content and the discussion of appropriate teaching/learning strategies.(Gift, 2001). It is in the development of the unit plans and suggested lessons that the emphasis on designing and making seems to be less evident than the discussion implies.

CHILDREN'S THINKING IN THE CARICOM CURRICULUM

Does technology education have a peculiar contribution to make to the development of children's thinking? In the review of literature on this issue that was presented in an earlier section of this paper, it was observed that relatively little is known about the way in which children think while engaged in technological activity. It has been suggested that technology is the area of the curriculum that best provides children with an opportunity to externalize their thinking and judge the outcomes of their thinking in concrete ways. Twyford and Jarvinen (2000) suggest that direct interaction with tools and models contributes to the acquisition of technological concepts. This outcome is another benefit that could be derived from increasing the practical component of the CARICOM curriculum.

DELIVERY MODES FOR CARICOM TECHNOLOGY

The decision to employ a multi-disciplinary approach to the delivery of the CARICOM primary technology education curriculum is very much in keeping with current trends in the research, although this was not always the case, and is still not uncontested. However, a recent Gallup poll conducted by the International Technology Education Association showed that while ninety seven percent of the poll respondents believed that technology education should be part of the school curriculum, two thirds said that it should be integrated into other subjects rather than taught as a separate subject. (ITEA, 2000). There are those who believe this to be true for all levels of the school system (National Academy of Engineering and National Research Council. 2002). The developers of the CARICOM curriculum based their decision to use the separate subject approach at the lower secondary level on two main premises the first is that integration might result in dilution of the content and the loss of important concepts and skills. The second is that technology is a discipline in its own right. Gift (2001) presents arguments in support of that position. An analysis of the literature on the nature of technology reveals anything but consensus on the question of whether or not technology has the structure of the " recognized academic disciplines" (Herschbach, 1995). I believe that the argument is largely an academic one and that as a recognized and pervasive area of human activity, distinct from other areas of human enterprise, technology needs to be part of the education of the young and that it should be presented in a manner that is true to its manifestation in society. This in my view, is justification enough for its treatment as a separate subject. The concern for the loss of important aspects of the subject if taught in an interdisciplinary manner is a compelling one. However, in a recent editorial in the International Journal of Technology Education the view was advanced that "a new paradigm for technological literacy is unfolding" in which the role of technology teachers and their "dedicated courses in technology" was uncertain. (Laporte, 2002, p. 4). The article suggested that widespread adoption of dedicated technology courses was unlikely and that in such a scenario the inclusion of technology subject matter in other academic areas was the surest way to increase visibility of technology. There are obviously conflicting viewpoints on this issue. Some constituencies of interest advocate the separate subject approach and others the integrated approach. Clearly the jury is still out on this issue.

ASSESSMENT

The CARICOM curriculum quite appropriately promotes the use of alternative assessment strategies, such as displays of students' work, group projects and portfolios. These approaches to assessment serve to externalize children's thinking and thus are integral components of instruction. They do however pose challenges when assessment is to be used for the more social purposes of certification and access to further education. The nature of technology is such that the strategies used to assess learning must be open-ended and highly contextualized, but these characteristics are often in conflict with the notions of validity and reliability that guide the design of assessment procedures used by the Caribbean Examinations Council and most other examining bodies. These issues have not been addressed by the CARICOM documents.Future modifications might incorporate some effort to assess creativity since this is an indispensable aspect of the technological product. It should be borne in mind that assessment should not be confined to technological products but that technological processes should also be assessed since these are indicators of children's thinking while doing technology.

VALUES IN THE CARICOM CURRICULUM

The discussion of the place of values in technology in an earlier section of the paper, suggested that values infuse every aspect of technology. Indeed every technological product is a reflection of the values of its creator. These values are however often hidden. The technologically literate person has the skills to unearth these values. For students in the CARICOM region this ability is vital. For reasons already adduced, countries like the CARICOM member states are inevitably going to be the recipients or users of transferred technology, and it is essential that Caribbean people are discerning of the hidden values in technology. The earlier section discussed some possible approaches to teaching values in technology. Subsequent iterations of the curriculum could make the treatment of values issues more explicit in the objectives and could spell out some strategies which teachers could employ as they seek to engage children with these issues.

TOWARD A RESEARCH AGENDA FOR CARIBBEAN TECHNOLOGY EDUCATION

The context-dependent nature of technology and hence technology education makes it imperative that curriculum development be informed by locally generated research. This is not a call for the reinvention of the wheel but rather a safeguard against outcomes that do not result in the preparation of citizens who possess the skills, attitudes and competencies to respond adequately to the challenges posed by technology. Following are some issues which represent the beginning of a research agenda for Caribbean technology education.

The design of a locally relevant technology education curriculum is dependent on a clear understanding of the range of technological applications that exist in the Caribbean and that are likely to exist in the future. The basic question is, **"What manifestations of technology influence Caribbean societies now and are likely to do so in the future?"** The CARICOM curriculum addressed a categorization of technology that recognized four fields, other curricula have used different categorizations, but the specific applications of whatever categories are used, need to be determined. In addition, categories of alternative technologies in use in urban and rural settings in the Caribbean are important examples of technological concepts and principles and should be documented for inclusion in Caribbean technology education curricula. A clarification of these technologies would provide a part of the answer to the question, **"What do Caribbean people need to know about technology?"**

The constructivist orientation to the teaching of technology in the CARICOM curriculum requires an understanding of children's prior conceptions about technology. It has been advocated elsewhere that the teaching of values might also be best accomplished using a constructivist approach which takes children's existing values as the point of departure in their learning experiences. Attitudes to technology might also be important determinants of children's learning of technology. These characteristics are almost certain to have a strong cultural component and research generated in other contexts might reveal little about Caribbean learners. The research issue here is **"What qualities with respect to technology characterize Caribbean learners?"**

With respect to children's learning in technology, it has been suggested that very little is known. This is also an area that is likely to be heavily influenced by cultural differences. The piloting of the units that have already been produced presents an opportunity for classroom-based research into the nature of Caribbean children's knowledge construction and skill acquisition in technology. In this regard comparisons of children at lower and upper primary and secondary levels would be extremely enlightening. The overall question would thus be, **" What are the nature and conditions of children's learning in technology?"**

"What is the nature of the design process as practiced in the Caribbean?" It would be extremely interesting to compare the methods of Caribbean designers with those of designers in other cultures. Such comparisons would also speak to the issue of what is appropriate technology education as well as what is appropriate technology in Caribbean societies. It has been suggested that professional designers do not adhere to the stylized process depicted in many technology textbooks. How do children in the Caribbean intuitively engage in the design process? These are questions with important implications for curriculum.

The piloting and implementation stages of curriculum development also offer opportunities to explore the effects of integrated units at all levels. **How can integration of technology with other areas of the curriculum be most effective?**

Another issue of high priority in our thrust to get technology education established in Caribbean schools is that of teacher education. The preparation of teachers to deliver the technology curriculum is of utmost importance. The best efforts of curriculum development can be frustrated if teachers are not adequately prepared, do not feel a sense of ownership or do not feel supported with continuing professional development and with resources. Research to answer the question, **"How can Caribbean teachers best be prepared to teach technology education?"** is of vital importance.

I am convinced that no other curriculum area has the potential to contribute to a reconceptualization of curriculum and schooling, as does technology education. It pushes us to the borders of our subject matter territorialism , it forces us to rethink the way that schools are traditionally organized and makes us think again about the relationship between schooling and work. The development of the unit plans for primary and lower secondary schools in the region is an important accomplishment for which the consultant, the project facilitators and the country participants are to be highly commended, but this is only the beginning of the process. It would take continued commitment of human and material resources to get the subject established, but the benefit to the region's education system and to its people would be incalculable.

BIBLIOGRAPHY

Akubue, A. (2000). Appropriate technology for socio-economic development in the third world countries. *The Journal of Technology Studies*, XXVI (1), 33- 43.

Anning, A. (1994). Dilemmas and opportunities of a new curriculum: Design and technology with young children. *International Journal of Technology and Design Education*, 4(2), 155-177.

Aukiewicz, P. (1995). The planning of technology education for South African schools. *International Journal of Technology and Design Education*, 5(3), 243-254.

Barnett, M. (1994). Designing the future? Technology, values and choice. *International Journal of Design and Technology Education*, 4(1), 51-63.

Barnett, M. (1995). Literacy, technology and "technological literacy". *International Journal of Technology and Design Education,* 5(2), 119-137.

Budgett-Meakin, C. (Ed.), (1992). *Make the future work.* London: Longman.

Cajas, F. (2000). Research in technology education: What are we researching? A response to Theodore Lewis. *Journal of Technology Educaiton*, 11(2), 61-69.

Cajas. F. (2000). Technology education research: Potential directions. *Journal of technology Education.* 12(1). 75-84.

CARICOM. (1998). *Blueprint for the introduction of technology education in the curriculum of primary and secondary schools.*

CARICOM. (2001). *A curriculum for technology education at the primary level.*

CARICOM. (2001). *Preparations for the introduction of a curriculum in technology education into the primary and secondary schools in the CARICOM.*

CARICOM. (2001). *Unit plans in technology education for forms in the lower secondary schools in the CARICOM.*

Childress, V. (1996). Does integrating technology, science and mathematics improve technological, problem solving? A quasi-experiment. *Journal of Technology Education,* 8(1),16-26.

Clark, A.C. & Wenig, R.E. (1999) Identification of quality characteristics for technology education programs: A North Carolina case study. *Journal of Technology Education*, 11(1), 18-26.

Conway, R. (1994). Values in technology education. *International Journal of Technology and Design Education.* 4(1),109-116.

Davies, D. (1996). Professional design and primary children. *International Journal of Technology and Design Education*, 6(1), 45-59.

DeVore, P.W. (1970). Discipline structures and processes. A research design for the identification of content and method. *Journal of Industrial Teacher Education*, 7(2).

Donelly J. (1992). Technology in the school curriculum: A critical bibliography. *Studies in Science Education*, 20, 123-159.

Dugger, W.E. (1998). Technology- The discipline. *The Technology Teacher*, 48 (1).

Dyrenfurth, M., Hatch, L., Jones, R. & Kozak, M. (1991). In M. Dyrenfurth & M. Kozack (Eds.), *Technological Literacy*, 40th Yearbook of the Council on Technology Teacher Education (pp. 1-7). Peoria, IL: Glencoe.

Eisner, E. & Vallance, E. (Eds.) (1974). *Conflicting conceptions of curriculum.* CA: McCutchan.

Erekson, T. (1992). Technology education for the academic rationalist perspective. *Journal of Technology Education,* 3(2), 6-14.

Feiman-Nemser, S. (1990). Teacher preparation: Structural and conceptual alternatives. In W. Robert Houston (ed.). *Handbook of Research on Teacher education.* New York: Macmillan Publishing Company.

Foster, P. (1994). Must we MST? *Journal of Technology Education,* 6(1), 76-84.

Foster, P.N. & Wright, M.D. (1996). Selected leaders' perceptions of approaches to technology education. *Journal of Technology Education*, 7(2), 13-26.

Foster, P.N. (1997). Classifying approaches to and philosophies of elementary school technology education. *Journal of Technology Education*, 8(2), 21-34.

Foster, W.T. (1992). Topics and methods of recent graduate student research in industrial education and related fields. *Journal of International Teacher Education*, 30(1). 59-72.

Franklin, U. (1992). *The real world of technology.* Ontario: Anansi Press.

Glaser, R. (1987). Toward a cognitive theory for the measurement of achievement. In Ronnig, R., Glover, J., & Conoley, J. (eds.) *The Influence of Cognitive Psychology on Testing and Measurement.* Vol. 3. Buros-Nebraska Symposium on Measurement and Testing.

Glaser, R., & Silver, E. (1996). Assessment, testing and instruction. Retrospect and prospect. *CSE Technical Report 379.* National Center for Research on Evaluation, Standards and Student Testing (CRESST).

Gloeckner, G.W. (1991). The integration of science, technology and mathematics. Myth or dream? *Journal of Technology Education*, 2(2), 1-6.

Gradwell, J.B. (1996). Philosophical and practical differences in the approaches taken to technology education in England, France and the United States. *International Journal of Technology and Design Education*, 6(3). 239-262.

Gustafson, B.J., Rowell, P.M. & Guilbert, S.M. (2000). Elementary children's awareness of strategies for testing structural strength: A three year study. *Journal of Technology Education*, 11(2), 5-21.

Gustafson, B.J., Rowell, P.M. & Rose, D.P. (1999). Elementary children's conceptions of structural stability: A three year study. *Journal of Technology Education*, 11(1), 27-43.

Hansen, J. (2000). Lessons from star trek: Examining the social values embedded in technological programs. *The Journal of Technology Studies,* XXVI(2), 2-8.

Hansen, R. (1993). A technological teacher education program planning model. *Journal of Technology Education*, 5(20.

Herschbach, D. (1992). Curriculum change in technology education. Differing theoretical perspectives. *Journal of Technology Education,* 3 (2), 31-42.

Herschbach, D. (1995). Technology as knowledge: Implications for instruction. *Journal of Technology Education*, 7(1), 31-42.

Hill, A., & Smith, H.A. (1998). Practice meets theory in technology education: A case of authentic learning in the high school setting. *Journal of Technology Education*, 9 (2), 29-45.

International Technology Education Association (1996). *Technology for All Americans.* Reston, VA: Author.

International Technology Education Association (2000). *Standards for technological literacy: content for the study of technology.* Reston, VA: Author.

Johnsey, R. (1997). Improving children's performance in the procedures of design and technology. *Journal of Technology Education*, 2(3), 201-207.

Johnson, S. (1992). A framework for technology education curricula which emphasizes intellectual process. *Journal of Technology Education,* 3 (2), 29-40.

Kimbell, R. (1994). Progression in learning and the assessment of children's attainments in technology. *International Journal of Technology and Design Education*, 4(1), 65-83.

Kozolanka, K., & Olson, J. (1994). Life after school: How science and technology teaches construe capability. International Journal of Technology and Design Education, 4(3), 209-226.

Lavonen, J., Meisalo, V., & Lattu, M. (2001). Problem solving with an icon-oriented programming tool: A case study in technology education. *Journal of Technology Education,* 12(2). 21-34.

Layton, D. (1992). *Values and Design and Technology.* Loughborough University of Technology, Loughborough.

Layton, D. (1992). Values in design and technology. In C. Budgett-Meakin (Ed.) Making The future Work. 3. London: Longman.

Lewis, T. (1991). Introducing technology into school curricula. *Journal of Curriculum Studies*, 23 (2).

Lewis, T. (1999). Content or process as approaches to technology curriculum: Does it matter come Monday Morning? *Journal of Technology Education*, 11(1), 45-59.

Lewis, T. & Gagel, C. (1992). Technological literacy: A critical analysis. *Journal of Curriculum Studies,* 24(2), 117-138.

Lewis, T. (1996). Contemporary technology education in the U.S. and U.K. *International Journal of Technology and Design Education*, 6(3), 221-238.

McCormick, R. (1996). Instructional Methodology. In .A. Williams, & P.J. Williams (eds.), *Technology Education for Teachers.* Melbourne: Macmillan.

Ogunmola, G. (2001). An assessment of technology education in the school curriculum in Nigeria. (Personal Communication)

Petrina, S. (1998a). The politics of research in technology education: A critical content and discourse analysis of the Journal of Technology Education. *Journal of Technology Education*, 10(1), 27-57.

Petrina, S. (1998b). Multidisciplinary technology education. *International Journal of Technology and Design Education*, 8(2), 103-138.

Petrina, S. (1992). Curriculum change in technology education: A theoretical perspective on personal relevance curriculum designs. *Journal of Technology Education*, 3(2), 37-47.

Prime, G. M. (1993). Values in technology: Approaches to learning. *Design and Technology Teaching*, 25(3), 30-36.

Prime, G.M. (1998). Tailoring assessment of technological literacy learning. *The Journal of Technology Studies*, XXIV(1). Winter/Spring, 18-23.

Ridgeway, J., & Passey, D. (1992). *Developing skills in technology: The theoretical basis for teaching*. ICTE.

Roswell, P.M., & Gustafson, B.J. (Eds.) (1998). *Problem solving through technology. Case studies in Alberta elementary classrooms*. University of Alberta: Center for Mathematics, Science and Technology Education.

Royer, J.M., Cisero, C.A., & Carlo, M.S. (1993). Techniques and procedures for assessing cognitive skills. *Review of Educational Research*, 63(2). 201-243.

Sanders, M. (2001). New paradigm or old wine? The status of technology education practice in the United States. *Journal of Technology Education*. 12(2). 35-54.

Savage, E. (2001). Technology curriculum organizers that could make a difference. *The Journal of Technology Studies,* XXVII(1),4-10.

Solomon, J., & Hall, S. (1996). An inquiry into progression in primary technology: A role for teaching. *International Journal of Technology and Design Education*, 6(3), 263-282.

Technology for all Americans Project. (1996). *Technology for All Americans: A Rationale and Structure for the Study of Technology*. Reston, VA: International Technology Education Association.

Twyford, J.,& Jarvinen, E. (2000). *The formation of children's technological concepts: A study of what it means to do technology from a child's perspective.* Journal of Technology Education, 12(1), 32-48.

Vincenti, W.G. (1984). Technological knowledge without science: The innovation of flush riveting in American airplanes, ca. 1930-ca. 1950. *Technology and Culture*, 25(3), 540-576.

Volk, K. (1997). Going, going,gone? Recent trends in technology teacher education programs. *Journal of Technology Education,* 8(2), 1-5.

Waetjen, W. B. (1989). *Technological problem-solving: A proposal.* Reston, VA: International Technology Education Association.

Waetjen, W.B. (1993). Technological literacy reconsidered. *Journal of Technological Education*, 4 (2), 5-10.

Williams, J. (2000). Design: The only methodology of technology? *Journal of Technology Education,* 11(2), 48-60.

Wolff-Michael, R. (1996). Learning to talk engineering design: Results from an interpretive study in a grade 4/5 classroom. *International Journal of Technology and Design Education*, 6(2), 107-135.

Wright, M. & Custer, R. (1998). Why they want to teach: Factors influencing students to become technology education teachers. *Journal of Technology Education*, 10(1).

Zuga, K. (1992). Social reconstruction curriculum and technology education. *Journal of Technology Education*, 3(2), 48-57.

Zuga, K. (1994). *Implementing technology education: A review and synthesis of the literature.* Columbus, Ohio: Eric Clearinghouse on Adult, Career and Vocational Education.

Zuga, K. (1997). An analysis of Technology Education in the United States based upon an historical overview and review of contemporary curriculum research. *International Journal of Technology and Design Education*, 7(3), 203-217.

Zuga, K. (1999). Addressing Women's ways of knowing to improve the technology education environment for all students. *Journal of Technology Education.* 10(2), 57-71.

GRAMMAR IN CONTEXT: FUNCTIONAL TEACHING FOR THE FRENCH CAPE

Béatrice Boufoy - Bastick
University of the West Indies
Jamaica

Chapter 3

MAJOR CHANGES have occurred over the last two decades in theories of Foreign Language (FL) teaching as practiced in the Caribbean. This paper examines, from a communicative language teaching perspective, how these changing theoretical emphases have transformed FL pedagogical practices. There is now an emphasis on developing effective interactional skills, resulting in valued competency outcomes such as learners' increased verbal fluidity and awareness of social norms. It is argued here that this heightened socio-linguistic FL performance could be further enhanced by including functional grammar teaching in the FL class. Functional in-context grammar teaching can promote FL competence by facilitating accurate linguistic transfer to wider contexts. Functional grammar input can also significantly improve both the accuracy and the fluency of learners' linguistic input. It is therefore suggested that functional in-context grammar teaching could now be beneficially introduced into French CAPE communicative activities.

Rapid changes have occurred over the last two decades in language learning and teaching in the Caribbean. This followed a shift, in the late 1970's in Europe and America, from concern with teaching methods to an emphasis on language teaching objectives, language content, and curriculum design (Stern, 1983, p. 113). In most Caribbean countries influenced by the British education system, the traditional grammar-translation methods have since then been gradually phased out and communicative foreign language (FL) teaching methodologies have been implemented. Emphasis on the development of oral/aural communicative skills is reflected by greater fluidity in verbal interaction and increased awareness of social mores. Notwithstanding the value of developing FL sociolinguistic performance, it is argued here that formal contextualised grammar teaching can improve linguistic competence and better prepare students for development of higher order linguistic skills (CXC A13/U2/98, p. 1; CXC A17/U2/99, p. 1) to facilitate accurate transfer of linguistic fluency to wider contexts (Huang, 1998; Lyster, 1999; Rott, 2000).

This article briefly describes changes in FL teaching in the anglophone Caribbean that have led to improved interactional skills, it then it explains the role of in-context grammar inclusion in promoting linguistic competence, and finally it shows how grammar can effectively serve the communicative aims of Caribbean Advanced Proficiency Examination (CAPE) FL syllabi.

INCREASED INTERACTIONAL LANGUAGE TEACHING

Today's foreign language learners in the Caribbean show much greater ease when participating in a variety of communicative activities and when interacting with one another in the target language. The relatively 'free communication' Caribbean Secondary Education Certificate (CSEC) language class is no longer limited to narrow linguistic instruction utilising peer input. The emphasis has shifted away from peer input for linguistic instruction towards interactive output to promote quality speech production (Green, 1987; Jones, 1992). This shift is essentially a de-emphasis from grammaticality and it is the result of two overlapping developments in FL teaching: i) lexis improvement , i.e. developing conversational ability using vocabulary-building, which leads to (ii) internalising interactive norms, e.g. using rote learning of idiomatic forms.

USE OF INTERACTION TO PROMOTE QUALITY SPEECH PRODUCTION

Communicative activities use teacher/student interactions and peer interactions, and sometimes 'peer teaching' (Togle & Bito, 1991, p. 279), to promote fluency in speech production, albeit by de-emphasising grammatical accuracy. This emphasis on developing verbal skills was seen in the revised CSEC FL syllabus (1995) which "emphasizes the speaking skill and situational responses" (Morris, 1997, p. 94).

The following three changes of emphasis in foreign language teaching have allowed this development.

(i) Acceptability of imperfect speech to build confidence and fluency

First of all, imperfect speech facilitates interaction has become more acceptable (Oxford, 1989). This approach encourages students to use meaningful language without focusing on correctness of form (Dieter, 1994; Holliday, 1994; Ratleff & McDonough, 1992). As students' apprehension about speech quality is overcome, their increased risk-taking confidence leads to greater willingness to communicate and this enhances their fluency in the language.

(ii) Participation in simulated activities

Secondly, participation in simulated activities gives learners the opportunity to become involved in a variety of interactional experiences (Boufoy-Bastick, 2001). Authentic communicative functions involve more than verbal utterances. They need to be accompanied by correct intonation and appropriate demeanour. These interactional experiences teach the correct intonation and appropriate demeanour that are essential to authentic communicative functions (Nunan, 1988, p. 78). This interactional competence is a major specific 'Speaking' objective of functional French CAPE which expects students to be able to: "1. produce French sounds and intonation patterns acceptable to native speakers; 2. ask and respond to questions relating to practical everyday situations, e.g. weather, directions, time; 3. participate in conversation on topics specified in the syllabus; 4. make a short oral presentation" (CXC A14/U1/98).

(iii) The communication-oriented dynamic

Thirdly, establishing a sound working relationship between the teacher and the students, and amongst the students themselves (Benson & Voller, 1997; Rodgers, 1988), is also essential for inducing a communication-oriented milieu. Without such rapport, the necessary dynamic environment cannot be achieved. These stimulating working conditions facilitate interaction which further enables the development of conversational skills. The communication-oriented dynamic is a positive feedback environment which builds conversation skills in the FL CAPE class.

DEVELOPMENT OF STUDENTS' CONVERSATIONAL ABILITIES

Total FL interactional skills improve with conversational ability. Communicative language teaching activities, therefore, aim not only to develop interactional skills but also at developing students' conversational abilities. Conversational ability is best developed by (i) first building a strong lexical base then (ii) by acquiring context-related speech functions (Al-Khanji, 1987).

(i) Building students' lexical base

Vocabulary is built gradually by word-recognition, learning routines, patterns and formulae which subsequently lead to acquisition. To serve conversational objectives, lexical items are presented in a communicative context. For example, ordinal numbers such as 'le premier/la première' (the first), 'le/la deuxième' (the second) etc... expressions such as 'à droite' (on the right), 'à gauche' (on the left), 'tout droit' (straight on) etc... are introduced in a relevant situation where directions need to be given. The significance of vocabulary-building in communicative FL teaching needs to be underscored as it enables students "to expand their range of interaction in the target language to new topics and new situations" (Krashen & Terrell, 1983, p. 156). Vocabulary-building in communicative contexts offers one of the most powerful ways of enhancing conversational ability in all CXC classes. However, it is argued here that grammatical structures - which are, after all, also formal patterns and formulae of word-recognition - are being under-utilised in this powerful enhancement of conversational ability (Celce-Murcia, 1990).

(ii) Acquiring context-related speech functions

Context-related functions are developed by providing a variety of speech situations where specific speech acts and speech events can be used, practised and expanded (Omaggio Hadley, 1993). Oral/aural tasks have a significant role to play in developing conversational skills. As Tschirner (1992) demonstrated, both input and output activities facilitate the expansion of both receptive (aural) and productive (oral) skills which are crucial for fluent conversation. Described in terms of information theory, these two-way processes aim at decoding and processing a message. Understanding involves meaning negotiation (decoding) whereas speaking requires response elicitation (processing a message). To result in an appropriate response, these processes require the ability to recognise the key lexical items of a cue as well as the ability to retrieve items previously learnt. Developing such communicative strategies result, on one hand, in improved conversational skills and, on the other, in establishing norms of interaction. It is part of the argument made here that grammatical structure relates lexis to context - e.g., gender, plural, person etc. - and so its de-emphasis detracts from the optimum development of conversational and interactional abilities.

NORMS OF INTERACTION

By exposure to a multiplicity of contextual situations, norms of interaction are internalised and CAPE students soon emulate native speakers' behaviour with undeniable authenticity. Both linguistic and paralinguistic features characterise these interactional norms. In the free communication language class, these features are typically highlighted in enjoyable dyad activities such as modelling through role-playing (Al-Arishi, 1994).

(i) Linguistic norms - Formulaic speech training

Models of speech acts formalise, fairly prescriptively, the sequence of a conversation. "The sequencing of speech acts in a given situation, for example, in a telephone call... are subject to definable rules of sequence..." (Stern, 1983, p. 228). These rules of sequence are the social rules of communication. Acquiring them necessitates both building a specific linguistic register and following conventional discursive patterns. For example, a French telephone conversation between three students role-playing a business telephone call will be close to the model below:

'A' answers the phone.

> *A - Allô. Compagnie Simenon. Puis-je vous aider?*
>
> *B - Bonjour, j'aimerais parler à la secrétaire de M. Larivière.*

A - Oui, un instant, s'il vous plaît.

C - Ariane Lamy , la secrétaire de M. Larivière, à l'appareil. Que puis-je pour vous?

This example illustrates the appropriate specific register and how it is structured into a conventional discursive pattern of a standard welcome initiating a telephone call. Such structures are the common content of first language social and business etiquette training which students taking the CAPE Functional French are expected to acquire (CXC A14/U1/98, p. 3).

Communicative FL teaching relies on such conversational models to impart defined interactional norms which students are required to memorise as part of "the experience of learning a language" (CXC A14/U1/98, p. 1). By using such formulaic speech patterns students appear to be fluent speakers without the need to understand the underlying grammatical notions. However, without resort to an underlying grammar, this appearance belies the flexibility implicit in fluency and makes it difficult "to *choose* the language appropriate to the context", a major specific objective of the CAPE 2-unit French course (CXC A13/U2/98). Notwithstanding the value of memorising formulaic language patterns for facilitating communication, these patterns are often "short-term substitutes" (Krashen & Terrell, 1983, p. 56) which may limit students' production to mere dyadic communication.

(ii) Paralinguistic norms - cultural sensitivity

The authenticity of the students' rendition is also exaggerated by their lavish use of paralinguistic features. The use of mimics, gestures, intonation or other idiosyncratic cultural features (e.g., "Oh, la, la..". or "oui, oui...") is even often taught before teaching verbal output. Such a reliance on easily acquired non-verbal communication gives students the feeling that they can 'get by'. This may encourage complacency and undermine some students' willingness to make that extra effort to acquire and use further verbal skills. This is not to berate the place of mimetic activities in language learning as they assuredly help "to arouse student interest and promote foreign language acquisition" as well as fostering greater cultural sensitivity in a stimulating FL learning environment (Seaver, 1992). However, by developing a grammatical awareness of the FL structures, the student is empowered and can make that extra effort to acquire and use further verbal skills.

In-context grammar inclusion for improved linguistic competence

PROMOTING POSITIVE ATTITUDES TOWARDS L2 LEARNING

Pure, traditional, rote grammar teaching may have suited a puritanical colonial work ethic that is less in evidence today in the former British colonies of the Caribbean. Such an ethic may have contributed to negative modern views of foreign language learning, namely French, as having been tedious and difficult. In contrast, modern expectations are that work should be interesting and personally rewarding. The communication-oriented dynamic environment fostering active participation certainly encourages a favourable attitude to a discipline formerly considered as difficult. Stern (1983, p. 386), for example, notes that in language proficiency "learners who learn well acquire positive attitudes". This is achieved in two main ways: (i) by acknowledging the learners' individual differences and (ii) by acknowledging their age-group similarities.

i) Acknowledging learners' individual differences - negotiating relevance

Valuing learners' particular abilities involves accepting their potentials and limitations. The linguistic objectives are no longer hierarchically set by the teacher alone, but negotiated between the teacher and the students (Carter, 1998; Nunan, 1988, p. 95). Although the teacher provides the materials, the learners decide what is relevant to their specific needs. The responsibility to know how and how much to use also lies with the 'informed' learner. As a result, a positive attitude is fostered promoting further achievement. However, in practice, teachers find low intrinsic motivation among students who do not choose to learn the language, but who are required to do so, as is often the case with secondary school-aged Caribbean males. These students are less 'informed' and consequently less able to direct their own learning. The result is that they learn little in the 'free' communication language class. Incorporating some direct grammar-in-context instruction in communicative class activities would better 'inform' these students, improving their learning and attitude, because of this added direction. Attitude is of such considerable importance in FL learning that Krashen and Terrell (1983) considered it to be an even more important factor than aptitude: "attitudinal factors are more important in second language acquisition than aptitude" (p. 40).

(ii) Acknowledging age-group similarities - validating students' need to talk

In student-centred classrooms, students have a proclivity to talk. This penchant can be utilised to promote the development of verbal interaction and language learning and teachers who recognise and validate this need through their teaching, can enhance their students' attitudes to learning. In brief, the major improvement brought to FL teaching by communicative activities is that they empower all learners, whatever their abilities, to function appropriately in a given social situation. It is argued, here, that grammar inclusion is far from being inimical to communicative language teaching, and that, conversely, it may extend students' abilities to function better and appropriately in other situations and help develop their reading and writing skills (Huang, 1998; Jean, 1999; Ke, 1992; Kennedy, 1990; Muranoi, 2000; Nassaj, 1999).

DEVELOPING READING AND WRITING SKILLS

Communicative language learning activities potentially enable all learners to become operational in the language by developing, first, listening and speaking skills, and then, reading and writing skills. The Communicative FL approach to reading and writing aims at encompassing the large range of linguistic abilities by using holistic learning methods while de-emphasising formal grammar teaching (Boyle, 1994; Ke, 1992; Wahl, 1999).

IGNORING THE GRAMMATICAL STRUCTURE OF THE WRITTEN MATERIALS

CAPE communicative language learning utilises a wide range of written materials - ranging from announcements to advertisements, news flashes, newspaper articles, reports (CXC A13/U2/98, p. 2; CXC A14/U1/98, p. 3). However, communicative FL teachers make cautious use of explicit grammar teaching to help students understand the structure of the written materials. As a result, some of their students fail to internalise the implicit, and often complex, language patterns (Efstathiadis, 1987).

(i) Additional reading proficiency from grammar learning

In communicative reading activities, the emphasis is on searching for clues to clarify text comprehension rather than understanding syntactic structures (Wahl, 1999). By using this method of language acquisition, students develop reading strategies which allow them to grasp the overall ideas of a text fairly adequately, and to demonstrate some intuitive feeling for the language. As Krashen and Terrell (1983) found: "the result of language acquisition is a 'feel' for grammaticality" (p. 40).

An intuitive feel for the foreign language is, indeed, essential. However, the more grammar-oriented methods that were used before the advent of communicative language teaching gave students some proficiency in the language - a proficiency based on language structure that was somewhat different from the proficiency based on communicative activities (Stern, 1983, p. 347). This does not suggest, in any way, reverting to traditional grammar-translation FL teaching methods, but rather including an examination of the specific syntactic structures of the FL language in order to add this additional dimension to students' FL proficiency..

(ii) Additional writing proficiency from grammar learning

Certainly, reading should focus primarily on content (meaning), but form (grammar) should not be sacrificed. The lack of stress on producing accurate syntactic structures also hinders the students' written performance. The linguistically able may extract the underlying rules from the texts presented by making explicit their tacit understanding of the grammar - as linguists do - but the less able students are satisfied with gross inexactitudes in their written communications.

Depriving students of explicit grammatical rules slows down progress in FL proficiency development. In the communicative classroom, this is hidden by the otherwise successful communicative methods of FL learning (Gschwind-Holtzer, 1990).

USING THE GRAMMATICAL STRUCTURE OF THE WRITTEN MATERIALS

Communicative language learners tend to use aural cues - 'it sounds like this'. This oral competence is the basis of false beginners' initial success, and resulting confidence, in FL learning. As indicated above, attitudinal factors, of which this initial confidence is a common example, are major influences on FL acquisition. The importance of this, is that it applies to most students. However, in the absence of any knowledge of grammar, this otherwise natural, useful and common strategy can actually mislead the student. On the other hand, some knowledge of grammar, used in conjunction with written/reading materials during communicative activities, would utilise this overlap between oral and written competence to greatly enhance the FL proficiency of all students (Muranoi, 2000). In illustration and, with relevance to the previous example, simply presenting to students verb conjugations as a whole enables them to use their visual memory in conjunction with an understanding of how a personal pronoun relates to a certain verb form.

Communicative language activities have, admittedly, succeeded in making language learners socially and culturally aware. By using formulaic speech structures and by copying the linguistic and paralingustic characteristics of normative interaction, students seem to emulate native speakers' behaviour with undeniable authenticity. However, the smallest change in context necessitating an appropriate variation in the student's linguistic and social behaviour, immediately gives the lie to such seeming authenticity by testing their ability to apply appropriate language structures to novel social situations. It is argued here that by obdurately excluding grammar, communicative activities fail to explicitly teach the transfer of linguistic accuracy, which is essential to the flexibility of authentically fluent speakers (Ke, 1992). Conversely, authentic fluency can be reached by integrating oral communicative competence with written grammatical competence. "Knowing a language - being a fluent speaker - presumes both communicative competence and grammatical competence. Neither one is sufficient by itself to constitute fluency in the full sense of the word - in the sense that encompasses both structure and use. Grammatical competence and communicative competence are needed together" (Finegan, Besnier, Blair & Collins, 1992, pp. 8-9). This issue of syntactic accuracy in CAPE communicative language teaching should now be addressed.

DEVELOPING SYNTACTIC ACCURACY IN THE FL CAPE

It is argued here that communicative skills can be further expanded by introducing functional in-context grammatical concepts in CAPE language learning.

COMMUNICATIVE ACCURACY IN CONTEXT

Prioritising communicative accuracy whilst downgrading grammar limits students interactional language skills to only a few informal communicative contexts which tend to be of limited importance.

(i) Prioritising communicative fluency

To date, communicative language teaching has prioritised communicative fluency at the expense of syntactic accuracy.

Communicative fluency, using linguistic and paralinguistic cues, is achieved when the communication matches the situation and the listener. The behavioural outcome, can be interpreted and evaluated against the aim of the communicative act. For example, to be rid of an unpleasant person who is making a personal enquiry, it is unnecessary to respond to the enquiry - or even to understand it. A successful communication need only be an aggressive expletive that sends him/her on his/her way. Communicative language instruction strives to reach this goal by encouraging students to use meaningful language in a holistic context without focusing on the correctness of the form (Ratleff & McDonough, 1992).

(ii) Limiting communicative contexts

However, there are many situations where linguistic accuracy is essential to the accuracy of communication. Furthermore, these situations tend to be most important for the student - formal, institutional, traditional and cultural communications. For example, a business letter or a CV which contains linguistic errors reduces communicative accuracy by communicating 'imprecision' by form which conflicts with the intended communication of 'precision' by content. Hence, some effort should be made to develop syntactic accuracy within communicative activities in order for students to achieve communicative accuracy in more varied, and often more influential, contexts.

(iii) Limiting interactional performance

Going beyond linguistic/interactional performance to linguistic competence seems difficult to achieve without a clear understanding of the rules governing the language. Knowing about the language enhances linguistic sensitivity and ensures greater linguistic proficiency. Although communicative approaches undeniably facilitate internalisation of salient linguistic characteristics they fail to equip most students with the tools necessary, not only to transfer their linguistic skills to totally different situations, but also to more rapidly extend their skills within familiar contexts. Introducing tools of syntactic accuracy would enable students to progress even faster within the 'free' communication language class (Munroi, 2000).

GRAMMAR AUGMENTS LOW IMMERSION FL LEARNING

In no way does presenting the intricate syntactic aspects of language imply a return to formal out-of-context grammar teaching (Ellis, 1999). On the contrary, what Bourdet (1992) calls a "textual" approach, identifying grammatical facts relevant to communication, would enable the learner to become aware of the governing grammatical rules and subsequently apply them to new linguistic situations in communicative activities. So, as a new lexical or syntactic structure is met, clarification and rule explanation help the student to formalise his/her intuitive understanding. Some educationists support this view and advocate the introduction of a 'functional grammar approach' which focuses "first on the function rather than the form of a given grammatical feature" (Jubb & Rouxeville, 1998), that is on "meaning and how meaning is built up in language" (Jones, 1993, p. 9). By developing an understanding of language construction, language use is facilitated and improved (Borg, 1999; Ellis, 1999; Jean, 1999; Kennedy, 1990; Nassaji, 1999) and "the acquisition of grammar and vocabulary embedded in context will be an easier undertaking" (Salmon, 2000, p. 65).

For instance, in French, as in other romance languages, use, choice and formation of tenses remain difficult to the English-speaking Caribbean student which is reflected in their inability to spontaneously produce the correct verb form. The insufficient input in the communicative FL class does not support intuitive internalisation of underlying grammatical rules. Although the student gradually develops a 'feel' for grammaticality, his/her lack of constant exposure to the target language does not allow him/her to bridge the gap to educe and apply the in-built rules as is the case of learning . A 'feel' for the language is not sufficient to produce linguistically accurate speech so grammatical input is necessary in order that "effective and satisfying communication can take place" (Bloomfield, 1992, p. 30). Bloomfield (1992, p. 30) also recommends reverting to "some form of structured or systematic teaching" to offset the lack of language exposure outside the classroom. She asserts that grammatical study has a beneficial effect on communicative skills as "this encourages real conversation, not artificial nonsense". This view was also shared by Celce-Murcia (1990, p. 212) who made the recommendation "to supplement the social-interactive work now accomplished successfully..." and "to move learners beyond that level of fairly superficial everyday communication...".

It is suggested here that conversational flow be facilitated by exploring this overlap between linguistic structures and their communicative values (Bourke, 1992). Developing both linguistically accurate and effective speech are not inimical (Celce-Murcia ,1990, p. 213) but contribute 'symbiotically' towards reaching higher degrees of linguistic competence. Language learning cannot be simplified to communicative performance but encompasses functional language use, conversational effectiveness and structural analysis which are all necessary conditions for reaching linguistic competence (Efstathiadis, 1987; Gschwind-Holtzer, 1990; Kaplan & Knutson, 1993).

Over the last two decades the grammatical approach to FL teaching in the Caribbean has been rejected in favour of communicative language teaching. This paper has briefly described some teaching techniques which build interactive competence in the target language by using communicative language teaching activities. These communicative activities, with their emphasis on social and cultural norms, indisputably yield exemplary results in terms of developing ability to competently interact in the target language. However, their under emphasis on grammar teaching robs the FL student of the tools necessary for more rapid language learning and transfer of language skills to wider and more influential contexts. It is, in no way, suggested here that we return to traditional language teaching aimed primarily at grammatical accuracy, but that some functional in-context grammar teaching can enhance communicative competence. What is recommended is inclusion of some functional grammar input with communicative activities so that linguistic proficiency will develop much further enabling the CAPE French student "to communicate clearly and appropriately in the target language with an educated native speaker" ((CXC A13/U22/98).

REFERENCES

Al-Arishi, A. (1994). Role-play, real-play and surreal-play in the ESOL classroom. *ELT Journal, 48*(4), 337-346.

Al-Khanji, R. (1987, April). *Strategic interaction: A method that enhances communicative competence.* Paper presented at the

Annual Meeting of the International Association of Teachers of English as a Foreign Language, Westende, Belgium.

Benson, P. & Voller, P.(1997). *Autonomy and Independence in Language Learning,* London: Addison Wesley Longman.

Bloomfield, N. (1992). Is the Communicative approach working? *Journal of the Australian Federation of Modern Language Teachers Associations, 27*(3), 28-30.

Borg, S. (1999). The use of grammatical terminology in the second language classroom: A qualitative study of teachers' practices and cognitions. *Applied Linguistics, 20*(1), 95-126.

Bourdet, J.F. (1992). Pratiquer une grammaire textuelle (To practise a textual grammar). *Le Français dans le Monde, 252*, 65-66.

Boufoy-Bastick, B. (2001). *Constructivist pedagogy for authentically activating oral skills in the foreign language classroom.* ERIC identifier: ED450596

Bourke, J.M. (1992). *The case for problem solving in second language learning.* Centre for Language and Communication Studies (CLCS) (Occasional Paper 33).

Boyle, E.M. (1994). This is the dictionary of Ivan Petrovich: Balancing the role of grammar in the Russian communicative classroom. *Theory into Practice, 33*(1), 10-15.

Carter, B. (1998). Fostering learner autonomy among mature language learners. *Caribbean Journal of Education, 20*(1), 102-116.

Celce-Murcia, M. (1990). What role for grammar after the communicative revolution? In S. Anivan (Ed.) *Language Teaching Methodology for the Nineties* (pp. 203-214). SEAMEO anthology series 24.

Dieter, W. (1994). New approaches to language teaching: An Overview. Centre for Language and Communication Studies, Trinity College, Dublin. *CLCS Occasional Paper No. 39.*

Efstathiadis, S. (1987). A critique of the "Communicative approach" to language learning and teaching. *Journal of Applied Linguistics, 3*, 5-13.

Ellis, R. (1999). Input-based approaches to teaching grammar: A review of classroom-oriented research. *Annual Review of Applied Linguistics 19*, 64-80.

Finegan, E., Besnier N., Blair, D. & Collins, P. (1992). *Language: Its structure and use.* Sydney, Australia: Harcourt Brace Jovanovich Group.

Green, P. (Ed.) (1987). *Communicative Language Testing: A Resource Handbook for Teacher Trainers.* Council of Europe, Directorate of Education, Culture and Sport, Strasbourg, France.

Gschwind-Holtzer, G. (1990). L'approche communicative en questions (The communicative approach in questions). *Le Français dans le Monde, 232*, 74-75.

Holliday, A. (1994). The house of TESEP and the communicative approach: The special needs of state English Language education. *ELT Journal 48*(1), 3-11.

Huang, L-y. (1998). *A new model of teaching pedagogy in CHISEL for the 21st century.* A New Model of Teaching Pedagogy in CHISEL for the 21th Century. Paper presented at the 32nd Annual Meeting of the American Council on the Teaching of Foreign Languages, Chicago, IL, November 20-22, 1998.

Jean, G. (1999). L'intégration de la grammaire dans une approche interactive/experientielle en français de base (The integration of grammar in an interactive/experiential approach in core French). *Canadian Modern Language Review, 55*(3), 315-338.

Jones, C. (1993, November 27-28). Grammar comes back into fashion. *The Weekend Australian*, p. 9.

Jones, F.R. (1992). A language-teaching machine: Input, uptake, and output in the communicative classroom. *System, 20* (2), 133-150.

Jubb, M. & Rouxeville, A. (1998). *French Grammar in Context.* London: Arnold.

Kaplan, M.A. & Knutson, E. (1993). Where is the text? Discourse competence and the foreign language textbook. *Mid-Atlantic Journal of Foreign Language Pedagogy, 1*, 167-176.

Ke, C. (1992, November) *Challenges to the proficiency movement: The issue of accuracy*. Paper presented at the Annual Meeting of the American Council on the Teaching of Foreign Languages, Chicago.

Kennedy, G. (1990). Collocations: Where grammar and vocabulary teaching meet. In S. Anivan (Ed.) *Language Teaching Methodology for the Nineties* (pp. 215-229). SEAMEO anthology series 24.

Krashen, S.D. & Terrel, T.D. (1983). *The Natural Approach*. Oxford: Pergamon Press.

Lyster, R. (1999). La négociation de la forme: La suite... mais pas la fin (The Negotiation of Form: The Next Stage... But not the End. *Canadian Modern Language Review, 55*(3), 355-384.

Morris, J. (1997). Foreign language teacher education in Trinidad and Tobago. *Caribbean Journal of Education 19*(1).

Muranoi, H. (2000). Focus on form through interaction enhancement: Integrating formal instruction into a communicative task in EFL classrooms. *Language Learning, 50*, 617-73

Nassaji, H. (1999). Towards integrating form-focused instruction and communicative interaction in the second language classroom: Some pedagogical possibilities. *Canadian Modern Language Review 55*(3), 385-402.

Nunan, D. (1988). The Learner-Centred Curriculum. Cambridge: Cambridge University Press.

Omaggio Hadley, A. (1993). *Teaching Language in Context*. Boston: Heinle & Heinle.

Oxford, R. (1989). Language learning strategies, the communicative approach and their classroom implications. *Foreign Language Annals 22*(1), 29-39.

Ratleff, J.E. & McDonough, R. (1992, April). *Instructional conversations out of the mainstream: Issues and accommodations for special education students.* Paper presented at the Annual Meeting of the American Educational Research Association, San Francisco.

Rodgers, T. (1988). Co-operative language learning. What's news? In B. Das (Ed.) *Materials for Language Learning and Teaching* (pp. 1-15). SEAMEO anthology series 22.

Rott, S. (2000). *Unterrichtspraxis/Teaching German, 33*(2)125-33.

Salmon, H. (2000). Two contrasting foreign-language teaching orientations. In T. Bastick *Education Theory and Practice* (pp. 57-70). Kingston: UWI, Department of Educational Studies.

Scarcella, R. & Oxford, R (1992). *The Tapestry of Language Learning: The Individual in the Communicative Classroom.* Boston: Heinle & Heinle.

Seaver, P. Jr. (1992). Pantomime as an L2 classroom strategy. *Foreign Language Annals, 25*(1), 21-31.

Stern, H. (1983). *Fundamental concepts of language teaching*. Oxford: Oxford University Press.

Togle, S. & Bito, R. (1991). Student empowerment: Peer teaching in ESL classes. In T. Le and M. McCausland *Language Education: Interaction and Development* (pp. 278-282). Proceedings of the international conference held in Ho Chi Minh City, Vietnam, March 30 - April 1, 1991.

Tschirner, E. (1992). From input to output: Communication-based teaching techniques. *Foreign Language Annals, 25*(6), 507-518.

Wahl, Y. (1999). Evaluer la compétence de lecture. (Evaluating reading competence). *Le Français dans le Monde, 301*, 31-33.

SECTION 2
TEACHING

CHAPTER 7:

COLLABORATIVE LEARNING IN CARIBBEAN HIGHER EDUCATION: EXAMINING THE PROSPECTS

Olabisi Kuboni, *University of the West Indies, Trinidad..*
Pages 217 - 250

FIVE WAYS OF TEACHING AND LEARNING IN HAITI

LeGrace Benson
State University of New York
USA

Chapter 4

ASK WHAT Haitians need to learn in school and college. Some will begin with the need for more and better-prepared teachers who can become effective school managers and administrators to insure the rapid increase of teaching basic skills of reading, writing, mathematics, and social studies in a country where literacy rates are the lowest in the hemisphere. Others will respond with a plea for professionals in forestry, agronomy, water and soil resource management, animal husbandry and farm product marketing. Still others implore the urgency to train doctors, nurses, midwives, physical therapists, and dentists. Many agree with each of those compelling needs but point to the necessity of developing an understanding of essential social structures that could support such programs. Hence they call for courses in social sciences, economics, quantitative and qualitative management principles. Some educators insist on the priority of pedagogical reforms. Most specifically, they urge replacing rote learning of texts as the almost exclusive means for instruction. In any room full of discussants, most will finally agree that every thing on all lists needs to take place. At once.

I. SOME ASPECTS OF THE EDUCATIONAL ENVIRONMENT OF HAITI AT THE BEGINNING OF THE TWENTY-FIRST CENTURY.

Common wisdom and observation says that education carries a high valuation in Haiti, sometimes even to the point of a salvific mysticism. With sufficient education, the children will escape poverty. A strong education for everyone will bring about true freedom and democracy. Once everyone knows how to read and write the farms will thrive, the politicians will be constrained to honesty, and the trees will once again cover the hillsides. People say so. More realistically but no less intensely, a Haitian educator notes

> Education remains the biggest national activity after that of food supply. It very much so since to educate is to develop all the life resources of a person or of a nation: identity, autonomie, relationships, values, aspirations, as well as economic, physical, social, intellectual, religious and cultural needs.
>
> [L'éducation demeure la plus grande activité nationale après celles qui ont trait à alimentation. Il en est bien ainsi puisque éduquer c'est développer toute les ressources de vie d'une personne ou d'une nation : son identité, son autonomie, sa vie de relations, ses valeurs, ses aspirations, ses besoins physiques, économiques, sociaux, intellectuels, religieux et culturels.][1]

Evidence that such hopes have credence appears in the sacrifices, often severe, that families make to send at least one child to school.

Such high regard for learning renders the actualities bitterly ironic. Some say literacy has actually decreased in the last decade. Others claim this is simply a problem of gathering and interpreting data. Figures provided in 1981 from the government claimed 20% literacy. A United Nations report of May 1997 reports a literacy rate of 43.4%.[2] The United Nations Human Development Index of 1999 records Haiti as 134th of a total of 162 nations with a rate of 48.8.[3] United Nations Human Development Reports for 2002 using year 2000 figures show an education index of .50[4] The same source sources shows an increase in adult (age 15 and above) literacy rates from 35.1 in 1985 to 49.8 in 2000, still low by global standards.

Statistics on literacy reveal an outcome of problems, not the primary source of them. Investment in public education is low relative to other expenditures of government (and in comparison with many other Caribbean nations). Since 1996, the central government has had a policy of decentralization to the nine Départments (provinces) of the country, so that the most relevant figures are from those sources. The government outlines its official positions in its magazine, *Transparans*.

While treating investments reserved specific to education, it is important to

> recall, in a general way, that the 133 communes of the country disposed for the school year 1996-1997 the sum of 160,558,552 gourdes: 95,334,527 gourdes originated from the Executive branch [the office of the president], and 65,224,005 gourdes were allocations originating from the communes [municipalities].
>
> [En traitant d'investissements spécifiques réservés à l'éducation, il importe de rappeler, de manière générale, que les 133 communes du pays disposaient, au cours de l'exercice 1996-1997...de la somme de 160,558,552 gourdes: 95,334,527 gourdes provenant de l'Exécutif, et 65,224,005 gourdes d'allocations provenant des recettes communales.][5]

The most recent available figures are from 1997 and show the heavily-populated Ouest, where the capital, Port-au-Prince and its metropolitan communes Delmas, Pétion-Ville, Carrefour and Croix-des-Bouquest with a population of 5,242,510 (out of a total population in Haiti of expends the equivalent of 659,338,800 gourdes (=$20,1252 at current exchange of 25 Gourdes to the dollar). This is about 12 to 13 gourdes per capita. The average does not show that affluent Pétion-Ville with 122,269 inhabitants expends 14,007,728 gourdes (= approximately $ 5,0309), or about 115 gourdes per capita, almost ten times the provincial average. Nor do the data show the high percentages of Pétion-Ville students attending its numerous private schools, in contrast to, e.g. Croix-des-Bouquets. Nor yet do they reveal that in a more rural neighborhood of the province, just beyond Croix-des-Bouquets, children of school age responded to a 2002 inquiry with, "*Nou pa genyen lekol.*" "We don't have any school."

Beyond the saddening statistics is the visual evidence anyone visiting the country can gather. Too many schools in cities and especially in the countryside are in disrepair There are often no toilets or supply of clean drinking water, classroom furniture is insufficient and in poor condition. Principals must make insistent requests for blackboards and chalk. Books are rare throughout the whole country.

How can this be in a country where education is held to be a key to personal and national freedom and development?

There are paradoxes nested inside this paradox. To begin with, if a democratic republic requires citizens who can gather facts and think through these for themselves, then schooling based upon rote memorization of texts, as it is in Haiti, is at odds with the health of the nation. French educator, Jacques Rancière, participating in a colloquium in Port-au-Prince on Haiti's transition to democracy remarked on the "myth" and "illusion" that schools (he especially referred to the public schools of Haiti) prepare students to think for themselves.[6] Numerous studies in critical thinking bear out the assertion that verbatim recall tested by ability to recite passages without error does not support the development of free, critical thought essential to the full exercise of citizenship. Observers of Haitian students from elementary school through college are struck by the experience of hearing what sounds like chanting rising up at dawn from nearby yards. They watch in wonderment the dozens of students criss-crossing Champs de Mars in the center of Port-au-Prince, book in hand, alternately reading and repeating the texts aloud. If there is one single stylistic mark of Haitian education up until now and in nearly all schools, public and private, it is this. The method has roots in the powerful oral traditions of Haiti. It has another set of roots in traditional French schooling methods, brought into Haiti primarily by missionaries who provided the greater portion of Haitian education until 1917 and still continue to support a significant number of schools. Rote learning has the merit of developing an ability to concentrate attention and to develop prodigious memory abilities. It is a virtue, but one that has and makes limitations.

A second paradox is that the greater number of schools, public or private, primary through college, have a curriculum better related to the development of a French writer or diplomat than to the immediate and obviously pressing professional and vocational needs of the country. Discussions about this began at least as early as the late nineteenth century and continue into the present. Contenders range themselves along a dichotomy between a presumed "vocationalism" in which one is prepared only for a job, and a presumed "elite classicism" in which one is prepared to talk and write eloquently and philosophically but without consequence in the world of work. The arguments are too often this simply and extremely posited. Some Haitian educators decry the situation. Yvon Joseph regrets that

> Everyone has only the traditional, classical education in mind.The symbol of the education for the government, for the associations, for the organizations, for the churches, for the remainder of the private sector, for the directors, the professors, the parents, the journalists is the traditional classical education, Instruction for technical and professional [work] is marginalized. As for informal or unstructured education, they are not, for all practical purposes, figured into the representations of education [usually] made. Such does not exist, except in some rare non-gouvernmental organizations that are preoccupied with this aspect.
>
> [Tous n'ont en tête que l'éducation tradionelle classique. Le symbole de l'éducation pour le gouvernement, pour les associations, pour les organizations, pour les églises, pour le reste du secteur privé, pour les

> directeurs, les professeurs, les parents, les journalistes, c'est l'éducation classique traditionnelle, L'enseignement technique et professionalisme est marginalisé. Quant à l'»éducation informelle ou non formelle, elle ne figure pas, à toutes fins pratiques, dans les représentations que l'on se fait de l'éducation. Elle n'existe pas, sauf dans quelques rares organisations non- gouvernementales qui s'en préoccupent.][7]

The third paradox is that of language. All Haitians speak Kreyol; a language developed during colonial times on a grammatical base that most linguists describe as derived from African languages. The lexicon is largely French-derived, but includes a sprinkling of words from the native Taìno and a rich assortment of terms acquired from West African languages and all the European languages arriving in the Caribbean after 1492. Until recent decades instruction has been in French with textbooks published in France for French schools. The sometimes peculiar outcome of this practice is that pupils in «The Black Republic» read «Nos ancêtres les Gaulois…» both in a history text and in a commonly-used French grammar, according to Haitians who graduated from high schools as late and the 1960's. (Not to single out the practice for Haiti only, the phrase also appeared in the schoolbooks used in French, North, West and Central Africa. Alfred Camus satirized this irony in his short story, «L'Hôte.)[8]"[9]

There have been many efforts to have instruction in the mother tongue, and to produce texts that reflect the history and actualities of the nations whose students use them. The "blue-eyed ancestors" seem to have returned to their own homes. There are now many more schools that teach the first three years in Kreyol, then move to French. The number of schoolbooks in Kreyol increases slowly.[10] There is resistance to the use of Kreyol at all levels of society, for it continues to be a matter of status and pride to speak and read French rather than Kreyol. This is especially to be observed among teachers in public schools. Yet, one research team found parents distressed because their children were "...ashamed to speak their language and ashamed to do manual labor."[11] There are also those who actively oppose using French as the language of instruction, identifying it with French colonial oppression of slaves. Moreover, they cite the continuing use of French as the official language of an élite and a state that in many respects, it is asserted, continues the same oppression. The literature concerning the issue is extensive, and the resolution of the dilemma requires sensitive approaches. A strong supporter of Kreyol, Haitian linguist, Yves DeJean, noted at a recent conference that ones mother language is the primary and fundamental tool of cognitive development. To marginalize this instrument is thereby to reduce the scope and complexity of a child's potential intellectual development.[12] Nearly all linguistic scholars urge instruction in the national language, but often key teachers, school directors and both urban and rural parents continue to lend their weight to French. The two most oft-encountered reasons stated are (1) the prestige of French both in Haiti and abroad, (2) the presumed greater usefulness of French in the contemporary global economy.

The fourth paradox may be the most significant in responding to the question of how a nation setting high valuation on education would have such weak results. Immediately after winning independence Haitian leaders, notably Christophe and Pétion, saw to the establishment of schools, academies of art and music and libraries. The reversal of these laudatory efforts seems to have come at the time of President Boyer's 1840 reparations paid to France. A depleted national treasury tightened its belt by discontinuing or significantly reducing the educational and cultural subventions. Subsequent history is one of long erosion of public sector support for education. The result is that now the government is by default the minority authority in the nation's educational efforts. Jacky Lumarque, a professor in the École normale supérieur of Haiti and an international education consultant, speaks of "un état sans école" –a nation without a school.

> In 1995[sic, 1985?], effectively, students registered in a public school represented only 33.5% of the population enrolled in any school. In 1988, the public primary schools constituted 20% of the aggregate of this category. This

> proportion is not more than 16.4% in 1995. The picture is not different for the other divisions of instruction, whether one speaks of the number of establishments or of students. The evidence is absolute. What it is conveniently called [in sum] the private sector constitutes a very heterogenous group of actors: NGO's, religious congregations, contractors motivated by profit-seeking, [and] not-for profit associations that exercise responsibility to educate the majority of citizens of the Republic.
>
> [En 1995[sic, 1985?], les effectifs d'élèves inscrits dans une école publique ne représentent que 33,5% de la population scolarisée. En 1988, les écoles primaires publiques constituaient 20% de l'ensemble de cette catégorie. Cette proportion n'est plus que 16,4% en 1995. Le tableau n'est pas différent pour les autres ordres d'enseignement, que l'on parle du nombre d'établissements ou des effectifs. L'évidence est absolue. Ce qu'il est convenue d'appeler le secteur privé qualifie somme toute un ensemble d'acteurs très hétérogène: ONG, congrégations religieuses, entrepreneurs motivés par la researche du profit, associations à but non lucratif, qui exercent la responsabilité d'éduquer la majorité des citoyens de la République.][13]

There are a few schools at secondary and tertiary level that provide instruction in trades, artisan skills and agriculture. Most of these are supported and directed by Christian missionaries, primarily from Roman Catholic orders. The Episcopal Church has an agronomy school combining secondary and some tertiary-level studies in Terrier Rouge in the north, and a tertiary-level institution headquartered in Port-au-Prince offering degrees in both agriculture and business. The Salesians have vocational schools in Cap Haitian and in Port-au-Prince combining instruction in trades and skills with studies in algebra, geometry, biological sciences related to agriculture, and teacher-training. The Salesians support study abroad in France, Canada and the United States for certain talented young men who then become master teachers in the programs. There is a state-supported program for agronomy, but it has suffered episodic closures in recent years.

An interesting part of the mix of private schools are what are called "community" schools, all of them serving elementary pupils, some with continuations into secondary level. The schools come into being as a result of efforts by parents and others in a district too poor to afford the fees, uniforms and supplies for a private or public school.[14] Many live on the edges of districts where the school is too overcrowded to accept more youngsters. They "bootstrap" with literacy program funds, private donations from affluent Haitians, and grants garnered from a range of Haitian and overseas foundations. Their students take the state exams for which they must pay a per capita fee of about $2.00 (about 90 gourdes). Most of the teachers are non-certified, but, when they are able to get outside subventions to pay for their attendance, go to in-service training programs provided by the national government. A recent training session cost a community school $55, of which $40 covered the fee for 19 teachers and one director, and the remainder went for the cantina noon meal served to visiting trainers and the local staff. The figures need to be seen in light of the $40 per month wages for the local teachers.

By 1991, the state did prescribe norms which all schools, public or private, were to follow. Comprehensive tests were designed to assess student learning, and schools which did not meet national standards were to be denied license to conduct classes.[15] In the observation of many, the expectation that all schools, public or private were to satisfy national standards has not been met.[16] A 1997 study of educational needs in the Central Plateau region found

> ...a clear absence of the National Ministry of Education, Youth and Sports (MENJS)...Teacher and administrator qualifications go unchecked because of MENJS's lack of presence and supervision. The schools are not licensed nor are they regulated or monitored and educators are not required to attend any professional development on the new educational plan...Thus, instead of teaching the standards outlined in the new reform plan, they are teaching what they had learned in schools themselves."[17]

Whatever the paradoxes, economic facts are incontestable. Classes are overcrowded. There is a shortage of both teachers and space. Many schools, especially in rural districts, lack the simplest hygienic facilities. Textbooks are in short stock or absent. Ordinary supplies such as paper and pencils are expensive or unobtainable. While one sees old Canadian and U.S. school busses carrying pupils to a private school, children in public or community schools provide their own transportation, usually walking. For some the daily journey is as much as three kilometers each way. Understanding the important connection between nutrition and learning, many private schools, especially those supported by overseas religious groups, have an adjacent cantina where a midday meal is offered. The Salesian vocational schools in Port-au-Prince distribute 25,000 meals to students each year.[18] Some community schools have been able to get matching funds from the United Nations to build cantina units by providing labor and local materials.

SCHOOL SPACE AND SCHOOL TIME IN HAITI

For any school, the space of the school and the time of the school are set apart from the space and time of all other aspects of ordinary life and the surrounding natural or built environment. The case of Haiti is a concentrated example characteristic of schools anywhere. That is, Haitians create and generally show great respect for sacred and dedicated (often quasi-sacred) spaces. Typical of these are Christian church buildings, cemeteries, *calvaires* (crosses or crucifixes with additional sculptures, pictures or ornaments placed in public localities); pilgrimage locales such as a grotto or the Citadel of King Henry Christophe; Vodou temples and wayside shrines, as well as public squares, bridges or battlegrounds where important historic events took place. People with arms upraised in supplications may be observed in any of these locales. (Yet it should be mentioned also that one sees picnics, even rowdy ones with secular or religious music, on these same sites.) The habit of giving honor to a particular demarcation of space carries over into the classrooms, which sometimes, moreover, share the same space as a church. This special quality of classrooms is unsurprising for anyone who in a moment of nostalgia has re-visited the school of his or her youth, sat in the now too-small desks, imagined being "back there." School in many countries does have qualities that resonate with those of religious experience. As Yvon Joseph tells us, the school is a place above all where we develop "...an identity, our autonomy, our way of relating to one another, our values, our aspirations..." There is an intensified sense of privileged set-apartness of the space of a Haitian school perhaps in part a result of lingering effects of the still-recollected time when slaves were forbidden school and learning. The late historian, Jean Fouchard describes in *Regards sur le temps Passe* the evidence for there having been clandestine schools and how these were surely related to the fervent hope for liberty.[19] School is still visibly a place where the privileged have free entry, hence, that space is also associated for many Haitians with possible liberation from poverty and its associated lack of honor.

School time is set apart as well. In Western industrial nations, school-time is one of the major organizing factors of societies. Just ask any traffic engineer. In sectors of Haitian society strongly connected with the "beat" of colleges and universities in North America, families arrange their lives accordingly. The October through June Haitian school year, with its longest tradition tied to the calendar of feasts and saints of the Catholic Church, marks time for a majority of families, even those who have no children enrolled. In the schools directed by or strongly influenced by foreign groups, whether secular or religious, the uses of time associated with the school day and year contrast in some important ways with those of ordinary life in the surrounding communities. A salient factor bears mentioning. Average unemployment in Haiti varies widely from district to district. Firm statistics are not available, but estimates by observers of certain districts range as high as 60%. In late October 2002, some 200 villagers from Acul du Nord tried to enter the United States from a district where unemployment was said to be 90%.[20] Complex factors in flux shape the time and pace of work for the nominally unemployed. The saying goes that "everyone is out of work but everyone is working." A family garden can be scratched out of the hillside the day the rains cease; an axle on the neighborhood truck must be repaired; there is a funeral; a woman with children is sick so someone goes to her side and another takes the children. It is like that day by day. Over the ancient order of events ordered by weather and the rhythm of planting and harvest; rainy season and dry; birth, marriage and death; sunrise, sunset lie the unforeseen exigencies of life on the edge that pull a day this way and that unpredictably. But school time begins sharply at the first bell ringing and ends exactly at the appointed afternoon hour. Assignments are due according to the teacher's plan, rather than when a student's ideas have matured and are ready for "harvest." The test happens ready or not. Punctuality is a greater virtue than readiness. The day is parceled out in clock hours, in contrast to holding discursive consultations with an elder in the family; or accompanying an experienced farmer in order to learn how to plant manioc. School classes start and end at pre-appointed moments, unlike the narrations of the woman who relates what just happened in the market to her neighbors; or the startling tire that creates havoc as it rolls away from under its truck. In school, beginning and ending "on time" is a greater virtue than playing out to completion. School time marches on whether the tire gets mended or not; whether a story is finished, or the way to plant manioc is grasped.

Foreigners who come to Haiti to teach are accustomed to what can be called the "industrial model" of time arrangements. They soon begin to speak of "Haitian time." The contrast between the arrangements inside the schooling framework and that of the surrounding community is an everyday constant. Teaching and learning must occur in this double consciousness of "school time" and "Haitian time." The two intersect and overlap in the observance of holidays, most of them also Holy Days. The official calendar usually has twelve holidays, sometimes more, sometimes less depending upon government decision. In addition to these standard schedules, most schools and many businesses observe Haiti's January 1 Independence Day;

Ancestors' day on January 2; Flag Day on 18 May; the Catholic and Vodou pilgrimage to the sacred site, Saut d'Eau in July; or Mid-August Assumption of the Virgin and commemoration of the Oath for Liberty at Bois Caiman.[21] There are also the movable feasts of Carnival, Holy Week and Easter. The last day of October and beginning of November see the observance of Christian All Saints and All Souls coupled with Vodou Gedè and remembrance of the dead. Both the secular and religious observances include processions, offerings, masses and ceremonies that may occur in the classroom and in the church space conjoined by processions. Teachers visiting from other countries, especially the U.S., are unaccustomed to this permeation of sacred and secular time so characteristic of Haitian life.

School itself from first grade through college graduation sets the learner apart as well. It is only a little exaggerated to say that schooling confers almost the same sort of invisible sacramental seal as preparation for holy orders. Sometimes they are the same for young men who will eventually go into the priesthood or young women who will become sisters. There is the social habit of honor and respect accorded to the teachers and professors, as well as to pupils and students. A person who has achieved a diploma has increased measure of honor and respect. A university degree is a mark of great honor indeed. If the degree is from a university in France, the honor is edged with an aureole slightly more luminous than that of degrees from Canadian and U.S. institutions. The obligations placed on nearly every person undergoing education, especially those from the poorer parts of society, are deeply felt. In fact, there are class differences to be observed. The children of the wealthy often have a range of almost nonchalant attitudes comparable to those one encounters among North American students. The sons and daughters of the old elite (sometimes wealthy but often not so by North American standards) customarily exhibit a sense of duty coupled with patriotism that appears to be handed down as a family tradition. Students from struggling or impoverished families manifest an intense dedication to studies, openly expressing fears about the possibility of failure. While one can see these attitudes in the United States or Canada, their pan-societal intensity and distinctiveness is notable in Haiti.

II. APPROACHES TO SCHOOLING AND THE FORMATION OF TEACHERS BY FIVE NON-GOVERNMENTAL ORGANIZATIONS

Faculty and supervisors in Haiti's public schools of Haiti are engaged in a monumental task, in general utilizing scant resources to advantage. Many put in uncounted extra hours, sometimes waiting longer for a paycheck than most educators elsewhere would tolerate. Their mission, support systems, curricula and results deserve special study and attention. In fact there have been some studies, which while critical of the lack of support from a government which is itself running in deficit, and of curricula and pedagogies that are judged to be either out-of-step or inadequate for the country's needs, do usually give the teachers "A" for diligence and dedication. Yet the public school system remains Haiti's minority educational provider. According to figures available in 2000, the state supported only 16.44% of primary schools, while 83.6% were in the private sector. At the secondary level the comparable figures were 16.85% public schools and 83.15% private.[22] The remainder of this discussion is thus devoted to the role of five private, non-governmental educational efforts, each with a distinctive approach to teaching and learning. The five were selected partly on the basis of opportunities to make direct field observations and partly in order to show a variety of possible modes. One focuses on development and implementation of community-generated plans for literacy, one on providing community library resources, one on artisanal skills development, one on direct provision of classroom instructional services, and one on the preparation of education professionals. Each also addresses the range of instruction, teacher preparation, ancillary services such as libraries and study centers as related to the central mission. All are oriented toward the increase and improvement of education of the youth of Haiti. They include Beyond Borders, FOKAL, Fondation Vincent, L'École L'Amitie, and the Faculty of Education of Regina Assumpta, "the FÉRA." The description of the FÉRA program incorporates a case study of a course designed to teach both content (history of art) and instructional strategies as yet infrequently used in Haiti. The case study provides specific instantiations of some of the opportunities and difficulties educators in Haiti face.

A. BEYOND BORDERS

Beyond Borders, an ecumenical Christian organization has as its central motif the "transformative"model for education. They "...foster transformative learning by supporting indigenous organizations in Haiti; placing volunteers who are seeking to learn from, and live out the gospel within Haitian communities; hosting short visits of small groups of people from industrialized countries who want to learn more about how to confront human misery and hunger in the world." The collaborating organization in Haiti is Limyè Lavi (Light of Life), whose mission statement is " Limyè Lavi is a group of Haitians and expatriates who cooperate as servants of God and Christ to cultivate knowledge and experience that lead to liberation."[24] The organization is greatly concerned with literacy in reciprocity with community development. There is an office in Washington, D.C., and another headquarters in Port-au-Prince. Their governing board consists of an equal number of Haitians living in Haiti and of North Americans. Projects are approved by reaching consensus. Proposals for projects come from communities in Haiti, or are generated by members of the board who have identified a need, or are brought to the board by interested others with experience in the Haitian educational environment. They have a long-standing relationship with Rotalpha, the literacy project of the Haitian division of Rotary International. In addition to promulgating their own projects, Beyond Borders sometimes acts as designated fiscal agents for other not-for-profit educational endeavors who need a 501(C)3 tax-exemption status.[25] The board must review the intentions of cooperating organizations and the Haitian members of the board make a site visits to assess feasibility of the project legitimacy of the organization, and congruence with the guiding philosophy of education of Beyond Borders.

Beyond Borders uses a technique they call *Wonn Refleksyon* (Reflection Circle) as a major component of their preparation of *animateurs* (instructors) for literacy programs. Small groups –ten to fifteen ¾ of potential animateurs sit in a circle with an experienced facilitator. The facilitator simply keeps the process moving, without initiating ideas. That is the responsibility of the others in the circle. What is needed in the community? How can we see that the need is met? How can we best implement the possible solutions we think of? How will we know things are working out the way they should? Along the way the new animateurs learn how to facilitate their own Wonn Refleksyon and are encouraged to use it as a main pedagogical strategy.[26]

Beyond Borders believes that local Haitian communities have a well-developed sense of their own needs and can devise locally appropriate means for meeting them. Financing is a constant issue, but often a part of this need is met by astute use of local resources. Beyond Borders expands the method for initiating basic literacy skills to the formation of teachers in the schools. Since most schools proceed with rote learning, "transformative model" is in some ways against the grain. So it is, if one looks only at the space and time of more formal schools. In the context of some of the oldest Haitian ways of teaching and learning and just getting daily tasks done it is familiar for generations. The governing board of the organization points to the long tradition of "*konbit*." [27] Throughout its history Haiti has been and remains an agriculturally-based society. The konbit (work group)[28] began as early as colonial times possibly as a retention of West African ways[29] and after the revolution became a major tactic for insuring good production. In the absence of taskmasters, but with the same production needs before them, Haitians would constitute themselves as a community to assist in the work of planting, cultivating and harvesting. At each small farm, the host farmer would provide food and drink, musicians from the community at large set the pace for work and everyone else pitched in. When the work for that family was complete, the whole community moved to the next family, repeating the process until all crops for the entire community were ready. With the enlargement of farms and the steady move toward industrialization of agriculture in Haiti, the konbit is passing away. Some have pointed to uneven and sometimes inequitable divisions of work and shared benefits as an even stronger factor in its near-demise. Yet it continues to thrive in principle in many of the women's cooperatives and other, mostly rural collaborations. The Wonn Refleksyon makes use of ways of learning and of collaboration toward the accomplishment of common tasks existing in Haiti from its beginnings. Yet, some observers of the method point out that traditionally there were also elders or strong personalities that guided or dominated community decision-making. Further, they assert that it has been rare to see a community in Haiti or anywhere that operates consistently and over long periods of time on a purely consensual system of agreement.

In any case, the formation of teachers (and of workers in other endeavors as well) in this manner makes new use of the old ways, gives them a name and a statement of the inherent principles and prepares instructors to interact in much the same manner in their own classrooms. The organization reports doing sessions for teachers from public and private schools, with a greater number coming from the latter source. It is a method well adapted to teaching and learning in technical, artisan skills, and equally suitable for teaching such basic skills as reading, writing and mathematics. Teachers who have learned to make use of the reflection circle are prepared to implement forms of collaborative education now infrequent in Haitian classrooms, but successful in many North American situations. Two strengths of the method are apparent. One, it engages the learners themselves in the identification and specification of what it is they need to learn. This process is itself a major step in grasping new materials and skills, laying out a clear foundation for the stages to follow. This strategy works for nearly any subject. Two, it is interactive, so that the insights and grasp of concepts by one is available to all. Thus, both individual and the cohort realize gains beyond what the most apt can accomplish alone. The chief limitation is strict adherence to the role of leadership as only facilitator, who may hold back a rich amount of knowledge and experience in favor of generating learning out of the less-informed members of the circle.

Wonn Refleksyon workshops may involve as many as three days of reflection and generation of needs, ideas and solutions in an on-going community "free-think" where everyone's ideas are put up for consideration, and the eventual management structure is an outcome of the process. In the end all must agree or the initiative is discarded. Literacy and schooling are among the perennial decision outcomes. The joint project Beyond Borders conducts with Haitian Rotary trains leaders in the interactive, non-hierarchical methods for the Rotary literacy program. The organization conducts its own annual board meeting in this open fashion, thus both setting an example and gaining direct experience of possibilities and limitations. In both the Wonn Refleksyon and the two to three-day retreat, every participant serves as both leader and follower. Potential teachers and leaders by observation and practice acquire skills for interactive teaching and learning in a non-hierarchical environment.

June 1, 2001 through June 30, 2002 report on activities of Beyond Borders and includes, among others: The Experiment in Alternative Leadership; literacy, school and leadership development activities in Cite Soliel; Port-au-Prince Discovering Resources Initiative, the Farmers' Association and the Lady of Grace Elementary

School in Mariaman; FAVILEK, a women's organization in Port-au-Prince; Louverture Cleary School in Santo, and Rotalpha.

A key feature of the literacy efforts is oriented at reaching older children who have missed out on opportunities to attend school. David Diggs describes the program as " is restricted to children who are 'sur age' or 'over-aged' for starting a traditional school. Hence the program only lasts four years. Some children who complete the program get the chance to be mainstreamed into private schools. Most do not, but finish the program being functionally literate."[30]

In 2001 there were 1686 children entering the fifty-seven centers in the Les Cayes region. Of these, 1486 completed the school year. Some of the non-finishers were children whose parents were able to move them into the several rural schools newly opened by the Haitian government. The program has four levels, and for the year cited there were 589 in level one, 535 in level two, 212 in level three and 150 in level four. Diggs estimates that in the last 15 years 300 to 400 have graduated from the program.[31]

B. FOKAL (FONDATION CONNAISSANCE ET LIBERTÉ/FONDASYON KONESANS AK LIBETE), A NON-GOVERNMENTAL, NON-SECTARIAN HAITIAN ORGANIZATION[32]

In 1995, building upon experience as Haitians, and from studies abroad, it seemed both needed and possible to create an organization to support the establishment of small libraries publicly accessible, to engage the neighbors in the planning, use and development of the libraries; and to provide apprenticeship and instruction in a range of academic and artisanal skills related to the library services. Initiators began with programs in literacy, teacher training and a debate group. A special concern was to "...integrate marginalized populations in the process of school reform as a way to structure communities around their schools and to interact with them." The dream was to create a "...just, democratic and open society" by means of making knowledge fully accessible to all Haitians. The partners in FOKAL's efforts included "peasants' associations, youth groups, women's organizations, parents' committees, specialized institutions, schools, universities and libraries" in Haiti and international partners from outside the country.

The principles undergirding the teacher-training program are to utilize and maximize interaction, collaboration, and critical thinking. The libraries, standing outside the school space and school time are more free to experiment with new methods of teaching and learning, with the introduction of new texts in a range of subjects which may be neglected or avoided in the structured public and private schools. (For example, basic nutrition, health, hygiene and human sexuality texts are absent from many Haitian classrooms. Recent Kreyol texts in such topics are now in the FOKAL libraries.) The efforts, especially centering around neighborhood libraries, were underway with successes to record when the work came to the attention of George Soros. His Foundation for an Open Society provided a significant subvention to advance the projects. The eventual aim is for FOKAL to become self-sustaining, financed entirely from within Haiti.

Teachers and potential teachers are drawn from all parts of Haitian social geography, but there is great attention paid to encouraging the development of teachers from districts and social groups least served under the present conditions. As with Beyond Borders, there is a presumption that those who, for the time being, may be illiterate typically have knowledge, skill, social insight, cultural and religious gifts, and wisdom to bring to the learning process –their own and that of the people they will eventually instruct.

The traditional classical education is honored and supported in the high regard for literacy, and in the treasuring of literary and philosophical works. One of the early projects was to rebind some choice Haitian books, joining physical and intellectual caretaking of a part of Haiti's cultural heritage into a single process. The word used in

Haiti for teacher –*animateur*, an "animator", describes the energy of such training processes.

The original two libraries and sites for creating cadres of literacy and school animateurs had by 2001 become over fifty sites in nearly every part of Haiti, with plans for more. There are requests from all parts of the country for FOKAL staff to come do in-service teacher training and to help establish community libraries. As the organization moves toward becoming self-sustaining, it must move more slowly than the expanding needs of the country. Meanwhile to the extent it is possible with careful husbanding of all financial and human resources available, the current goals include an emphasis on "...providing quality education, teacher training, on encouraging parent involvement in the schools, and on enhancing economic, social and cultural development of the community. We have deliberately chosen children and youth as our target group, and have the great ambition to provide access to knowledge, books, the Internet, tools of scientific learning, and a full and equal life as citizens."[33]

For FOKAL, then, teacher training is conceived of as centered in a community and as generated out of the particular qualities and needs of a community. Librarians, parents and youth all participate in joint efforts. Hence, in some way, each is a learner engaged in processes of gathering both book- and experiential knowledge. In some sense everyone is an apprentice, and everyone is a giver of information. A "teacher" so designated is simply one who has taken on special responsibility for a set of leading duties.

C. FONDATION VINCENT, A SECONDARY-LEVEL VOCATIONAL, AGRICULTURAL SCHOOL[34]

Fondation Vincent, one of the educational programs provided by the Salesian Missions in Haiti, occupies several hectares of land at Haut de Cap just south of Cap Haitian. Buildings include administrative offices, classrooms, dormitories for students, the several vocation-specific workshops, a plant nursery, animal barns, poultry houses and land devoted to crops, pasture and forestry. Students have classes in traditional school subjects, and in the studios directly integrate such subjects as algebra, trigonometry and geometry, and biology into the actual production of iron work, furniture making, automobile repair, agronomy and animal husbandry.

Many of the instructors are former students who showed interest and aptitude for teaching. One of them described his career trajectory as having begun when, orphaned, he came to the Salesians for shelter. He enjoyed learning, and was especially interested in engines. He made good progress throughout his school years then spent some apprentice time in another, larger Salesian mission in Haiti. Having acquitted himself with distinction there, he received a scholarship to do an apprenticeship in an automobile factory in France. He did some studies in educational theory with the Salesians, and is articulate and voluble about the guiding philosophies of the Fondation.[35]

He and the other instructors interviewed see the program as appropriate for the current needs of the country and as sound preparation for students. They see strength in the integration of, for example, geometry and welded iron work; algebra and the design of tools for furniture making; botany and the care of the plant nursery. Graduates from the school are able to follow an artisan trade, and nearly all graduates are fully employed in a locality where there is up to very high unemployment. Some of the employment is at the Fondation itself that has a steady local clientele especially for the production of school- and office furniture, and is a major supplier of vegetable and decorative plants. These students have also acquired habits of attention, persistence, and problem solving that enable them to move into management positions or to change employment when necessary. They are admired in the community for these accomplishments, and the instructors themselves are accorded special regard.[36] While instructors admire the classical education offered in the private and public schools of the district, they view the philosophies and practices of Fondation Vincent as more strongly related to Haiti's current needs.

Nearly all instructors have come up through the ranks. They themselves begin their teacher training as youngsters in the classrooms. Thereafter, those whose duties will include teaching begin to receive class- and hands-on experiential instruction in the workshops. Some undergo further studies in post-secondary institutions in Haiti and abroad. The program includes both theoretical and apprentice aspects. The director of the school holds an advanced degree and also teaches educational studies in another institution. All instructors' training is heavily weighted toward interactive learning in which induction, deduction and discovery play strong roles. The program and the teacher training thus contrast sharply with the rote instruction more common throughout the country, and with the classical education in French common in many private schools.

D. L'ÉCOLE L'AMITIÉ, A COMMUNITY SCHOOL

A painting from the time when Haiti was St.-Domingue depicts the French colonist who owned a stretch of bay shore known as "La Fossette" enjoying a picnic with his elegantly dressed family. The little inlet is now a landfill and L'École L'Amitie occupies the site, a municipal demarcation between two so-called "popular" districts on the south side of Cap Haitian. "Popular" is a euphemism for destitute bidonvilles. Houses share common walls with one or two neighbors. Sometimes the cheek-by-jowl cubicles surround a central space or "lakou" used by the ubiquitous pigs, goats and chickens and by homeless adults and children who have no other place to sleep. Descriptions of mediaeval European cities at their population zenith and of the swollen port cities of Asia that sprang up in the wake of the first waves of international shipping are apt. Most houses are without electricity, and toilet facilities are rudimentary. Many doorways, often the only opening of the dwelling, serve as informal vending "shops." Everyone seems to be selling something to everyone else in a scarcity economy of exchange and recycling.

The school is an island of relative spaciousness, although as many as ninety children may occupy one of the nine classrooms. Sometimes the overflow children stand outside the window, straining forward to hear and see. There is a schoolyard, but it is bisected by a drainage canal that, after a heavy rain, looks more like an open sewer. There are active plans to cover the canal and to place large containers of potherbs on top. The children will soon learn to plant and care for the herbs, which will be used to flavor the midday beans and rice. In a way the school is an institutional "squatter," but when the municipal authorities were about to put the drainage ditch right against the school wall, parents of the thousand youngsters who study there occupied the ground until a better decision came about. Since late spring of 2001, there is a cantina where the children have a noon meal prepared by women from the community. A UNESCO organization matched the local "sweat equity" and bags of cement to enable the community to build the kitchen and covered eating place.[38] Additional spaces to accommodate the increasing flow of children are either planned or in progress, which incidentally insures paid formal employment for approximately 20 men in the district. Materials used are also locally procurable.[39]

There are nineteen teachers and a Director, each with classes of 80 and more children. There are few books, none for take-home. The blackboards are barely usable. So minimal are the accommodations that visitors looking to see what might be done shake their heads in disbelief that learning can take place under such circumstances.

Learning does take place. When informally queried about some basic elements of early schooling, children will eagerly and with great pride do a recitation. Despite the dependence –probably necessary in this instance –on rote learning, the youngsters are able to play number and word games sprung on them unexpectedly by a visitor. A review of their national exams examination scores shows a high percentage of passing grades. At the end of the 2001-2002 school year, 120 of the 130 youngsters completing the final year of the school (equivalent to sixth grade in the US) passed their certificate exams. One hundred got places in two public schools with scholarship subventions. In spring of 2002, the sixth grade entered the Cap Haitien academic competition, held for all schools, public, private and community. The whole neighborhood rejoiced as the youngsters went from round one to round two, to quarter finals and then took one of the two places at semi-finals. They could not attend the final competition. There is a fee for each student participating and contestants must wear "clothing suitable for this important occasion." They think they would have won.

The teachers all lack a college degree. Most also lack the two-year certificate that many public school teachers have. Yet, in extensive conversations about their methods and strategies for teaching so many pupils in such crowded circumstances, unquantifiable factors emerge that, at least in part, explain their success. They are all dedicated to the task before them. They all care about the children. Each has a repertory of ways to insure that attention stays focused and that learning takes place.[40] When there is any opportunity to do in-service training they scrabble around to find the money to pay for the sessions the government offers. They collaborate with each other to share experiences, thus learn from each other. They all live in one or the other of the two neighborhoods in which the pupils live, so they are sharply aware that their task is one of the most important in the nation. They may go as many as four months without pay, as the people they serve are unable to scrape the funds together. So far, over a period of several years, at desperate moments, resources appear and the teachers and school go on.

The neighborhood is too poor to provide steady salary to the staff; too poor to send their children to the public school. That school is far away, is already even more overcrowded than L'Amitié, and the required uniforms and fees are more than most of these families can manage. Some Cap Haitien artists[41] who knew the district well and had friends and family there began to press for a solution to the problem. Thus encouraged by enthusiasm and some small donations, the community pulled themselves together in a sort of "konbit" to see what could be done. The collaboration of all the parents has created a source of donated labor, and sometimes of donated materials which then is matched by one or another donor organization. There is a board of directors, a budget that is open for review, and administrative means to receive, use and account for resources. L'École L'Amitié is as clear an example as can be presented of the school as a near-sacred civic institution and teaching as a consecrated duty.

Viewing teacher training for the staff at L'Amitié from the point of view of the elaborate and sophisticated programs in Europe and North America and through a disciplinary lens of recent advances educational theory and practice obscures its actualities. Beyond the blinding enlightenment of modernity one can nevertheless see enough happening to keep a thin little string of learning in place, some fragile anchor to secure the future. The oldest ways of all are in place and active. The teachers remember how they were taught and put that into practice, for good or ill. They are constantly attentive to their students, hence find ways to connect what needs to be known with the potential knower. They are there every day as embodied witnesses to the importance of learning. They immediately respond to any chance to learn from other teachers who have more experience and training. They are people from the community, hence tacitly and profoundly identified with those they teach.

E. FACULTÉ DES SCIENCES DE L'EDUCATION , REGINA ASSUMPTA - "THE FERA"[42]

The FERA is a private post-secondary school, accredited through College of Notre Dame, Manchester, New Hampshire, currently administered by Canadian and United States Holy Cross Sisters.[43] The mission is to prepare teachers and other education professionals for primary and secondary schools of Haiti and to promote the development of studies in educational theory and practice focused on the needs of Haiti. Graduates receive a baccalaureate degree from both the Haitian institution and the college in the United States. The degree (a "license" in education in Haiti) is valid in Haiti, Canada and the United States. The license indicates broader and longer preparation than the certificate of education. Many of the students become principals, superintendents, and district supervisors even before completing the degree.

The objectives of the program in addition to the granting of the degree is

"...to give to the persons engaged in educational work:

- the occasion and the means to analyze their educational experience and confront [and learn from] the experiences of others;
- the theoretical and methodological knowledge to enable them to best apprehend the complexity of educational situations to the end that they can move in the direction of innovations;
- an initiation into and practice of research in the sciences of education.

With the knowledge acquired, the students are invited to participate to articulate different theoretical and methodological approaches with their own projects and [school] personnel."[44]

The FERA deliberately seeks to encompass diverse approaches and methods of instruction. Faculty and students have computers available and by 2001 they were able to access the web and to send and receive electronic mail. This is far more expensive than such means are in North America hence the initial utilization was modest. By fall of 2002 more computers were installed, consistent access to the internet was available and each faculty and staff member had an email address. Faculty seek to present and make direct use of the whole range of traditional educational methods, and have periodic in-service training to become acquainted with recent educational thinking and practice. There are lectures, but many classes are interactive and the laboratory sessions engage students in "bench" experience. The laboratories are said to be the best in the Department du Nord. Many on the faculty emphasize the skills of observation, analysis, summary and explication, and make specific efforts to overcome the exclusive use of rote memorization. There is a small library, and students have opportunities to do short research papers making use of the resources available there.

Students pay tuition fees equivalent to US$35.00 per course to attend. This is small by North American standards but often represent a significant sacrifice for the students. There is some scholarship assistance for unusual circumstances. Nearly all students come from modest to poor situations, and nearly all have full-time or part-time jobs, many in public and private schools. For nearly all it is a serious, even sacrificial, financial investment.

FERA STUDENT LIFE

Classes commence at 5:00 in the evenings and end at 8:00, with most students coming straight from work. There is no food on the campus, so most have no supper on the days they attend classes. Many drive or take the "tap-tap" bus from as far away as Fort Liberté, a town over 60 kilometres away over roads that are dangerous and scarcely passable. One supervisor of a parochial school in a small village near Port-au-Prince journeyed the distance each week (some 200km., half-hour by plane but up to 8 hours by highway) to Cap Haitian for two days of classes. The degree is a heroic physical achievement.

Students enrolled at the FÉRA had attended public or private schools where all instruction was in French despite the fact that Kreyol was their home language. The dominant, nearly exclusive, teaching method they had experienced was lecture and rote memorization. All had strong abilities to listen or read and recall. They had no prior instruction and practice in library or archive uses and none reported ever having done a book report or term paper before coming to the college. Nor had any done fieldwork. Many had a range of "hands-on" skills learned at home or in their community. Of the sixty students taking a course in art history, one had studied art and was actually a painter. With three exceptions, students were the first in their family to enroll in college. With five exceptions, each was teaching and/or supervising in a public or private school in the *Departement du Nord*. Exceptions were a journalist, a secretary, a auditing volunteer at the school with advanced degrees from Canadian universities, an airline pilot, and a bank teller.

III. TEACHERS LEARNING ABOUT THE HISTORY OF ART

COURSE DESCRIPTION, RATIONAL AND THE DUAL SYLLABUS

How and why did the FÉRA institute a study of art history as a requirement for the degree and license for educational sciences? This particular study is viewed as a "frill" by many who see a greater need in Haiti for "more practical" courses. A part of the story has to do with liberal arts sciences distribution expectations in traditional degree programs in North America where art history usually fulfills all or part of the humanities requisite. Notre Dame in New Hampshire as an accredited college has its version of those requisites. A more weighty factor included the educational philosophy of a crucial administrator who saw a study of the arts as a means by which the future teachers could acquire a range of intellectual abilities by-passed in the lecture/memorization mode of instruction. Moreover, she and others agreed that it was important on several counts for students to learn about the significant heritage of Haitian painting, better known outside the country than within it. To have this important cultural contribution recognized would promote a sense of cultural and personal worth among students while providing richer information about their own heritage.

The course catalogue description is brief:

> "AR201 History of Art. The course introduces the student to the evolution of art through the centuries. Attention will be given to: the history of Haitian art, naïve painting and its ties to Vodou and social and political realities; how Haitian art developed, is developing and how it is situated in international art. 3 credits."

Six to nine hours of instruction each week for a total of 45 classroom hours met U.S. norms for a three-credit study. There were homework assignments, projects due at the end of the term, examinations during the term and a final examination of three hours duration. The syllabus, lectures, additional print materials handed out for classes, copies of tests, copies of assignments, attendance and grades records permanently filed for review by accreditation officials. The bibliography included books on reserve in the library. There were no texts since comprehensive art history texts must be imported from France at costs far beyond any student's ability to pay. (Typically the cost is US$90.00 plus shipping costs.) Until late in 2001, there was no text for Haitian art history that included colored illustrations. Had it been available, the US$150.00 cost would have been prohibitive.

Students were heavily dependent upon time in class and the library for their acquisition of the art history survey portion of the study.

THE DUAL SYLLABUS

The curriculum committee of the sister college approved a syllabus meeting their guidelines and the requisites for United States accreditation. The syllabus met the conditions of this approved document in every respect, but really served as the substrate for the important perceptual/cognitive studies. The parallel syllabus included a range of strategies for teaching and learning to be demonstrated, with attention called as to how these could be used in the classrooms where the students were or would be teaching. Furthermore, course "content," methodology and structural design had to take numerous factors into consideration that normally do not form part of the conversation of United States curriculum committees. Some of these were anticipated in the double syllabus, but others emerged in the interactions between students and professor.

. With a wide and rich number of possible selections, the course focused on those art works most likely to open up opportunities for analysis and discussion. Diversity of periods and styles and the many ways artists related to the circumstances of their times and places were at issue as well. The selections included works from Cave of Chauvet, France; Egypt; Ancient Greece and Rome; selected eras from China; selections from Byzantine, Gothic and Renaissance arts and architecture; selections from West African works; nineteenth and twentieth century French art from the time of the Haitian Revolution through mid-twentieth century; and Haitian art of the same historical period. The parallel syllabus added:

- development of observation skills in the actual environment and in the arts;
- development of visual recall of environment and arts;

- ystems for organizing reports of observation (text and graphics);
- methods for analysis, summarizing, comparison and contrast (text and graphics);
- methods for engaging students in the discovery and explication of the material being studied;
- strategies for collaborative study and report;
- information search, retrieval and organization, centered on library work;
- identification and documentation of arts and artists in the region, using cameras, sound tape, video and note-taking as teaching/learning tools.

In the second year of the course, students also created twelve-page, bilingual schoolbooks using Haitian art to illustrate key historical events.

Development of observation skills in the actual environment and in the arts

Unlike their North American counterparts, the Haitians had not grown up with crayons, coloring books, paper, markers, scissors and other arts and crafts materials. Nor had they had any of the instruction in arts or museum visits so common outside Haiti.[45] Since all their school instruction had been by the rote method, the skills in the parallel syllabus were unfamiliar and proved a challenge to all. As sessions began, it became apparent that the students lacked a range of vocabulary either in French or Kreyol for describing and discussing color, shape, and composition. This was a surprise and entailed the speedy creation of graphic charts and the use of some classroom exercises with crayons, markers and paper. The students learned rapidly, and regretted they would not be able to do the same in their own schools due to the lack of materials.

In the process of learning to make thorough, accurate observations, students encountered their own habits of attention and noted the limitations these placed upon comprehensiveness. They were all skilled at gathering information related to daily necessities and the vicissitudes of life in a difficult place. They easily described facial expression, gesture and posture of individuals, and the disposition of groups in the market or in the central plaza. They had much greater difficulty describing the surrounding environment, tending to report response to it rather than a description of what was there to be seen. The lack of art materials and lessons meant that the process of looking at an object or a landscape and then drawing it was completely outside these students' experience. Students appeared not to recognize sections of their own countryside in photographs, and had difficulty describing what they saw there. They quickly recognized but had difficulty describing city scenes. They all recognized the regional historical sites, such as the Citadel, or Milot near Palais San Souci, but not Milot Centre Ville through which one passes to arrive there. Many had surprising difficulty in distinguishing photographs from paintings, while others seemed to make the distinction but to have to struggle for the descriptive language. In class the slides of art works presented some problems in this respect, with the slide itself understood as the work by some. Actual works viewed in class presented no such problem. It emerged that the complaint of the science teachers that their students did not know how to make observations was well taken. Students simply had had no experience or instruction in how to use and increase their own powers of looking, discriminating, detecting, grasping and analyzing higher-order visual relationships, and then putting the results into their own words.

In each class session students themselves had to describe the works viewed before receiving any information from the instructor. This plan was met with groaning and complaints but over time moans yielded to pride in being able to complete the task. It annoyed them greatly at first, became a sort of on-going joke, and finally came to be a pattern at which they were more and more skilled. Every gain in ability was mirrored back to them. The instructor made some positive use of every accurate description, and errors simply received a request to try again. The only way to learn how to do this unfamiliar task was to do it. Patience and positive reinforcement were the requisites. By the end of the term, all students had made significant gains, about 10% had become adept, and most could do an acceptably complete and specific description.

The great difficulty these dedicated and intelligent students had with observation points to a serious problem in the educational system. The art history course was an appropriate place to work toward amelioration. Teacher education and in-service training that develops the skill *and* leads teachers to understand how to include it in their own classrooms is essential. *This need cannot be overstated in its fundamental import.*

Development of visual recall of environment and arts

Students received praise for their prodigious memory of text and oral presentation, but that skill was excluded as a learning strategy for the purposes of the course. Instead they learned some simple systems of enhancing visual recall of large amounts of detailed material –all those art objects from 35,000 Before the Present until now. Students expressed dismay at the lack of a text about the works to memorize, and at the fact that the examinations would test visual recall, and ability to describe, analyze and compare rather than memorized names, dates and titles. Many complained loudly. However, from the first day, they began to use a visual technique of recall by location first described by ancient Greek philosophers. Students had studied Greek history and philosophy (but not Greek art) in lycée so had respect for the source. This enabled them to go along with the game long enough to discover that it worked.

All the art presentation sessions were to be thought of as "galleries," with each student imagining a gallery into which one could walk and imagine seeing the works along the walls. This simple but efficacious strategy enabled most students quickly to arrive at strong recall ability for the works seen in each class session. Those who had difficulty were exactly those who were inattentive during the presentation. (It should be reiterated that many students in the class were almost certainly sleep-deprived and hungry, two deterrents to attention.)

Recall of environmental features seemed more challenging. This may well have been in part due the fact that environment is by definition continuous rather than clearly framed as in photos or paintings, and in part because students were accustomed to focusing on only those aspects of their environment needed for immediate action. (Thus "framing" it.) Class discussions included information about the complex ecologies out of which art works arise, and into which they return as part of the continuing human conversation.[46] There were some practice exercises in description and some attention to how students could engage their own pupils in observation and description of aspects of their enveloping local ecologies, and even how that might connect with art study directly.[47] As with arts, ecology is an uncommon study in Haitian schools and the environmental field trips usual in North American schools are rare or altogether missing. No FERA students had participated in such sessions. Courses in both biological sciences and in art history tried to begin to redress this lack.

SYSTEMS FOR ORGANIZING REPORTS OF OBSERVATION; Methods for analysis, summarizing, comparison and contrast

Since many students were teachers or supervisors, they were familiar with reporting to the next levels up in a managerial hierarchy on official forms. None had generated such forms. Many had perhaps pondered as they filled out a form, "Why are they asking for this?" But none had pursued either question to get at the issue of the relation of information gathered to the gatherer to the eventual reader/user. In the art history course they were to gather information, organize the report for their own future use and for the use of eventual students to whom they might teach something about art.

In the case of the documentation of artists/craftspeople, questions and reports were in part for their own use and in part to become records kept in the Regina Assumpta library for use by others. None, including the journalist, had ever before systematically organized information gathering from observation, and the analysis, summarizing and possible comparing and contrasting. None had garnered information with the probable end-use or user in mind. Their information gathering had consisted of the famous rote memory of givens, to be reiterated as response to examination questions. This is opposite to the process of gathering and using information for purposes integrated into larger studies - or indeed of life - outside the classroom.

Imagination came into play as students tried to figure out how they and other interested persons might need or use their observations. They envisioned specific audiences and their particular interests, present and future, then began to shape their processes accordingly. This strategy, a commonplace in secondary and post-secondary writing courses elsewhere, is practically unknown in Haiti. In order to make their observations clear to others they began to make use of outlines, charts and graphs, most of them closely following models seen in class as part of the instructional techniques. For some the process of organizing observations had interesting consequences, as it led them to see and understand relationships in their larger environment heretofore overlooked. Students all made progress, and some reported that this had made some of their other studies easier to understand and remember. Some of the organization took place in the teams, where they assisted each other in the increase of skill and knowledge. The process was similar to the kinds of mutual assistance interactions in the Wonn Refleksyon, the informal group sessions in FOKAL libraries, or in the workshops at Fondation Vincent. The mutual generation of ideas with each member of the team serving various roles as needed worked well for most. There were a few complaints that "X" or "Y" was not pulling the load, but they resolved this among themselves. Overall, their progress in using these new study, communications and knowledge acquisition skills indicated a high potential for development along these lines in other types of studies. These ordinary study and communications skills are left underdeveloped in rote systems, hence the diminishing fullest use of the considerable body of knowledge thus acquired.

FORMAL INFORMATION SEARCHES; The library assignments

For many students, a library was a new experience. Until the FOKAL efforts of the last decade, libraries were private, except for the national library, or open only to the students and faculty of the few schools that were strongly supported by outside donors. The Regina Assumpta Library is open to all students and for a time was also open to the public. A Holy Cross priest trained in library science set up a Dewey Decimal System catalog and provided instruction to library assistants. Students often were learning to use library information resources at the same time they were studying art history. Only two knew how to "mine" the catalogue or a book for information. The first book reports revealed that only two had ever done such an exercise. They did not know how to arrange bibliographical information or make a citation. With the same two exceptions plus one, they did not understand the concept of summarizing major points, and presented instead a personal reaction and opinion of what they had read. By the end of the term, with six short reviews turned in, each student showed improvement. However, the notion of summary eluded many of them. They would select an idea that especially interested them as the "main" point then give a long disquisition of personal reaction and opinion mode. Much more instruction was needed in this important area. Using the illustrations as a basis for improving visual analytical skills showed progress by only three students. This too needed many more hours of instruction and practice. When these teachers know ways to maximize use of libraries and books, they will be in a position to create a rapidly expanding surface of knowledge wherever they are throughout the country.

Many educators make the claim that information search, retrieval and organization skills at any level of technology from books to the World Wide Web are fundamental and essential. The case of this cohort of Haitian students gives an alert. North American educators coming from a situation where libraries and general use of informational resources both in schools and in public facilities may be surprised to find a significant difference of information search skills in areas of the Caribbean where comparable systems do not exist. It may be that the introduction of web-based information search and retrieval habits will render this lack irrelevant. Yet the book culture seems if anything sturdier than ever, indicating that the need to enhance the teaching of how to use a book and how to use a library continue to be pivotal to community development.

DOCUMENTATIONS

Many students expressed positive opinions about the documentation project. They had the option of doing or not doing the project, and chose unanimously to participate. Most apparently enjoyed working in a team to accomplish the project. They worked diligently to complete the projects and present them attractively. They formed their own teams, did their own searches to locate artists and craftspeople, and made their own arrangements with the subjects, all of whom were pleased to participate. Most students were surprised to discover so many good artists and craftspeople nearby.

The equipment used was simple: some one-time use 35mm. cameras, one-time Polaroids used to give each artist or craftsperson a photo, sound tape recorders, borrowed video cameras and their own notebooks. They received instruction on the use of the equipment, some rules of courtesy to follow, and check-in procedures. They were to devise their own questions, but it became evident that they needed some instruction as to a range of possible questions. None except the journalist had made such inquiries prior to the course assignment. The instructor was available to attend studio interviews, but served as simply as observer and sometimes as technical assistant. There was a high degree of cooperation, and every team completed at least two documentaries. This aspect of the course generated the most enthusiasm, was conducted by students themselves with the least prodding or prompting, and was the locus where some of the most sturdy acquisition of the techniques and strategies for teaching and learning occurred.

SCHOOLBOOK PRODUCTION

Just as with the documentation option, students taking the course the second year it was offered agreed to participate in the creation of twelve-page books for pupils in their own schools. Having agreed, they all resisted doing the books in Kreyol, so the compromise was to do the texts in both Kreyol and French. None had ever engaged in such a project, and again saw how they could do something similar in their own schools, were the materials to be provided. At the FERA, they had the advantage of color laser reproductions brought in from outside and the capacity to print text at the college. (Solutions are at hand to enable teachers to make a few of their own texts, perhaps with collaboration with their students and with their parents were modest financial provisions to be made.) The books they created used Haitian paintings as illustrations for the short texts. Some focused on the heroic deeds, some on the battles and some on consequences. They drew upon their own knowledge of Haitian history, a favorite topic in the northern part of Haiti, and on their recently-acquired understanding of the School of the North Haitian History Painters. The illustrations were all by Haitian painters with international art reputations. The students thought such books would send a whole group of positive messages to their pupils.

Because this was a new kind of task, students were not aware of the desirability of shaping the text to a particular grade-level vocabulary. Texts sent to their schools are selected at worst by outsiders with no knowledge of the eventual users, or at best by a school official who may have little range of choice. More are printed in Kreyol now, and there are some concerted efforts to create primary books that are attractive and carefully designed to support the advancement of the young pupils. The idea that they as teachers could collaborate to create even some small texts was an encouraging notion.

IV. RESULTS AND QUESTIONS RAISED

There were positive outcomes in knowledge acquired on both parallel syllabi. Students who found themselves greatly puzzled could make appointments for personal tutorials with the instructor and many did so each week. They also could review the slides, and they organized themselves into group sessions without the instructor present several times a week for this purpose. Those who lived and worked at some distance made special efforts to come in for tutorials and slide reviews. The library was less used than would have been hoped, but there, too, one could observe twos and threes using the books together. A shift from professor at the front, echoed by rows of seated pupils was thus accomplished, as was a shift from individual learning all alone and competitively to collaboration toward a significantly higher achievement for everyone. In this respect, methods like those of Beyond Borders's Wonn Refleksyon literacy projects were at work.

The students were all worried about grades, even more intensely it would seem, than North American students. For several, only an "A" was an acceptable grade. Fortunately, these were also the ones who worked hard and well enough to achieve that.

Supported by individual tutorials, no student failed the course either term it was taught. The lowest final grade was a "C-." The aim was to make sure everyone learned as much as possible, and the instruction was devised to make sure that could happen. Class attendance was excellent and those who missed a class always made it up later in an individual tutorial. All turned in all assigned work, and all showed progress toward the many knowledge and skill goals. They understood at the beginning that progress would be factored in, and were understandably disconcerted when the school was informed that under their United States accreditation conditions only numerical scores could be used, and that progress could not be factored in. There was the further expectation from the United States that final grades should show a statistical distribution. Given the parallel syllabus, a way was found to legitimately use only the grades from exams on the academic content examinations. By happenstance there was an acceptable distribution of grades. The notion of mutual assistance enabling all to reach similar high goals has a way to go to achieve acceptance in our hierarchical, grade-point schools and colleges.

QUESTIONS CONCERNING THE USE OF PERCEPTION/COGNITION METHODS

The use of methods that are based on recent understandings of perceptual/ cognitive learning contrasts with the traditional ones common in most Haitian schools. There are few teachers or professors beyond such institutions as Quiskeya University in Port-au-Prince who have much study or practice with such concepts. It is true as well, that many college-level professors in the United States outside departments where these investigations and their applications are conducted are either unacquainted with or distrustful of this approach. For both, there is something about text-based learning that

renders it nearly sacrosanct. This is as true in the discipline of art history as it is in some departments of history or literature or even economics. Given traditionalist constraints, there was a risk that the students' richest learning achievements would be discounted. However, since they were able to pass traditional examinations at specified moments, and presented in the accepted format, their other considerable progress could be noted as a "nice option" that did not unsettle traditionalists. Other faculty and administrators within the school saw advantages to the perception/cognition-based model and supported the course and its methodology.

Students themselves found the double syllabus demanding, some of them thinking it was too much so. They were perhaps correct. The kinds of intellectual skills that they were acquiring take time to assimilate, and a two-term course arrangement would have worked better. It would also be advantageous to implement the skills program systematically across the disciplines. There were students who thought a study of art history was a waste of time for a prospective teacher, since he/she would never be teaching that specific topic. They were of the opinion that more courses in educational administration would have been better for their program. Some thought more text-based classes in theoretical pedagogy would have been preferable. On the other hand, many remarked on their evaluations that they had learned many valuable techniques they could use themselves and pass along to their pupils, and had been able to have their eyes opened. To quote the late artist-teacher, Josef Albers, the central purpose had been "...to open eyes."

In subsequent semesters, the course has reverted to a standard history of art course using lectures with slides, and with testing of artists' names, dates, country and the identification of works. It is comparable to most courses in this subject taught in the United States and Canada and students would be prepared to pass tests in those institutions. The reversion was based upon practical matters. There are apparently only two or three art historians in Haiti, all living in or near Port-au-Prince. The faculty come from traditional art history departments, and are highly trained in the discipline, but have little or no background in perceptual/cognitive studies or the pedagogy that results. Additionally, they would not have a background in Haitian art (there is no existing doctoral program in Haitian art), hence the section on Haitian art was offered in just two class sessions by one of the Port-au-Prince art historians. This visitor is skilled in interactive and field-based methodologies, but was not able to be on the FERA campus for the length of time needed to implement the requisite style of teaching. This points to the second problem, which is that this, like many other schools in Haiti is somewhat dependent upon foreign or Haitian Diaspora instructors who volunteer for one term at a time. Creating a consistent cross-curricular collaboration such as was fortuitously possible for two terms, is difficult where there is a high turn-over of staff. The third problem is that a mode of teaching involving student teams, a range of types of assignments, and substantial fieldwork is highly labor-intensive. Like Wonn Refleksyon it also takes more time for both teacher and students than lectures, reading assignments and assessment of learning based on whole-class testing. The science courses may be the locus for development of observation, analysis and critical thinking that can be more easily accomplished and more immediately and obviously fruitful under the circumstances. Still the notion of a liberal arts study that has a strong focus on Haitian culture should be seen as desirable enough to solve the current problems.

V. IMPLICATIONS AND CONCLUDING REMARKS

Serious questions concern the transferability of North American methods, expectations and norms to a situation in which there are large and subtle structural and cultural differences. To prepare all Haitian students as though they were eventually to be functioning in France, Canada or the United States, and to expect that those who arrive at the first year of tertiary education are ready in the exactly the same ways as their North American and European counterparts is entirely to discount and even disfigure the Haitian reality. There is a rich learning taking place among the most unschooled populations of Haiti. There are lycée (classical high school) graduates who write eloquently, and are skilled in debate. They know Plato and Racine, but unlike Plato or Racine, they do not easily link the concepts to the environment beyond the classrooms. There are also unschooled people whose ignorance is more deeply abysmal than it would have been in colonial times; and there are lycée graduates who become distinguished analysts of the true conditions of Haiti and fluent spokespersons for ameliorative change. In any case, the comprehensive Haitian educational environment is incomparable with that of Europe and North America.

Strategies such as the Wonn Refleksyon, Open Circle group-generated learning methods and priorities, the local library open for reading, study and internet access; integration of academic learning with vocational training; community action efforts to support education outside the public sector; and the preparation of new teachers and administrators in educational strategies radically different from those obtaining up to the present each have valuable models to propose. In each case except the community-based school, the people generating these projects include educators from outside Haiti as well as from within it. Sustaining the efforts of all five are outside funding agencies and sponsoring individuals. At the same time each program includes significant contributions of time, labor, wisdom and even funds drawn from the local society. The workers and contributors from outside are respectful of local ways, and, indeed, repeatedly experience new learning gained from their Haitian counterparts. Thus there is a crucial reciprocity.

Some of the imported methods may be discarded as inappropriate or too expensive in time, or personnel or resources for local ways and means. Some, and we have tried to indicate the most promising, will be woven into the continuing fabric of communities. It is likely that the descendants of the people who created themselves a new language out of all the structures and lexicons that converged on Hispaniola will create out of the unfamiliar material a fresh, perhaps advanced range of methods and topics for their educational enterprise. This will be welcome instruction for those outside Haiti.

There is undeniably a present and pressing need for Haiti to receive new concepts and extensive material support from outside. This reality and the obligation that both Haiti and the world outside must share should be taken into account in any educational projects. While it is true that an authentic and durable Haitian education can only grow out of Haitian earth and climate and people, the words of a Haitian educator best close this chapter:

> Effective education can only take root in Haiti and become useful to the Haitian majority if Haitians reevaluate familiar forms of indigenous knowledge, modes of information-storage, and channels of information-transmission, while appropriating the best foreign ideas about teaching and learning.[48]

ENDNOTES

[1] Joseph, Yvon, «Problématique de l'education dans une perspective de development endogène, in *Livre Ouvert sur le Dévelopment Endogène d'Haïti*, by Webster Pierre, Gabriel Nicholas and Wilfred Joseph. Port-au-Prince: Imprimerie ArnéGraph, 1999. P. 255.

[2] UNDP-UNCDF Microfinance Assessment Report-Haiti. 1/1/2002,(*www.uncdf.org/sum/reports/assessments/country_reports/haitidb.html) p.* 1

[3] United Nations Development Programme. Human development index. (www.undp.org/hdr2001/indicator/indic.html) , p. 3.

[4] UNDP Human Development Reports, 10/30/2002, http://hdr.undp.org/reports/global/2002/en/indicator/indicator.cfm?File=cty_f_HTI.html, p 1.

[5] "De l'État aux collectivités locales et territoriales/L'Éducation: Nos obligations constitutionelles," in *Transparans* vol II, No 3, Oct. 1998. P.52.

[6] Rancière, Jacques, "Transition Démocratique et Éducation (Debat)" in *Les transitions démocratiques,* Laënnec Hurbon, ed. Paris: Syros, 1996. P. 380.

[7] Joseph, op.cit. p.255.

[8] Camus, Albert, "L'Hôte," in *L'Exil et le Royaume.* Paris:Gallimard, 1957.

[9] A double check with a number of Haitians on the "Corbett" listserve yielded numerous recollections of grammars and history texts that included this phrase. I am indebted to Professor Carrol Coates of State University of New York at Binghamton for the reference to Camus.

[10] A major Haitian publisher, Imprimerie Henri Deschamps, now has a policy of publishing more books in Kreyol for school use.

[11] Haitian Studies Association, *Education and Development Project Needs Assessment, Thomonde, Haiti*, 1997. P. 12.

[12] DeJean, Yves, speaking at Quiskeya University in a session of the Haitian Studies Association annual conference, "Haiti: Images and Realities," Port-au-Prince, October 2002.

[13] Lumarque, Jacky, «Éducation et Transition Démocratique,» in *Les Transitions démocratiques*, sous la direction de Laënnec Hurbon. Paris: Syros, 1996. P. 253.

[14] Inquiries yielded a range of costs. The equivalent of $17 for public elementary school fee in Cap Haitien, and $70 for the least expensive of the private schools. The least expensive uniforms are about $10 for shirt and skirt or slacks and $4.00 for a pair of shoes. With average incomes estimated at $100 to $500 per year, these are significant family budget allocations.

[15] As of October, 2002, there were no such accrediting examinations for tertiary programs. However, the Ministry of Education, Youth, and Sport has prepared a bill providing for this, planned to be presented to the national parliament.

[16] Requests to the Government of Haiti and to the Ministry of Education for official data regarding this question made in 2001 and 2002 received no response. A request in October of 2002 yielded the information that the figures were not yet available.

[17] Haitian Studies Association, op.cit. P. 13.

[18] Figures from www.salesiansmisions.org/aroundtw/lamerica/haiti/ha5.htm, 2/4/2002

[19] Fouchard, Jean, "Les écoles clandestines," pp. 83-87 in *Regards sur les temps passé*. Port-au-Prince: Editions Henri Deschamps, 1988.

[20] Dodds, Paisley, "Haitians flee in desperation." *Ithaca Journal* (Associated Press release), 2 November 2002. P.2A.

[21] Bois Caiman is a site several kilometers southwest of Cap Haitien traditionally thought to be the site of a ceremony in which a large number of slaves, led by Boukman, and the priestess Cecile Fatiman took a blood-oath to free all slaves and expel the French from St.-Domingue. This took place in August of 1791, and ,though the slaves were initially routed, is held in honor as the beginning of the only successful salve uprising in history.

[22] Joseph, op.cit., p.254.

[23] Information for the preparation of this section is based upon the1998 founding mission statement of Beyond Borders; from the newsletter BEYOND BORDERS, Spring 2001; from discussion with David Diggs, a staff member since the founding of the organization; and discussion and interview with Todd Sadler, member of the board now in the U.S., formerly working in Haiti with Beyond Borders.

[24] Dokiman LaKay ofisyel; Limyè Lavi misyon. 24-11-98 Unpublished.

[25] The 501(3)C status is a US Federal status that allows non-profit organization with certain educational or other eleemosynary intentions to forego payment of internal revenue taxes and to provide tax deductions for donors. Many such organizations also act as fiscal agents for smaller organizations.

[26] The Wonn Refleksyon technique is derived from Open Space Technology, developed by Gabriela Enders in Germany, and now accessible on Internet at www. OpenSpace-Online. The website provides opportunities to enter on-line discussion sessions on selected topics, and proceed in much the same way as a face-to-face Wonn Refleksyon.

[27] This information is from interviews in 2001 and 2002 with David Diggs and Todd Sadler of the Board of Directors.

[28] A reviewer of this chapter in draft notes that the word is from Benin, in the Fon language of that West African nation.

[29] See, for example, Paul, Emmanuel C., *Panorama du Folklore Haïtien (Présence Africaine en Haïti)*. Port-au-Prince: Imprimerie de l'Etat, 1962. P.205-220.

[30] Email communication from David Diggs, Board of Directors, Beyond Borders, November 2002.

[31] Diggs, op.cit.

[32] Sources for this section include the 2001 "Letter from the Executive Director", Michèle D. Pierre-Louis, Executive Director; an unpublished draft report describing the work of the organization, Michèle D. Pierre-Louis and Lorraine Mangonès, Coordinateur Général des Programmes; conversatons with the Executive Director and Coordinateur in advance of the formal foundation and over the six years of its work; observation of sites; conversations with the leader for library services, and with two teachers of English as a Second Language associated with the program both as teachers and as consultant-trainers for other teachers.

[33] Pierre-Louis, Michèle D., "Letter from the Executive Director," unpublished letter circulated to the organization and other interested, 2001.

[34] Fondation Vincent was one subject for documentation by advanced students in the teacher education curriculum of F.E.R.A. (see below). Students made video tapes of workshop instruction, of the instructional sites in general, and did interviews with several instructors. The author paid additional visits and spoke with faculty and the director of studies. Additional information has been supplied by the Salesian Order.

[35] Interview with automotive repair/mathematics instructor, Fondation Vincent, March, 2001.

[36] One indication of this regard was that students in the professional educators degree program selected Fondation Vincent as a locale for doing documentation on artists, artisans and teachers in the region. January and February, 2000.

[37] On several visits in the spring of 2001, the author observed classes in session, and photographed the site and many of the pupils. There were discussions with a guiding member of the Board of Directors and with the Director. Budgets for the two most recent years were available as were official scores from the National exams. The school receives no assistance from the government. All descriptions are based upon data gathered from this group of visits. Disclosure: the author was invited to sit on the Board of this school as its United States Representative in October of 2002,

[38] Information from copies of UN documents supplied by the school directorate.

[39] Information supplied by Pierre Wallace, director of the school, interviewed October, 2002.

[40] In extended interviews in which teachers were asked how they maintained their pupil's attention they described a number of techniques that teachers anywhere would find familiar. Notably, none reported using punitive measures as a means. They have an advantage in that these particular children all seem to be aware that their being in school is enormously important. In observing classrooms in several places in Cap Haitian and in the neighboring countryside, keeping attention did not appear to be a problem.

[41] The artists were at the time members of the Arc en Ciel (Rainbow) group. Several of them had been students of the internationally known Capois artist, Philomé Obin, a man dedicated to the education of his compatriots.

[42] Information concerning the FERA was developed over a period of nearly two years, including a term in 2000 and one in 2001 during which the course n question was given. Administrators, faculty, staff and students were all aware of the alternative nature of the course, and cooperated fully in providing informative, responses to inquiries. School files and records were made available, as were archives of news articles, community events and the like.

[43] This accreditation arrangment runs until December of 2003. A joint announcement by the FERA and a Canadian university was expected by the end of 2002.

[44] *Annuaire 1999-2000, FÉRA*, p. 6. Privately printed document.

[45] In 2000, the FÉRA was apparently the only tertiary-level institution in Haiti offering a course in art history, despite the strong presence on the world art scene of Haitian painting and sculpture. Since that time, other schools are beginning to offer such studies. At College (high school level) St. Pierre in Port-au-Prince, which is closely associated through the Episcopal Church and the College St. Pierre Musée d'Art new courses that include visits to the museum are in the process of development.

[46] The ecological approach to the teaching of art history (or any history) is in this case based upon studies in perception and cognition and related linguistics theories. The supposition is that all aspects of life within an encompassing natural and built environment furnish the motivation and the means for creating arts and technologies. Hence attention is paid to the particular

mix of elements from among all that are selected by the artist, and therefore what this resulting *style* can reveal about environment and attitude and response.

[47] Florence Etienne Sergile and co-workers have prepared extensive environmental study materials coupled with a teacher in-service training program. The program is part of the work of the Florida Museum of Natural History, University of Florida-Gainesville under grants from the John D. and Catherine T. MacArthur Foundation, with an office in Port-au-Prince and outreach programs in other towns. The program has commissioned posters by such major Haitian artists as André Normil, and these are available for school classrooms. Materials for pupil use take advantage of things that might be handy and free, but there are also some attractive coloring pages for schools that have crayons and markers.

[48] Prou, Marc, Executive Director, Haitian Studies Project, University of Massachusetts-Boston, private communication, October, 2002

CARIBBEAN TEACHERS IN U.S. URBAN SCHOOLS

Jo-Anne L. Manswell Butty
Howard University
USA

Chapter 5

SCHOOLS IN THE United States will need an estimated 2.5 million new teachers over the next 10 years due to expected increases in retirement, growing enrollments, and reductions in class size (National Center for Education Statistics [NCES], 2000; Recruiting New Teachers, 2000). This burgeoning teacher shortage has led to the aggressive recruitment of teachers from around the world. Large urban school systems such as New York, Chicago, Atlanta, Houston, and Cleveland are today recruiting teachers from the Caribbean, Canada, Austria, Italy, Spain, and Germany. Most of these teachers are needed to teach mathematics, science and technology, special education, and bilingual education. Though the bulk of the research on foreign teachers in the United States focuses on their recruitment, development, retention, challenges, and diversification, scant information exists on their perspectives and experiences as well as their abilities to transcend bicultural domains.

[1] The research was made possible with support from the Walter and Theodora Daniel Endowed Educational Research Fund. The author would like to acknowledge the assistance of graduate students Sheralyn Dash and Jennifer Lee, School of Education, Howard University.

Highlighting teachers' perspectives and experiences is key to knowing how teachers feel in the classroom and how they believe their students adjust and perform. Toward this end, this chapter presents a portrait of U.S. urban schools, reviews the literature on foreign teachers in these schools, and examines the experiences and perspectives of foreign teachers who teach in public and private urban school settings in the United States. It further describes the findings of a qualitative study involving focus group interviews with a group of Caribbean-born U.S. teachers. These findings provide U.S. educators and their foreign teacher recruits with a portrait of the urban classroom ecology from the Caribbean perspective. It is hoped that they will assist teachers and administrators, their colleagues, family members, and students in facilitating positive attitudes and performance in U.S. urban schools. The chapter closes with a discussion of the implications of this study for future research and practice.

A SNAPSHOT OF U.S. URBAN SCHOOLS

Educating children from all backgrounds is one of the main responsibilities of school systems in major cities throughout the United States. On the one hand, the diversity of academic institutions that can be found in the urban setting is impressive. Most U.S. metropolitan areas flaunt public schools of every size and type; alternative, magnet, and charter schools; private, religious schools (e.g., Catholic, Muslim, Episcopal, Seventh-Day Adventist); and nonsectarian schools (e.g., college preparatory, Montessori, military). On the other, the diversity of these schools' administrators, teachers, students, families, and community members is exciting as well as daunting (Banks, 1998; Berlinger & Biddle, 1995; Cuban, 1990; Heath & McLaughlin, 1994). Urban schools provide a wide array of experiences for all and present a range of diverse perspectives on education.

The social conditions of the neighborhoods and communities in which many urban students live create serious challenges for educators in the United States. The challenges encountered in some urban schools relate in part to the poverty, crime, and other social problems that many inner-city families confront (Kozol, 1996). Contributing to these challenges are other issues such as student inequity (Kozol, 1991; 1996), and problems related to school governance (Smith & O'Day, 1993). Russo and Cooper (1999) have identified six themes emerging from efforts to solve the large, nearly intractable problems associated with urban schooling: (a) the failure of centralized bureaucracies, (b) conflicts due to racial and social inequality, c) the exploitation of teachers, (d) parental noninvolvement in children's schooling, e) a reliance on outdated and incomplete data, and (f) low expectation and standards

Additionally, U.S. urban schools are responsible for educating a large majority of the nation's neediest children. This education typically takes place in environments characterized by decaying and overcrowded buildings, inadequate resources, high staff turnover, "out-of-field" and non-certified teachers, student tracking and sorting, low family involvement, separation between school and community, and a host of safety issues (Boykin, 2000; Casserly, 1994; Haycock, 2000; Kozol, 1991, 1996). Moreover, students of color are expected to constitute a majority of all K-12 students by 2035 (U.S. Department of Commerce, 1996), yet almost 90% of the current U.S. teaching force is White (NCES, 1997). In high-poverty urban schools, students of color currently make up 69% of the total enrollment compared to a percentage of teachers of color of only 29% (NCES, 1996). As a result, recruiting persons of color into the teaching profession has become a high priority particularly in the nation's urban school districts.

GROWTH OF FOREIGN-BORN POPULATIONS IN U.S. URBAN AREAS

Foreign-born populations in the United States have been steadily on the rise. For example, in Miami, the West Indian population—now 48% of the city's Black community—is expected to surpass the native-born African American population within eight years (Perry & Mackun 2001). As Fears (2002) notes, nearly one-third of the Black population in New York City is foreign-born One-third of the Black population in Massachusetts is foreign-born (Schworm, 2002). In Washington, D.C., nearly 8% of the Black population is foreign-born, up from 1% in 1970 (Frey, 2002). Similarly, in Maryland, more than 5% of Black adults are foreign-born compared with 0.5% three decades ago (Frey, 2002).

With this steady increase in foreign-born populations comes the need for new teachers. Recent data projects a shortfall of about 2.5 million new teachers by 2010 (Recruiting New Teachers, Inc., 2000; The Urban Teacher Collaborative, 2000). High-minority urban schools will suffer a particularly alarming shortage of teachers due to their higher teacher turnover rates and the reluctance of certified teachers to take jobs in urban settings, even when financial incentives are offered (National Commission on Teaching and America's Future, 1996; Villegas & Clewell, 1998). Therefore, the resulting increase in racial and ethnic diversity in U.S. classrooms makes the need for teachers who are culturally diverse and aware even greater.

WHAT DOES THE LITERATURE SAY ABOUT FOREIGN TEACHERS IN THE U.S.?

Traditional and nontraditional strategies are being employed to recruit and retain teachers from within the United States (Brown, Hughes, & Vance, 1999; Brown & Manswell Butty, 1999; Kelly, 1998) and abroad (McCoubrey, 2001; Urban Educator, 2001). Examples of recruitment from abroad include the Global Educator Outreach Initiative of the Chicago Public Schools and the recent international recruitment initiative launched by New York City's Board of Education's Teach New York Program. Within the last two years, a large-scale recruitment drive has been undertaken by the New York City Board of Education to select teachers from other countries (e.g.,

Guyana, Jamaica, and Trinidad and Tobago) to begin meeting the teacher shortage need (see www.teachny.com/news_events.html). As a result, foreign-born teachers from many countries in the Caribbean can now be included as part of the U.S. urban school landscape at all levels. These efforts have led to some speculation about the experiences, perspectives, and behaviors of foreign-born teachers recruited to U.S. classrooms (Carter, 2001; Rossi, 2001a, 2001b).

Research conducted in the areas of teacher interpersonal interactions (Good & Brophy, 2003), discipline (Levin & Nolan, 2000), classroom management (Emmer & Stough, 2001), instructional practices (Good, 1996; Manswell Butty, 2002), and orientation (Brooks & Brooks, 1993) has focused primarily on U.S.-born teachers. Other U.S. studies have examined the behaviors and perspectives of African American teachers (Delpit, 1995; Foster, 1997; Ladson-Billings, 1994), documenting specific constraints and supports in these teachers' professional lives as well as how their experiences and careers have changed over the years. Callendar's (1997) study explored the behaviors and styles of Caribbean and African teachers in British urban schools to determine whether or not these teachers' practices differed from those of their White, British-born colleagues. She concluded that the most important difference between Black and White teachers was their use of rewarding and reprimanding strategies. Mansell (2001) found that foreign-born teachers in British schools were also more likely to report that "standards of student behavior in the tough schools where they were placed were far worse than in their own countries. (p. 3)"

Goeff (2001), however, conducted a study of Caribbean-born teachers in poorly performing schools in the Brooklyn section of New York City. He reported that the local educational leaders felt that the Caribbean teachers provided students with a model of Black achievement and brought a traditional, no-nonsense approach to teaching. By contrast, McCoubrey's (2001) study found that many foreign-born recruits have difficulty adjusting to U.S. students and teaching styles. One of the biggest challenges facing teachers from foreign lands, according to Rossi (2001a, 2001b), is classroom management. Many of these teachers, she concludes, come from countries where they are accorded great respect and obedience, and they are often stunned by U.S. students' freer use of foul language as well as their tardiness, absenteeism, laziness, vanity, apathy, and general disrespect for teachers. However, no course on that topic is required for these foreign-born recruits.

METHOD

DESCRIPTION

In February 2002, one moderator (female, Caribbean, Ph.D., project director for research and evaluation) and two graduate students (both female, doctoral students in educational psychology; one Caribbean and the other African American) from Howard University conducted two focus-group interview sessions with Caribbean-born teachers who were teaching in both public and private U.S. urban school settings. Three teachers participated in the first interview, two in the second interview, and one teacher completed her interview by electronic mail. The 14 focus-group questions, developed by the study's moderator, examined the following three areas: (a) teaching background, (b) teacher training and preparation, and (c) teaching experiences and perspectives. The three categories of questions were neither mutually exclusive nor exhaustive. These questions and the collective responses obtained served as probes for identifying areas of challenge and interest among Caribbean-born teachers in U.S. urban schools (see Table 1). They also served as a compass for providing direction for future research.

Table 1: Focus-Group Interview Questions

Background

1. State your country of birth, years teaching in the US, years teaching at your present school, type of school (public or private), grade level presently teaching, subject areas presently teaching.
2. Did you teach in your home country?
   A. If so, what classes/grade levels and for how long?

Training & Preparation

3. Did you receive any teacher training in your home country (e.g., teachers' college, etc.)?
   A. How did that training prepare you for your teaching experience in this country?
4. How much further teacher training did you receive in this country (e.g., undergraduate or graduate degree)?
   A. If so, how did that training prepare you for your teaching experience in this country?

Experiences & Perspectives

5. As an international/Caribbean teacher, how would you describe the professional interaction/relationship you have with your colleagues (e.g., administrators and school staff)?
   A. How does your Caribbean heritage positively affect that interaction/relationship?
   B. What challenges do you face in that interaction/relationship because of your Caribbean heritage?
6. As an international/Caribbean teacher, how would you describe the interaction/relationship you have with your students?
   A. How does your Caribbean heritage positively affect that interaction/relationship?
   B. What challenges do you face in that relationship because of your Caribbean heritage?
7. As an international/Caribbean teacher, how would you describe the interaction/relationship you have with your students' parents / family members?

A. How does your Caribbean heritage positively affect that interaction/relationship?
B. What challenges do you face in that interaction/relationship because of your Caribbean heritage?

8. How would you describe your teaching style (teacher-directed, student-directed, other)?
A. How much did you have to change or adjust your teaching style to accommodate the needs of students in this country?
B. How do you feel about this?

9. How has your dialect/accent affected your interactions/work with administrators, staff, and students?

10. How would you rate yourself in terms of managing your classroom and disciplining your students?
A. Have your experiences been positive, have there been challenges?
B. In what ways have the school helped you in developing/strengthening these areas?

11. What are your challenges as an international/Caribbean teacher in a US urban school?
A. What are the areas in which you would like more training or support?
B. What are the areas in which you feel competent?

12. As an international/Caribbean teacher, what are some the individual or group strategies you use to support yourself (emotionally, socially, professionally) in your career?

13. How much <u>cultural difference</u>, <u>conflict</u>, and/or <u>compatibility</u> have you experienced among administrators, staff, students, and family members? Can you give examples?

14. Is there any other issue(s)/comment(s) you feel is important as a foreign/Caribbean teacher teaching in an urban US school?
A. If so, what is it and why is it important?

The participating teachers' responses to these 14 items were transcribed verbatim, and several common themes were identified from them. The following section summarizes those responses by themes. The teachers' names and identities have been omitted to ensure confidentiality.

RESULTS

PARTICIPANTS

Of the six participants, four taught in private schools and two taught in public schools. Five participants taught single grades– one each in pre-kindergarten, kindergarten, first, and third grade; and two in fourth grade. The sixth participant taught fifth through eighth grades. The teachers who taught single grades taught all subject areas. The lone teacher who taught multiple grades specialized in mathematics but also taught reading and religion. Their length of time teaching in U.S. schools ranged from 6 months to 12 years (see Table 2).

Table 2: Demographic Table of Caribbean Teachers in the Study

ID	Country	Gender	Years Teaching U.S.	School Type	Grade Teaching	Subject Area Teaching
1	Trinidad	F	2	Private	3	All
2	Trinidad	F	12	Private	4	All
3	Jamaica	M	3	Private	5-8	Math Reading Religion
4	Trinidad	F	‰	Public	4	All
5	Trinidad	F	8	Public	Pre-K	All
6	Jamaica	F	‰	Private	K	All

Teacher 1 was originally from Trinidad and Tobago and had 30 years experience teaching at various grade levels in that country. She attended a teachers' college in her homeland, where she later earned a degree in history and government at the University of the West Indies (UWI). At the time of this study, she had been teaching in the United

States for two years, exclusively at a private school, teaching subjects across the full curriculum at the third-grade level.

Teacher 2 was also born in Trinidad and Tobago. Collectively, she had 35 years of experience teaching in Trinidad and Tobago, England, and the United States. She received her four-year teacher training in England, after which she returned to Trinidad to teach at the high-school level. She had been teaching in U.S. schools for 12 years, spending 3 of those years at a private school. At the time of this study, she was teaching subjects across the full curriculum at the fourth-grade level.

Teacher 3 was from Jamaica and had 10 years experience teaching mathematics and the sciences in that country. He too had attended UWI, where he earned a business degree. After teaching for a while in Jamaica, he obtained a Diploma in Education at UWI. At the time of the study, he had been teaching in the United States for 3 years and had spent all of that time at a private school, teaching fifth through eighth grades and specializing in mathematics. He also taught religion and reading.

Teacher 4 was from Trinidad and Tobago. She attended a teachers' college in her homeland and later earned a degree in history and sociology in the United States. At the time of the study, she had 12 years teaching experience in her homeland and 6 months experience teaching in the United States at the fourth-grade level in a public school. She taught all subject areas.

Teacher 5 was born in Trinidad and Tobago. She did some informal teaching in her homeland at a private church school. She later earned her bachelor's degree in early childhood education and her master's degree in counseling and guidance in the United States. She had 8 years experience teaching in U.S. schools. At the time of the study, she was teaching all subject areas at the pre-kindergarten level at a public school.

Teacher 6 was born in Jamaica. She had four-and-a-half years of teaching experience in her home country. She attended teachers' college there and later earned a degree in early childhood education and general psychology from UWI. At the time of the study, she had been teaching all subjects at the first-grade level in a private school for 6 months.

THE PARTICIPANTS' TRAINING AND PREPARATION

All but 2 of the 6 participating teachers received formal teacher training in their countries of origin. When asked if the training received "back home" in the Caribbean prepared them for their teaching experience in the United States, one Caribbean-trained teacher aptly summed up her feelings:

> Definitely not, because this is a different world. I don't think anybody or anything could prepare you for here unless you were born in this culture, but if you come from a different culture you are definitely not prepared.

Although the majority of participants indicated that they felt ill prepared for the social and cultural differences with which they were confronted in U.S. classrooms, they were unanimously confident that their previous training had prepared them academically to teach in the United States. As one teacher commented:

> When we get prepared back home, we are prepared content-wise. That's not the problem. The problem is this whole social thing and the behavior of the children. And it's a different thing here.

The one teacher who received teacher training in this country claimed she also felt prepared in terms of content but expressed that "behavior management" was her biggest challenge.

Each of the participants relayed experiences of "culture-shock" upon coming to the United States, and each indicated that the

U.S. culture was very different from those of their homelands. Most agreed, for example, that there were too many disruptions and differences in expectations and rules in U.S. classrooms, and that students' lack of attention made it very difficult to teach efficiently. Some participants claimed that U.S. children seemed "so angry" and unsmiling. The schoolchildren "back home," in their view, were relative angels compared to children in the United States.

According to the Caribbean-born teacher participants, respect for teachers and other school figures was one of the features absent from U.S. schools. Several mentioned feeling frustrated and ineffective, and some noted experiencing physical pains at times as a result of this absence. As one teacher indicated:

> ...let us say you planned six subjects for the day, sometimes you could only deliver four, you don't get through, and at the end of the day you feel drained, your chest hurts, you feel frustrated.

Although all of the participants, at the time of the study, were participating in ongoing teacher training programs in the United States, they each expressed concern that the strategies and methods in which they were being trained to handle discipline and classroom management (i.e., time-out, suspension, rewards, and reinforcement) did not work. None indicated that these strategies were effective in the classroom. According to one teacher,

> [The strategies] are nice on paper, and they have certain points, but when you go back to your classroom and try to use these things, you meet up on the same thing. So no matter how you try you like you're beating your head against a wall.

The participants also identified many cultural differences insofar as disciplinary techniques were concerned, with several noting that in their U.S. classrooms they were unable to practice the disciplinary techniques they believed would be most effective. As one teacher explained:

> I suppose our expectations in the Caribbean are high, so our children know that we expect them to be good. But these children know they are expected to be bad! That's the difference: the expectations. We know [that] very well in the Caribbean, and every mother knows when she sends her child into that classroom, she says to that child, "I am working hard to send you to school, so I expect you to learn, and I expect you to behave." I was a child growing up in the Caribbean, and my mother told me that all the time: "I expect you to be good! I don't expect you to give your teacher trouble!" And nobody rewarded me because I was good.

PARTICIPANT EXPERIENCES AND PERSPECTIVES

Professional Interactions with Colleagues

A variety of interactions take place in schools every day between teachers, administrators, students, and students' family members. All of the teachers participating in the focus groups indicated that they believed their interactions with their teacher colleagues were good, yet clearly those interactions were very different in nature. One teacher claimed that her upbringing and her family ties helped her to foster a good relationship with her colleagues. When asked to rate her professional relationship with her fellow teachers and school personnel, she stated:

> I think it is great. Because of our family ties and the way we associate back home, the kind of bonds we [Caribbean folk] form with friends and relatives, that really takes us a long way toward working with others, especially in this society.

Another participant added the following comment:

> The respect that I have for authority and the cooperative attitude that I express toward my coworkers is a direct result of my being pre-exposed to this type of working environment while in Jamaica.

The participants concurred that being a professional and displaying a solid level of maturity was critical in this regard. According to one teacher:

> Back home we learn that even though you might be worst enemies but you are still in the same school, you work together. We know that it is the right thing to have a professional relationship. So even though you and your principal could be disagreeing with everything whatsoever, you know, you come and you say "good morning," and you do what you have to do. And that's how we work it, and that's how I know it back home. So it's the same thing I apply here, and it helps with my relations. I haven't had any disagreements or falling outs with any others so far.

Professional Interactions with Students

Many of the participants indicated that, given the current socio-political climate, they were unable to allow themselves to become too close to their students. In their view, this did not augur well for the teacher-student relationship. As one teacher explained:

> In Jamaica, the teacher is allowed to reward a child by hugging, and you are not judged if you ask very personal questions. However, being in America, I have to refrain from personal contact and be tactful not to ask questions which can be interpreted as being too personal. It is a fine line that I have to tread, and the challenge is finding the right balance, which is appropriate.

Another participant explained that he felt compelled to "keep a little distance" between himself and his students "because if you get too close to a kid professionally, they don't know when to stop." One teacher articulated the following about her relationship with her students:

> You cannot joke with them. I remember with my class, after they settled in for a little while, I would joke with them sometimes in the morning. Like if they come and they don't look happy, I would say, "Why you don't feel like coming to school today?" Everybody would smile. It never got out of hand, but we can't take it too far.

Professional Interactions with Students' Family Members

The professional interactions most of the participants had with their students' parents and family members varied. Although in many cases, the teachers felt that they had the support of some parents, one teacher claimed that teachers "need more support from home, especially for those children who are disruptive." Another teacher stated that the challenge was "to help parents realize that they need to take responsibility to help their children cope with the demands that are placed on them in order to succeed."

Some participants stated that their U.S. students often manipulate the parent-teacher relationship, and indicated that this can lead to conflict and even confrontation between the teacher and parent. For example, according to one Caribbean-born U.S. teacher:

> You are a teacher, a professional, and when you say that this child did something wrong, why [is it that] you as a parent can't believe it? You don't have any malice for anybody beforehand. You come to school with a blank slate, as it were, you accept what is there, but if they behave badly, that's it. You have to deal with it.

Another participant agreed, adding:

> That's a weapon that the children use. They put the parent against the teacher. And boy, they are good at it!

The participants also noted cultural differences with regard to childrearing strategies. Whereas children in the United States are encouraged to speak up, they pointed out, West Indian children are trained to show respect for their elders by not answering back. According to one teacher:

> You know another difference I have noticed in the American culture and the Caribbean culture? The American parents and teachers encourage the children to speak up—not necessarily to speak back, but to speak up, whereas in the Caribbean, we tend to say you don't answer.

Participants' Teaching Style

Although the teaching styles of the participating teachers, based on their own self-description, were found to vary, most claimed to have adjusted their teaching style to accommodate the needs of their U.S. students. One teacher initially claimed that he had not changed his teaching approach from the one he had in Jamaica. He later admitted that his teaching style had changed, although he had not yet found a "happy medium." He described his current U.S. teaching style as one of laissez-faire. He further stated that he did not like teachers to be too authoritarian and that although he liked being seen as approachable, he also expected his students to be mannerly and respectful.

Another participating teacher admitted outright that she had adjusted her teaching style to suit the demands of U.S. culture, with some success. She stated that in her U.S. classrooms, she tries to maintain the required student-centered approach while simultaneously insisting that her students behave more like Caribbean students—that is, sit still and listen to her or know that they will be asked to leave the class or miss recess. Yet another participant maintained that her teaching approach in U.S. schools was neither student-centered nor teacher-centered but rather a combination of the two approaches. She noted, for example, that when introducing a new topic, she would utilize the student-centered approach; but when developing the topic further, she reverted to the more Caribbean-like teacher-centered approach. She described this concession as her "happy medium."

Only one participant held fast to the claim that the student-centered teaching style she had used in her homeland had not changed much upon coming to the United States. That teacher further maintained that the resources and materials that are so readily available in the United States enhanced her style of teaching. She indicated that she felt she could work wonders with her U.S. students. Another participant, who claimed to have used a teacher-centered approach "back home," described her U.S. teaching style as "sometimes teacher-centered and sometimes student-centered." As she indicated:

> Now I have to adjust it where I always have some student-centered activity in every lesson....It was not like that before.

Issues Related to Participants' Accents and Dialects

Generally, the Caribbean-born U.S. teachers participating in this study maintained that their various accents and dialects had not been problematic for them in their interactions with fellow school staff, students, and students' family members. As one teacher stated, " I think they <u>like</u> the accent. It's different." In only a few instances did the participants indicate that their accents had caused a problem among their peers or students. Most ascribed to the following participant assessment: "If you laugh at somebody's accent or somebody's pronunciation, all you are doing is showing yourself as ignorant."

In most cases, these teachers indicated that their U.S. students were very accepting of their Caribbean accents and dialects. On only a few occasions did their accents and dialects cause problems with family members, they claimed. In one instance, a participant stated that a parent requested the transfer of her child to another class because "she was uncomfortable with the foreigner." In another, a parent reportedly challenged a participant and "said [she] should not be allowed to teach subjects like phonics because [her] accent was different."

Participants' Perspectives on Classroom Management

Only two of the participating teachers (the prekindergarten and first-grade teachers) indicated that they would rate themselves highly in classroom management and discipline. The other participants stated that these aspects were problematic areas for them. Some in the latter group felt that they had "come a long way," while others conceded that they needed improvement and support. One teacher explained that she posts a list of rules on the board and insists on compliance. Another stated that "with the younger children you have some control" but "the older the children become, the harder it is to control them."

The majority of this study's Caribbean-born U.S. teachers confirmed that one of the reasons they experience difficulty in classroom management can be attributed to within-school inconsistencies regarding discipline. As one participant explained, the rules about discipline may be agreed upon at the general staff meetings, but teachers may or may not reinforce these rules, or they may do so only for those students who are in their class. Another participant indicated that school disciplinary problems in the United States stemmed from the fact that very few U.S. children "come from stable families where there are no serious emotional and behavioral issues." As she stated:

> The experience here cannot compare to back home. In all my 12 years teaching experience back home I have never

> had a child throw a temper tantrum and knock down my library!

Another teacher humorously explained her method of keeping her students in check. She stated:

> In Trinidad, there was a term called santiwa. If, for example, anybody is misbehaving or sick, you may want to give them a bush bath. You fill the bath pan, and you put all these different kinds of bushes or herbs and you santiwa them. You say, "That one was a real santiwa!" But I know for myself I have already brought into the school, not this year, holy water. Yes, I have reached that stage when I was saying, "God please, and especially this one." (Laughter)

Participants' Perspectives on the Additional Challenges Facing Caribbean-Born Teachers in the United States

An additional challenge mentioned by the Caribbean-born teachers participating in this study was that U.S. parents are sometimes quick to question the grades assigned to students. One teacher explained that she found it puzzling that U.S. parents would question the grade "given" to a student as opposed to the grade "earned" by the student. Another participant stated that the greatest challenge facing her as a Caribbean-born teacher in the United States, in addition to becoming accustomed "to the social values that are transmitted by this society," was "to maintain who I am and my values and beliefs in an environment that exhibits such a high level of indiscipline and unacceptable behavior."

Participants' Perspectives on Their Sense of Competency

All of the study participants stressed that the teacher training they received in the Caribbean served as an enriching experience. That training, they claimed, further led them to believe that they were quite competent regarding the content areas as well as the methodologies of the subjects they taught in the United States. It also helped them to adapt and adjust their curricula to better suit the needs of their students. As one teacher explained:

> You know, we, as teachers, we are all experienced people. We know how to teach, that is not the problem!

Sources of Support for Caribbean-Born Teachers in the United States

Interestingly, a few of the teachers who participated in this study stressed that they did not have any formal group supports. The majority, however, included among their support networks other colleagues, family members, and a supportive principal. As one teacher maintained, "Older teachers who are ready to retire and who come from the South, like South Carolina, have experiences and advice that are familiar that we can share." Another claimed that, "The older teachers from the South, I find I can relate to....They are different from the younger teachers." Others held that their religious beliefs provided them with a critical means of support. Yet another way of coping identified by one teacher was to "leave school behind at 3:30 p.m." and go "home to my family." Some of the participants also indicated that the "good students" in their classes provided them with the encouragement they needed to continue their efforts.

Other Concerns

The need for teachers to be very careful in terms of the amount of physical contact they have with students was especially emphasized by the male teacher in the sample. According to the one male teacher, these concerns had "reached a stage where [he had] an automatic reaction." "Maybe some of them [colleagues, students, and students' parents] think I am mad, but don't touch me!....I kick off their hand!"

Another concern expressed by the participating teachers was that U.S. parents too often blamed teachers for the failure of students.

One teacher stated that this was unacceptable because she firmly believed that parents should share in the responsibility for educating their children. Other participants claimed that their students whose parents were from either the Caribbean or Africa behaved very differently from those whose parents were African American, who were sometimes described by these Caribbean-born teachers as loud, obnoxious, and discourteous.

The participants also stated that U.S. schools should provide more counseling services and more social workers on school premises. According to one teacher, "All of these behavioral problems we are experiencing as teachers start in the home." According to another:

> I wouldn't mind if a counselor comes in one morning and says, "Good day, so and so, let us have a good day," [or if a counselor comes to] speak to the child, [and asks him or her], "How do you feel today? Do you think you can work today?" We need that kind of interaction. [The schools in the U.S. today] don't have it.

Yet another advocated putting into place in U.S. urban schools preventative methods like conflict management skills, coping skills, study skills, and sex education. As she saw the situation, U.S. schools "allow things to happen before acting."

Despite the many challenges described by this group of Caribbean-born teachers working in U.S. urban schools, all of the study participants agreed that it is necessary for teachers to love children and the teaching experience. As one teacher summarized:

> You really have to love children! What we give them is invaluable. You must love children and the whole teaching and learning process.

DISCUSSION

LIMITATIONS

The findings of this study are limited to teachers in the mid-Atlantic region of the United States who were employed in urban schools. Care should thus be exercised in generalizing the results of the study to other groups of Caribbean teachers working in other regions of the United States. Further, these findings may not be descriptive of male Caribbean-born teachers in U.S. urban schools because only one male participant was included in this study. Another limitation of the study was the use of an email interview for the participant who was unable to join the others in person for the focus-group interviews. Though this participant's comments were included in the study, this procedure did not allow for thorough probing of the responses that she offered.

IMPLICATIONS FOR RESEARCH AND PRACTICE

The findings from this study's focus groups revealed several broad themes related to the important experiences and perspectives of foreign teachers working in U.S. urban schools. These themes were: (a) teacher training and preparation; (b) interactions with colleagues, students, and family members; (c) teaching styles; (d) dialect and accent; (e) classroom management and discipline; (f) teaching challenges; (g) teacher competencies; and (h) teacher support systems. The findings related to these themes confirmed the existence of Caribbean-born U.S. teachers' feelings of competence and mastery of both subject-matter content and methodology, their feelings of culture shock upon arrival in the U.S. urban school setting, their cautions with regard to teacher-student interactions, and their concerns about U.S. students' tendencies to manipulate the parent-teacher relationship. The findings further highlighted these teachers' belief that the differences in the child-rearing philosophies of the United States and their Caribbean homelands and the inconsistent disciplinary practices within U.S. schools have an impact on student learning.

Although the teachers participating in this study's focus groups were confident that their training and preparation had equipped them well for the content they were charged to teach, many indicated that the social milieu of the larger U.S. society negatively affected those to whom they were to impart and facilitate that knowledge: their students. Yet, even against such a debilitating social backdrop, these teachers were attempting to carry out their teaching duties. They all agreed that they wanted to do a good job, but each expressed concern that he or she had to contend with powerful social forces at every turn and at every level—and as their students got older, they maintained that teaching them became more of a challenge. Findings from several reports and studies in the areas of discipline, classroom management, and respect for teachers support the findings of this study (Callendar, 1997; McCoubrey, 2001; Rossi, 2001a, 2001b). Indeed, classroom management and discipline were key areas that many of these teachers felt needed to be addressed in their orientation training and preparation for U.S. urban classrooms. Most indicated that this was a problematic area.

Despite support from their principals and colleagues, these teachers further noted that they had to keep adjusting and adapting to situations that they were not used to and that they many times did not want to become used to. Some found it very hard to adjust their Caribbean-based teaching values and beliefs. However, most confirmed that the values and richness of their native cultures had provided them with a unique fighting spirit as well as vital teaching competencies that had helped them thrive in the U.S. urban school setting.

The implications from these findings point to the utility of designing professional development workshop programs for current teachers as well as newly recruited teachers from the Caribbean who are teaching in U.S. urban classrooms. In addition to workshops addressing classroom management and student discipline, these teachers need to familiarize themselves with areas that examine the social, political, and economic context of U.S. society. As one participant claimed:

> I see myself as an ever-learning person and would therefore like to study the social aspects of this country to see how I can identify ways and means to direct children in a positive way that would allow them to make better decisions in the future.

Teacher training and professional development in mainstream and African American culture, schooling, and socialization are critical for both veteran and newly recruited teachers from the Caribbean. Forums in which Caribbean-born U.S. teachers can meet and express their success and challenges will also aid in their ongoing development and growth. Given the wide range of years and types of experience evidenced by this sampling of teachers, informal and formal mentoring and dialogues should be encouraged at different levels at the school and district levels.

The purpose of the study was to explore and describe the perspectives and experiences of Caribbean-born teachers teaching in U.S. urban schools. The qualitative research methodology of focus group interviews was used to collect data for analysis, synthesis, and evaluation. These focus group interviews garnered information along several dimensions.

In attempting to answer the research questions, suggestions for future research have emerged. These include suggestions for examining the experiences and perspectives of male Caribbean teachers only, and for examining the experiences and perspectives of female Caribbean teachers in public and private schools at different levels (e.g., middle school and secondary school) to compare and contrast the data obtained. Future researchers might also consider comparing the experiences and perspectives of Caribbean teachers with teachers from other groups (e.g., African American or Hispanic American) to determine any similarities or differences across and between these groups. Furthermore, broadening the research questions to address other areas that may specifically affect Caribbean-born U.S. teachers such as student motivation, assessment, instruction, and questioning may prove enlightening. These areas include issues related to professional and personal support; cultural differences, transitions, and adjustment; professional development; and the need to maintain linkages "back home."

CONCLUSION

Insights gained through inquiry into the thoughts, feelings, and experiencing of others is important for many reasons, not the least of which is the extent to which such insights improve one's ability to understand another's actions, inactions, perceptions, and intentions. Knowing the styles, orientation, and perspectives of all teachers, especially foreign-born teachers in the United States, will give U.S. educators a better feel for the attitudes, beliefs, and actions of those who will increasingly affect the cognitive, social, and emotional outcomes of students in this nation. A firmer understanding of the styles, orientations, and perspectives of all teachers, especially foreign-born teachers, will give U.S. educators a better picture of the emerging classroom ecology. The findings from this study expand the body of knowledge on Caribbean-born teachers in urban U.S. schools. This knowledge can help in facilitating positive attitudes among these teachers as they interact with administrators, colleagues, students, and students' family members.

REFERENCES

Banks, J. A. (1998). The lives and values of researchers: Implications for educating citizens in a multicultural society. *Educational Researcher, 27*(7), 4-17

Berlinger, D. C., & Biddle, B. J. (1995). The manufactured crisis: Myth, fraud, and the attack on America's public schools. Reading, MA: Addison-Wesley.

Boykin, A. W. (2000). The talent development model of schooling: Placing students at promise for academic success. *Journal of Education for Students Placed At Risk, 5*(1&2), 3-25.

Brooks, J. G., & Brooks, M. G. (1993). Becoming a constructivist teacher. In Association for Supervision and Curriculum Development (ASCD) (Ed.), *In search of understanding: The case for constructivist classrooms.* Alexandria, VA: ASCD.

Brown, J. W., Hughes, G. B., & Vance, P. L. (1999). The new face of teaching in the 21st century: Are we ready for the challenge? *Journal of Negro Education, 68*(3), 241-243.

Brown, J. W., & Manswell Butty, J. L. (1999). Factors that influence African American male teachers' educational and career aspirations: Implications for school district recruitment and retention efforts. *Journal of Negro Education, 68*(3), 280-292.

Callendar, C. (1997). *Education for empowerment: The practices and philosophies of Black teachers.* Staffordshire, London: Trentham Books.

Carter, R. (2001). School watch: Foreign teachers put accent on learning. *Atlanta Constitution,* p. 5JK.

Casserly, M. (1994). Problems facing aging urban schools. *Detroit News*, 5 October. [Available: http://www.cgsc.org/services/onissues/oped4.htm]

Cuban, L. (1990). Reforming again, again, and again. *Educational Researcher, 19*(1), 3-13.

Delpit, L. (1995). *Other people's children: Cultural conflicts in the classroom.* New York: The New Press.

Fears, D. (2002, February 24). A diverse–and divided–Black community. *Washington Post,* p. A01.

Foster, M. (1997). *Black teachers on teaching.* New York: The New Press.

Frey, W. H. (2002). *Census 2002 reveals new native-born and foreign-born shifts across U.S.*

Report No. 02-520). Ann Arbor, MI: Population Studies Center, University of Michigan.

Goeff, L. (2001, May 11). Caribbean staff can make it in New York. *The Times Educational Supplement,* p.18.

Good, T. L. (1996). Teaching effects and teacher evaluation. In J. Sikula (Ed.), *Handbook of research on teacher education* (pp. 617-665). New York: Macmillan.

Good, T. L., & Brophy, J. E. (2003). *Looking in classrooms* (9th ed.). New York: Allyn and Bacon.

Haycock, K. (2000). No more settling for less. *Thinking K-16, 4(*10), 2-5, 6-8, 10-12. [Available: http://www.edtrust.org/documents/k16_spring2000.pdf]

Heath, S. B., & McLaughlin, M. W. (1994). *Possible selves: Achievement, ethnicity, and Gender for inner-city youth.* New York: Teachers College Press.

Emmer, E., & Stough, L. (2001). Classroom management: A critical part of educational psychology, with implications for teacher education. *Educational Psychologist, 36,* 103-112.

Kelly, L. S. (1998). Urban districts inventing new teacher recruitment strategies. *Urban Educator, 7*(6), 7-9.

Kozol, J. (1991). *Savage inequalities: Children in America's schools.* New York: Crown Publishers.

Kozol, J. (1996). *Amazing grace: The lives of children and the conscience of a nation.* New York: HarperPerennial.

Ladson-Billings, G. (1994). *The dreamkeepers.* San Francisco: Jossey-Bass.

Levin, J. R., & Nolan, J. F. (2000). *Principles of classroom management: A professional decision-making model.* Boston: Allyn & Bacon.

Mansell, W. (2002, July 20). Schools accused of modern slave trade. *The Times Educational Supplement*, p. 3

Manswell Butty, J. L. (2002). Teacher instruction, student attitudes, and mathematics performance among 10th and 12th grade Black and Hispanic students. *Journal of Negro Education, 70*(1&2), 19-37.

McCoubrey, M. (2001). Recruiting teachers from abroad. *Techniques, 76*(5), 33-34.

National Center for Education Statistics. (1996). Urban schools: The challenge of location and poverty (NCES 90-184). Washington, DC: U.S. Government Printing Office.

National Center for Education Statistics. (1997). Public elementary/secondary school universe 1993-1994 [On-line). Available: www.ed.gov/NCES/pubs/96212bt.html

National Center for Education Statistics. (2000). Projections of education statistics to 2010. (NCES 2000071). Washington, DC: U.S. Government Printing Office.

Perry, M. J., & Mackun, P. J. (2001). *Population change and distribution 1990 to 2000: Census 2000 brief* (Report No. C2KBR/01-2). Washington, DC: US Census Bureau.

Recruiting New Teachers, Inc. (2000). *A guide to today's teacher recruitment challenges.* Belmont, MA: Author.

Rossi, R. (2001a, February 11). No course required in class control. *Chicago Sun-Times,* p. 12.

Rossi, R. (2001b, February 11). Rude Chicago students stun foreign teachers. *Chicago Sun Times,* p. 9.1, 10.

Russo, C. J., & Cooper, B. S. (1999). Understanding urban education today [Prologue]. *Education and Urban Society, 31*(2), 131.

Schworm, P. (2002, June 2). Immigrant population increasing. *The Boston Globe,* p.4.

Smith, M. S., & O'Day, J. (1993). Systemic reform and educational opportunity. In S. H. Fuhrman (Ed.), *Designing coherent policy.* (pp. 1-34). San Francisco: Jossey-Bass.

The Urban Teacher Collaborative. (2000). *The urban teacher challenge.* Belmont, MA: Author.

Urban Educator. (2001). *Cleveland turns to India for teachers.* Washington, DC: Author.

U.S. Department of Commerce. (1996). *Current population reports: Population projections of the United States by age, sex, race, and Hispanic origin: 1955 to 2050.* Washington, DC: U.S. Government Printing Office.

Villegas, A. M., & Clewell, B. C. (1998). Increasing the number of teachers of color for urban schools: Lessons from the Pathways national evaluation. *Education and Urban Society, 31*(1), 42-61.

TEACHING A READING FRENCH COURSE AS A FOREIGN LANGUAGE REQUIREMENT [1]

Lillith Barnaby
Kingston College
Jamaica

Hugues Peters
University of the West Indies
Jamaica

Chapter 6

SINCE 1991, the University of the West Indies (UWI) has developed a reading course as a foreign language requirement for those first year students who enter the Faculty of Humanities & Education (formerly the Faculty of Arts & Education) at the bachelor level with little or no background in any foreign language. It has seemed useful to the authors, who have had first hand experience with this course as instructor and coordinator between 1996 and 1998 to assess a course that has been in existence for the last decade.

[1] This article was presented at the Southeast Conference on Foreign Language and Literature, Rollins College, March 5-7, 1999, as well as at the Staff-Postgraduate Seminar, Department of Modern Languages & Literatures, UWI, Mona, April 8, 1999. It has benefited from comments from the respective audiences. We would also like to thank Professor Bragger as well as two anonymous referees for their detailed and insightful comments.

This assessment is based on a critical review of the objectives of the reading course and on a survey administered to the students enrolled in the course in French at the Mona Campus of UWI, Jamaica. We propose to examine students' reactions to the course and some of the problems that they encountered. We will first give the historical background and examine the rationale behind the establishment of such a reading course as an undergraduate foreign-language requirement, presenting and evaluating its objectives. Following a brief presentation of the course itself, we will introduce the questionnaire administered to the students, and discuss its results. We will finally give an idea of possible pedagogical implications of these results.

1. BACKGROUND AND RATIONALE.

According to Dr. Sheila Carter, who drafted the first proposal for the introduction of a foreign language requirement, the original rationale was the need for students to "have a facility in at least one of the languages of the region", and she emphasized the "inescapable responsibility" of the University to ensure that this objective was reached (Minutes of the Faculty Board, UWI [Mona], February-March 1990). Her position was that learning a foreign language would help to promote an awareness of different cultures, and that this broadening was an essential part of a liberal education (ibid.).[1] Dr. Carter's original concept was for a year-long course, developing all four communicative skills (personal communication). However, it is a one-semester reading course in French or Spanish that was first made compulsory in 1991 at all three campuses of the University through an initiative of the Mona Campus, Jamaica.[2]

The first question one may ask is whether such a reading course constitutes an adequate foreign-language requirement at the undergraduate level within the UWI system. This does not appear to be the preferred choice among universities in the United States: On the one hand, the institutions that actually have undergraduate foreign-language requirements usually propose a two- or three-semester programme, corresponding approximately to three years of foreign-language learning at the high school level. On the other hand, reading courses are usually designed as specific purpose courses, either to reinforce reading and translating skills of intermediate- to advanced-level learners (Dowling & Mitchell 1993; Grenier-Winther 1999), or as a foreign-language requirement at the postgraduate level (Solomon 1979 describes a reading course for students of the graduate Institute of International Relations of the UWI, Trinidad).[3] The second question that one may ask is whether a reading course is adequate to make the students aware of the cultural diversity of the Caribbean region. After all, as pointed out to us by Professor Bragger (personal communication), the promotion of such an awareness could be taught entirely through culture and civilization courses. These questions will be examined in light of the answers given to the questionnaire administered to the students.

2. PRESENTATION AND EVALUATION OF OBJECTIVES.

2.1. OFFICIAL COURSE OUTLINE.

The official course outline for both French and Spanish found in the Humanities and Education Regulations and Syllabuses reads as follows:

> F10R / S10R Reading Course in French / Spanish (3 credits): This course is for students with little or no background in French / Spanish and who are studying French / Spanish for the development of reading skills in the language. It is designed for those students who do not have the Faculty's foreign language requirement. Prerequisite : None.

This course is therefore designed as an introductory course for students with little or no background in the foreign language. Certain students are exempted, and even barred from taking the course for credits: Native speakers and students with a pass in a foreign language at the Caribbean Examinations Council (CXC) Secondary Education Certificate (C-SEC) or General Certificate of Education (GCE) Ordinary level. These certificates are the culmination of five years of studies at the secondary level.[4] Those who registered for an intensive beginners' course in French or Spanish were also exempted. This one semester 10-hour-a-week beginners' course in French or 6-hour-a-week beginners' course in Spanish is in fact another choice given to students to fulfill the language requirement.[5]

A consequence of the requirement is that the students described by the expression "with little or no background" allowed to register for this course could perfectly well have up to five years of studying the language without, however, having passed the examination. Therefore, although the course is designed for absolute beginners, the level of experience of the students is always varied, and can be quite high. This can affect the pace at which the course is taught.[6] As suggested by Dr. Elizabeth Wilson, an entrance exam granting exemption from the course could be organized and this would certainly make the class more homogeneous.

Although the word "culture" is not mentioned specifically in the official description, it was part of the original rationale for introducing the foreign language requirement. We do believe that it is an important aspect of language learning in general (Byram 1992), and of this course in particular, especially when one of the benefits of this course is to promote cultural awareness and regional integration.

2.2. DESCRIPTION OF THE COURSE MATERIAL.

The place of reading in the teaching methods of language courses has undergone considerable changes over the years: from being central for the grammar-translation method, then ignored in audio-lingual methods focused on the spoken language, it has now regained a more balanced position within communicative methods centred on the acquisition of the skills needed to survive in a foreign society (Cicurel 1991; Omaggio-Hadley 1993). Thanks to the development of research on cognitive processes, reading is no longer considered to be a passive skill, but rather a process by which readers actively "produce understanding" using linguistics as well as contextual knowledge (Byrnes 1985: 78). The communicative approach taken is notably reflected in the use of authentic texts likely to be encountered in realistic situations.

As coordinator and instructor between 1996 and 1998, we have had the opportunity to redesign the course materials and, in keeping with the official outline, we have proposed the following revised course description in our syllabus:

> This is an intensive reading course in French (13 weeks - 4 hours a week) designed for those who want to acquire an intermediate reading level in French (ability to read texts on topics familiar to you), but have never studied French or whose background in French is weak. You will acquire the fundamentals of French grammar and develop a basic reading French vocabulary with an accent on comprehension (rather than strict translation) of French texts. Although translation is not the primary concern of this course, it is a useful tool that will be used to verify your understanding of the meaning of texts in a foreign language. This course is NOT designed to teach you to write or speak French. (*Reading Course in French*, revised edition 1998).

As stated explicitly, the accent is on comprehension of reading material through the development of a basic knowledge of French grammar and vocabulary. From the beginning, it is made clear that only one language skill, reading, will be developed.

The course is based on grammatical progression. Discrete points of grammar are presented by the instructor and followed by sentences to be translated by the students. In principle, students are supposed to prepare grammar points in advance of the lecturer's presentation with the help of a reference grammar. In the syllabus outline, we present the manual in the following manner:

> This manual is composed of sentences focused on specific grammar points that you have to translate accurately into English, and of various types of texts (news items, short stories, articles, advertisements, literary texts, letters, recipes, maps, etc.) that will familiarize you with the culture of countries in which French is spoken. It is important that you have access to a French reference grammar and a good French / English dictionary. (ibid.)

Apart from sentences used to illustrate specific grammar points, more than half of the booklet is devoted to a variety of authentic texts followed by different types of comprehension questions.[7] We have used texts of general interest on recent topics of discussion as well as texts which describe the culture (including literature) of various French-speaking countries or regions (texts not only on Martinique, Haiti, or Guadeloupe, etc., but also on Burkina Faso, Senegal, etc.) in accordance with our objective of increasing the knowledge of the *francophone* world with an emphasis on the Caribbean region.

There is a variety in the type of texts (including non-prose texts such as maps, ads for apartment rentals or wedding proposals, menu at a restaurant, etc.) which takes into account the actual diversity of texts which are likely to be encountered in realistic communicative situations. We have tried as much as possible to have a progression in the level of difficulty.

There is also a variety in the type of questions set: open questions, multiple choice questions, yes-no questions, matching exercises, and summary questions. For example, we asked the students to match headlines taken from newspapers with the corresponding summary of the articles. The idea behind varying the type of questions is to develop different reading strategies, as well as making the activities more interesting. (Phillips 1984; Wahl 1999). For instance, learners with limited knowledge of the language should be able to scan a given text for relevance before reading it for content.

At the beginning of the manual, based on the idea that students know more than they think, we start by a presentation of different types of cognates because both languages share many words or expressions (Sandberg & Tatham 1968; Solomon 1979). This feature can be exploited immediately in various types of exercises, for example, matching exercises, comprehension questions and even translation of simple texts. A simple survey done in January 2001 shows that, after only four hours of instruction, even students with no background at all in the foreign language are able to answer comprehension questions and even translate an authentic text, with the help of their contextual knowledge and of their interpretation of cognates, once they are provided with function words such as auxiliaries, determiners and some prepositions (Annex 1). We feel that this approach is quite successful and motivating as an introduction to reading in a foreign language.

In principle, it is also helpful for understanding more complicated texts. However, the ability to recognize cognates depends on the extent of vocabulary in the first language. A number of students have difficulty recognizing vocabulary which is not basic, everyday vocabulary, and which we consider transparent. For instance, in a text on a Martinican prison, one can find the following sentence:

> Cette prison, les concepteurs **l'ont voulue** (*wanted it*) aérée, communautaire, conviviale pour améliorer les conditions de vie des détenus. (From *Antilla*, October 1996). [The prison's designers wanted it to be airy, communal, cheerful (convivial) so that the prisoners' living conditions would be improved.]

The adjectives *communautaire*, *conviviale*, and the infinitive verb *améliorer* are not readily understood by several students despite fairly similar English words *communal*, *convivial*, and *to ameliorate*.[8] This means that, in practice, the level of English vocabulary cannot be taken for granted, and a way of facilitating comprehension is to review morphological rules of word formation (affixes, suffixes, word compounding…) and to encourage students to study vocabulary in families of words, for instance : *commun/ communauté/ communautaire; meilleur/ améliorer/ amélioration…*[9] One wonders, in fact, if this sort of exercise in the foreign language does not lead to an improvement in knowledge of English.[10] We will return to this issue when examining the results of the questionnaire.

3. ORGANIZATION OF THE SURVEY, AND DISCUSSION OF RESULTS.

We asked the students to complete a questionnaire on the course at the end of the semester, over a period of two consecutive semesters during the 1998-1999 academic year. A random sample of sixty-six students (out of a total of 84 students registered during these two semesters) answered the questionnaire anonymously.

The survey was designed first to gain some basic information on the student population taking this course, second to gain some basic knowledge of their perception of the course, and finally to give them the opportunity for free commentary.

3.1. CHARACTERISTICS OF THE STUDENT POPULATION.

This questionnaire allowed us to define the students' background more precisely in terms of their level of exposure to a foreign language, and of their major at the University of the West Indies:

Question 1: Have you studied a foreign language before? If so for how long?

a. French b. Spanish c. Other d. None.

Question 2: Have you spent any time in a non-English-speaking country?

Question 3: What is your area of study?

When analyzing the responses to question 1, it appears that fewer than a quarter of the students have no exposure to a foreign language (15 out of 66), and that 39 students out of 66 had 3 years or more of exposure to a foreign language, whether French or Spanish (see table 1). Considering the similarities between French and Spanish, this means that our goal of reaching an intermediate level of reading proficiency in French on the ACTFL scale is a very reasonable one for these students who, hopefully, will emulate the rest of the class. Additionally, these figures allow us to point out a major difference with the situation encountered in the United States that might justify the introduction of a reading course as an undergraduate foreign-language requirement at UWI. These students with 3 years of learning a foreign language would very likely receive an exemption from the foreign-language requirement.[11] This immediately points out to the fact that the level of the exemption from the requirement at UWI is quite high (it requires 5 years of learning the language), and this might give another indication, given the sheer number of students who are likely to be concerned by it as to why a reading course was preferred in terms of cost efficiency.

Table 1: Answers to question 1

Number of students with no exposure to a Foreign Language: 15.
Number of students with formal exposure to a Foreign Language: 51.

1. Number of students with exposure to French (FR) alone: 17.							
FR 2 years:	3	FR 4 years:	3	FR 3 years:	9	FR 5 years:	2
2. Number of students with exposure to Spanish (SP) alone: 32							
SP %oyear:	2	SP 2 years:	5	SP 4 years:	6	SP 9 years:	2
SP 1 year:	2	SP 3 years:	13	SP 5 years:	2		
3. Number of students with exposure to both FR and SP: 2							
FR 2 years & SP 2 years:	1			FR 3 years & SP 4 years:	1		

Responses to question 2 show that there is relatively little contact with non-English speaking countries: only 15 students (out of 66) spent some time in a foreign country. The goal of fostering the awareness of the cultural diversity of the region becomes even more important.

Finally, responses to question 3 indicate that we have 16 students from History (HI), 12 from Linguistics (LI), 10 from English (EN), 7 from Mass Communication (MC), 7 from Sciences[12] (SC), 5 from Library Studies (LB), 3 from Philosophy (PH), 2 from Theology (TH), 1 from Literacy Studies (LT), 1 from International Relations (IR), and 2 of unknown major.

3.2. STUDENTS' PERCEPTIONS OF THE COURSE.

The second part of the questionnaire was designed to evaluate students' perceptions of the course:

> **Question 4:** Do you feel that learning to read and understand written French could be useful in your studies? Yes / No.
>
> **Question 5:** Do you find the course useful for acquiring general knowledge? Yes / No.
>
> **Question 6:** Has studying French made you more aware of the English language and how it functions? Yes / No.
>
> **Question 7:** How important is it for West Indian students to study one of the languages of the region? Very important / Important / Not very important.
>
> **Question 8:** Do you think it is worthwhile to learn to read a foreign language instead of learning to speak and write it as well? Yes / No.

Both responses to questions 4, 5, and 6 were overwhelmingly positive (respectively 61 out of 66, 60 out of 66, and 56 out of 66) (See table 2). As far as question 6 is concerned, all the students majoring in English, that is, students involved in the study of literature and therefore particularly aware of the difficulties of literary reading in their first language, answered 'yes' to this question. This last feature of developing the literacy skills of Caribbean students might be useful at a time when the democratization process brings the University to open itself to more and more students of varied educational backgrounds. For question 7, 61 students chose the answers 'Very important' or 'Important' (See table 2).

These responses are not surprising: the humanistic benefits of learning about another culture and the benefits for intellectual and linguistic development in the native language are among the traditional motivations that draw students to French (Sieloff-Magnan & Tochon 2001).

Table 2: Answers to questions 4, 5, 6 and 7.

1. Distribution table for question 4: usefulness for domain of study.

	Frequency	%
Yes	61	92.4
No	4	6.1
No answer	1	1.5

2. Distribution table for question 5: usefulness for general knowledge.

	Frequency	%
Yes	60	90.9
No	5	7.6
No answer	1	1.5

3. Distribution table for question 6: usefulness for improvement of English.

	Frequency	%
Yes	56	84.8
No	8	12.1
No answer	2	3.0

4. Distribution table for question 7: the usefulness of learning a foreign language.

	Frequency	%
Important	22	33.3
Very important	39	59.1
Not very important	5	7.6

Students seem to recognize the academic value of the course as far as the development of general knowledge, and the impact on the first language are concerned, and they are generally convinced that it is useful to learn a foreign language. However, when asked in question 8 whether it was worthwhile to learn "to read" a language, over half of the students (38 out of 66) answered positively, but 21 answered "no", 3 were without opinion, and 4 gave the answer 'both', one student explaining her answer by saying that "You will not always be able to read it, you need to be able to speak / write it" (see table 3).

It seems therefore that students feel that reading in a foreign language could indeed serve a purpose, but they would prefer to acquire the full range of skills.[13] When analyzing the responses major by major, we further noticed that although there was no clear tendency in the majority of cases, two disciplines showed opposite trends, namely English and Linguistics. While English majors (8 out of 10, and 1 'no response') clearly saw the benefits of reading in a foreign language, only 4 out of 12 Linguistics majors agreed. One explanation for this difference might be that students of linguistics place more emphasis on speech as opposed to students of English who are more focused on literature and on the written word.

Table 3: Answers to question 8

Distribution table for the usefulness of learning to read a foreign language.

	Frequency	%
Yes:	38	57.6
No:	21	31.8
Both	4	6.1
No answer	3	4.5

The answers to question 8 show that it is necessary to spend some time convincing the students of the usefulness of a course that does not teach how to speak or write. This could be done by emphasizing the fact that electronic means of communication such as the Internet facilitate as never before access to up-to-date texts written in a foreign language and increases the amount of reading that professionals might have to do in a foreign language.[14]

3.3. OPEN-ENDED QUESTIONS.

The last two questions offered the opportunity to students of giving open-ended answers concerning their reactions to the course itself. This part was very useful in interpreting answers given by students to other questions.

Question 9: What do you like about the course?

Question 10: What don't you like about the course?

As far as question 9 was concerned, students generally appreciated information they received about other countries, and about the language itself. Other points mentioned were the fact that they were not required to speak, the quality of tutoring, and the opportunity to participate. Here is a sample of significant answers:

- I am able to read some things written in French.
- Good exposure to learning another language.
- The challenge of learning to translate a recently obscure language.
- The chance I get to learn about other French countries while learning about their language ; I can learn the language without speaking/writing it.
- It is excellent as it helps to improve my knowledge of not only French but English.
- It gives you power to feel like a true West Indian person.

As far as question 10 was concerned, the most common negative points were that the course was too intensive and that one semester was not enough (27 out of 66 had this complaint). A certain number complained about the difficulty of French grammar, especially about the number of tenses, and also the amount of vocabulary (15 out of 66). Interestingly, 9 complained of not learning to speak, although it had been made clear in the course description and in class that this was exclusively a reading course. Of course this complaint leads us back to the discussion of question 8. According to one student, "It is a bit difficult to learn another language without being able to speak and hear the pronunciation". This seemed to be a matter of concern for a number of students who had to be reassured that accurate French pronunciation is not absolutely necessary in order to understand a written text. However, further research, on this particular issue is needed.

We can now address the questions of the adequacy of a reading course as a foreign language requirement at the undergraduate level, and the adequacy of a reading course for promoting an awareness of other cultures. As far as the first question is concerned, two points must be considered: One, it would be difficult to require all students to do a complete beginners' course due to time limitations (not all students can fit a 10-hour (or even a 6-hour) course to their schedule) and staffing restrictions. Two, offering the course at the undergraduate level means that a larger number of people can be exposed, albeit minimally, to a foreign language, and acquire reading skills that they can actually nurture and develop by themselves. Similarly, Omaggio-Hadley (1993: 163) cites Barnett (1989), who identifies among the specific advantages of reading, the fact that it is a skill that can be maintained after students complete formal instruction, and a skill that fosters the development of general literacy skills. As far as the second question is concerned, the use of authentic material will play a part in "fostering cultural insights and understanding", as mentioned in Omaggio-Hadley (ibid.), especially when the texts chosen speak about regional Caribbean issues, from a Caribbean point of view, for which adequate background knowledge exists.

4. PEDAGOGICAL IMPLICATIONS.

One challenge to be faced in periodically reviewing and modifying the manual is to make it even more manageable without sacrificing the content. We want the learners to acquire the fundamentals that will allow them to become independent readers. The intensity of the course has already been reduced, but apparently the process needs to be continued, based on students' answers to the questionnaire. In line with current conceptions of reading as a cognitive process involving the continuous interaction of bottom-up and top-down processing (Rumelhart 1980), we feel that the cultural, contextual and the linguistic aspects of texts should be taught simultaneously by providing different types of texts, by developing content to which students can relate, and by proposing tasks that will require different reading strategies (Phillips 1984; Omaggio-Hadley 1993).

If the course is to make students more aware that they live in a multilingual region, we need as much as possible to use texts which are relevant at the regional level. The use of the Internet as well as access to regional magazines in French (such as *Antilla*) will be especially useful in that regard. It could be possible, for instance, for students to consult a news site in order to have access to the French or Haitian point of view on matters of current interest in the region.

The use of the Internet could also help us find material directly geared towards the academic specialization of the students. This is a feature that should not be neglected since students overwhelmingly find the course interesting with respect to their own studies. This is also a way to develop a more student-centred type of instruction by providing students with different texts according to their major, and encouraging them to find additional texts by themselves. Other developments might include the setting up of a Web site on which recapitulative exercises would be available along with corrections. This again would encourage the students to take a more active role in the learning process. As a possible future development, it might be that such a course could lend itself easily to be taught entirely or partially in a distance mode. (See Grenier-Winther 1999 for the development of a distance reading proficiency course). This could be the ideal solution, especially for part-time and returning students.

CONCLUSION

The questions that we have examined in this paper are whether a reading course can constitute an adequate foreign language requirement at the undergraduate level and whether it can contribute to achieving the goal of developing cultural awareness with Caribbean French-speaking neighbours in particular, and the French-speaking world in general. The ideal is obviously that students learn to speak and write the various languages of the region in order to communicate fully. Within limits, however, taking into consideration the limited resources of the University, and the limited time that students can spend on studying a language, if they have not done so at high school, it seems that a reading course can be useful as seen in the students' responses to the questionnaire.

First, reading is a skill that learners can nurture and develop by themselves once they have received the basic elements of vocabulary and grammar. Second, literacy in a foreign language is a skill that becomes even more important today. It is now a 'lieu commun' to say that the new technologies of communication, such as the Internet, far from sounding the death knell of reading, have in fact opened new avenues for written communication. Finally, as confirmed in the students' answers to the questionnaire, learners can reflect on and develop their first language literacy by comparing it to another language of culture, such as French, which shares so many words with English, either by history or by reciprocal borrowings. As far as the teaching of culture is concerned, students recognize that this course allows them to become aware of the linguistic and cultural diversity of the region.

The cultural aspects are introduced by using authentic material in context.

Even though one cannot deny that, if given the choice, most students would rather learn a language in its entirety, and that students who are especially motivated to do so have the possibility of taking intensive foreign-language courses, we hope to have shown that there is a place for the reading course within the curriculum, by giving students, in a very short time, a foreign-language skill that can be immediately useful in their studies, and in their future professional life.

ENDNOTES

[1] Such an objective is particularly meaningful, within the context of growing regional political and economic integration. Indeed, special emphasis is placed within the Caribbean territories of the Commonwealth on developing cultural and economic relations with French- and Spanish-speaking neighbours. The emphasis on foreign language education is therefore important for UWI, a regional university with three main campuses in Jamaica, Trinidad and Barbados, funded by the English-speaking territories of the region, and Belize.

[2] The reasons for this decision are not mentioned in the minutes. It is reasonable to assume that considerations of cost efficiency and maximization of limited resources must have played a prominent role, especially for a course that is an end in itself and does not lead to further study of the language.

[3] The preference for reading courses as foreign-language requirements at the graduate level is revealed by a search on the Web at institutions such as Harvard, Stanford, Pennsylvania, York, etc. At Boston University, for example, the course 'French

for Reading' is described as 'Rapid acquisition of reading skills in French for graduate students intending to take departmental reading exams.' However, we have found one instance of a reading course in French as a foreign language requirement offered at Tel-Aviv University (Wahl 1998).

[4] Besides, the Faculty of Humanities and Education "strongly recommends" its applicants to have a CXC in at least one foreign language.

[5] The difference between the 10-hour-a-week course in French and the 6-hour-a-week course in Spanish is that, the beginners' programme in French, but not in Spanish, automatically allows students with a final grade of B (50 %) or higher after a second 13-week intensive semester to enter the level I programme in French. This 260-hour programme in French covers the programme of the whole CXC Secondary Certificate of Education level and helps to boost the enrollment in French.

[6] Notice that students who have a CXC-level in another foreign language are already prevented from taking a reading course for credits.

[7] In the examinations, translation of discrete sentences used to account for between 45 and 50 % of the marks, the other questions being various types of comprehension exercises. We are now reducing the weight given to translation, which is kept solely as an additional way to check reading comprehension of texts. The aim is to translate in order to show comprehension.

[8] The difficulty in guessing the meaning of these words might also be linked to a failure to activate the right schemata associated

with penal institutions (Omaggio-Hadley 1993: 134-137; Rumelhart 1980).

[9] See Mirhassani & Toosi 2000 for the benefits of developing knowledge of word formation on reading comprehension.

[10] The situation is even more complex when taking into consideration that the native language of most Jamaicans is an English Creole (Christie 1996, 2001).

[11] Eventually upon completion of a standardized test (such as SAT-2 as at Stanford).

[12] We included Biochemistry, Geography, Computer Sciences and Mathematics in a single 'Science' category.

[13] Remember that there exists the possibility of taking a French or Spanish Beginners' course, and therefore that the students enrolled in the reading course have chosen, for different reasons, not to take this latter course.

[14] Recent studies on the place of Romance Languages on the Internet have shown that French accounts for 4,61 % of the total number of Web sites on the Internet (as opposed to 52 % for English, 6,97 % for German, and 5,69 % for Spanish) (*Observatoire des langues et des cultures* par FUNDREDES).

REFERENCES

Barnett, M. A. 1989. *More than meets the Eye: Foreign Language Reading*. Language in Education: Theory and Practice 73. CAL/ERIC Series on Languages and Linguistics. Englewood Cliffs, NJ: Prentice Hall, Inc.

Byram, M. 1992. *Culture et éducation en langue étrangère*. Paris, CREDIF-Hatier/Didier.

Byrnes, H. 1985. "Teaching towards Proficiency: The Receptive Skills." in Omaggio, A. (ed.) *Proficiency, Curriculum, Articulation: The Ties that Bind. Reports of the Northeast Conference on the Teaching of Foreign Languages*. Middlebury, VT: Northeast Conference: pp. 77-107.

Christie, P. (ed.) 1996. *Caribbean Language Issues: Old and New: Papers in Honour of Professor Mervyn Alleyne on the Occasion of his Sixtieth Birthday*. Kingston: University of the West Indies Press.

_____ (ed.) 2001. *Due Respect: Papers on English and English-Related Creoles in the Caribbean in Honour of Professor Robert Le Page*. Kingston: University of the West Indies Press.

Cicurel, F. 1991. *Lectures interactives en langue étrangère*. Paris: Hachette.

Dowling, C. & A. Mitchell. 1993. "Reading in a Specific Purpose Foreign Language Course: A Case Study of Technical Japanese." *The Modern Language Journal* 77(4): 433-44.

F10R - Reading Course in French. UWI, Mona. Revised June 1998.

Grenier-Winther, J. 1999. "Real Issues in the Virtual Classroom". *The French Review* 73(2): 252-64.

Minutes of Faculty Board, UWI, Mona. February-March 1990.

Mirhassani, A. & A. Toosi. 2000. "The Impact of Word-Formation Knowledge on Reading Comprehension." *IRAL* 38(3/4): 301-12.

Observatoire des langues et des cultures. Cinquième étude sur la place des langues latines sur l'internet (août 2000-juin 2001). FUNDREDES *www.funredes.org*.

Omaggio-Hadley, A. 1993[2]. *Teaching Language in Context*. Boston, MA: Heinle & Heinle Publishers.

Phillips, J.K. 1984. "Practical Implications of Recent Research in Reading." Foreign Language Annals 17(4): 285-96.

Rumelhart, D. 1980. "Schemata: The building blocks of cognition." Chapter 2, in R. Spiro, B. Bruce and W. Brewer (eds.) *Theoretical Issues in Reading Comprehension*. Hillsdale, NJ: Lawrence Erlbaum Associates: pp. 38-58.

Sandberg, K. & E. Tatham. 1968. *French for Reading*. New York : Prentice-Hall.

Sieloff-Magnan, S. & F.V. Tochon. 2001. "Reconsidering French Pedagogy: The Crucial Role of the Teacher and Teaching." *The French Review* 74(6): 1092-112.

Solomon, D. 1979. "The Construction of a Specialised Reading Course in French". *Caribbean Journal of Education* 6(2): 147-58.

Walh, Y. 1999. "Évaluer la compétence de lecture." *Le Français dans le Monde* 301: 31-3.

ANNEX 1: BERMUDES : TOTALE INTEGRATION AU CARICOM.

A. Read the following paragraph and answer in English the following question : Why were Caricom representatives recently on a visit in Bermuda?

Un groupe de travail du (*A workgroup of the*) secrétariat **du** (*of*) Caricom, **comprenant** (*including*) Edouard Greene, assistant **du** (*of the*) Secrétaire général **au** (*in*) développement humain et social, **s'est rendu aux** (*went to*) Bermudes **du** 11 **au** (*from... till...*) 13 juillet 2001 **pour** (*in order to*) engager **des** (...) discussions **au plus haut niveau** (*at the highest level*) **avec** (*with*) le premier ministre de Bermuda, Jennifer Smith, **à propos de** (*about*) la demande d'admission **de ce pays auprès du** (*of this country to*) Caricom **comme** (*as*) membre associé de l'Organisation.

B. Translate into English the second paragraph:

Le cabinet **du** (*of the*) premier ministre, le leader de l'opposition, l'Association **des hommes d'affaires** (*of businessmen*) de Bermuda, l'Association hôtelière de Bermuda, le directeur de la police, **des** (*some*) représentants **des** (*of*) affaires sociales et de la culture, la chambre de commerce de Bermuda et la presse locale **ont** (*have*) participé **aux** (*to the*) discussions. La coopération **est** (*is*) spécialement **attendue dans** (*expected in*) les domaines de l'éducation, **de la santé** (*of health*), de la culture, **du** (*of*) sport, **du** (*of*) tourisme et de la sécurité régionale. [...] (From *Antilla* 949, August 2001, p. 16).

COLLABORATIVE LEARNING IN CARIBBEAN HIGHER EDUCATION: EXAMINING THE PROSPECTS

Olabisi Kuboni
University of the West Indies
Trinadad

Chapter 7

Within recent times the newer information and communication technologies (ICTs) have brought with them increased potential for two-way communication on both a one-to-one and a many-to-many basis. Within the education sector, this new technological capability has given rise to new thinking about teaching and learning and a focus on learning rather than teaching. A lot of emphasis is now placed on learning as an activity that entails the active participation of learners as they construct meanings that they validate through negotiation within the collective. This outlook on learning forms the basis of what has come to be known as collaborative learning.

This paper notes the increasing use of the ICTs in Caribbean higher education and the implications of this development for teaching-learning practices in the sector. Consequently, the paper examines current approaches to teaching and learning with a view to analyzing factors that are likely to impact on the possible emergence of collaborative learning (CL) strategies within the higher education sector of the region.

This examination is based on data derived from an observation study conducted in 1995 among in-service teachers pursuing the Certificate of Education programme offered via the audioconferencing facility of the (former) University of the West Indies Distance Teaching Enterprise (UWIDITE).

Arising out of the analysis of those data, the paper argues that there are several aspects of the teaching-learning interaction in higher education that can militate against the emergence of CL strategies. At the same time, it notes that there are pockets of good practice that can provide a platform for building more participatory teaching-learning exchanges.

The paper concludes by drawing attention to three broader issues related to the socio-political, organisational and cultural underpinnings of Caribbean higher education that warrant consideration in any thrust to introduce CL strategies into the sector.

INTRODUCTION

The idea of collaborative learning is gaining increased recognition in some sectors of the higher education community of the developed world. While no claims can be made about widespread practice, considerable headway is being made in small pockets. Teachers in higher education, both collectively and as individuals are recognising and taking advantage of the capabilities of the telecommunications and networked technologies to build environments to facilitate learning as a shared, mutually-supporting activity in a group setting (Harasim, Hiltz, Teles and Turoff, 1995; Valery and Lord, 2000).

While acknowledging the part played by these technologies in providing the setting for this approach to learning, advocates agree that operating within the networked environment does not necessarily imply that participants are collaborating to learn. Thus collaborative learning is receiving considerable attention as an area of study and practice in its own right.

This paper seeks to examine the prospects for the incorporation of this type of learning into the higher education sector of the Caribbean, given the fact that the University of the West Indies (UWI) and other tertiary level institutions in the region are investing considerable resources in the acquisition of the new interactive technologies with the intention of using them to enhance teaching and learning in the respective institutions.

COLLABORATIVE LEARNING – EXPLORING THE CONCEPT

The notion of collaborative learning brings into focus a more fundamental debate about the nature of learning. To what extent is learning an individual activity, and to what extent is there need for a group setting in order for it to take place? In an earlier work, commenting on the debate that was very much in focus at the time, I took the position that,

> While much learning actually takes place in group settings, it is being argued… that the social context is not a necessary condition for it to take place. Individuals do not necessarily need to be part of a collaborative group process to be able to activate and make use of their cognitive resources. Moreover, it is often the case that in a group setting, it is the contribution of the individual that propels the group forward. At the same time, one cannot deny the role of social and other environmental factors in influencing cognitive activity. (Kuboni, 1997, pp. 110-111)

What is evident in the above statement is that, at the time, I had resolved the issue of the individual/social dichotomy by leaning more in the direction of learning as an individual activity. Five years later, it seems to me that no useful purpose is served by highlighting one above the other. Further, in the Caribbean as elsewhere, professionals are more and more finding themselves being required to function in a team environment in the work place. Thus, while I remain opposed to the notion of learning as a social activity (Nipper, 1989; Garrison, 1990), I would concur with the position advanced by Kaye that "learning is simultaneously a private and a social phenomenon" (Kaye, 1992, p.4).

Harasim, Hiltz, Teles and Turoff (1995), in setting the stage for their definition of collaborative learning (CL), express the view that "learning together can be much more engaging and effective than learning alone" (p.4). In explaining further, they state, "collaborative learning refers to any activity in which two or more people work together to create meaning, explore a topic, or improve skills". It is against this background that they offer their definition of CL as "any learning activity that is carried out using peer interaction, evaluation and/or cooperation, with at least some structuring and monitoring by the instructor" (p.30).

Kaye, cited earlier, goes further in his analysis of the concept. In the first instance, he considers it important to distinguish between collaboration and communication. He asserts,

> Clear communication, and effective communication tools and channels, may be necessary pre-requisites for effective collaboration, but they are not sufficient … A lecture or a meeting may be an effective way of transmitting and sharing information, but it would be a mistake for the participants to believe that they are - in a real sense – 'collaborating' with each other in the process (Kaye, 1992, p.2).

Kaye shares the view of Harasim et al. that "to collaborate means to work together". Working together, he says,

> ... implies a concept of shared goals, and an explicit intention to add value – to create something new or different through the collaboration, as opposed to simply exchanging information or passing on instructions. (p.2)

Also of note is his further proposition that

> Collaboration involves synergy, and assumes that, in some way, the 'whole is greater than the individual parts', so that learning collaboratively has the potential to produce learning gains superior to learning alone. (p.4)

As if to reinforce his position that not all communication is collaboration, he refocuses on conventional classroom practice in order to emphasize the extent of the gap between that practice and CL. He asserts,

> Much educational practice is based on a transmissive model, with all authority and knowledge assumed to be invested in the teacher; as a result, it is notoriously difficult to initiate and maintain constructive group discussion as a learning medium in a traditional educational context. (pp. 3-4)

Ultimately, as a result of his wide-ranging exploration, Kaye defines CL as "... the acquisition by individuals of knowledge, skills, or attitudes occurring as the result of group interaction ... individual learning as a result of group process" (p.4).

Two factors are to be noted about Kaye's analysis. The first is his insistence that CL cannot take place in a conventional educational setting with its emphasis on the transmission or even sharing of information. What is worth noting about his comments about the transmissive model is that, even though the teaching-learning transaction is taking place in a group setting, group processes are not drawn on to facilitate learning. Rather learning, or more accurately information acquisition, is primarily carried out at the level of each individual. The second is the re-affirmation of his basic thesis that learning itself is both a private and a social phenomenon. Both these concerns will re-emerge as we delve more deeply in the examination of the Caribbean formal education sector.

While Kaye's analysis certainly extends on the definition provided by Harasim et al., it can be argued that it focuses heavily on overt intellectual activity and does not pay enough attention to the covert cognitive processes that must support these activities. For example, he talks about "shared goals", "creating something new" and "producing learning gains superior to learning alone".

By introducing the notion of learning as knowledge construction into their interpretation of CL, other theorists have taken the discussion of the concept beyond a focus on learning outcomes and into the area of the process of learning. Gunawardena (1991) alludes to this added dimension to the concept in her statement that

> Collaborative or group learning is premised on a learner-centred model that treats the learner as a participant who is active in the learning process and who constructs knowledge through a process of discussion and interaction with learning peers and experts. (p.16)

What then of learning as knowledge construction? Stated otherwise, what of the constructivist view of learning? Candy (1991) provides a useful starting point for dealing with this question in his proposition that,

> One of the central tenets of constructivism is that individuals try to give meaning to, or construe, the perplexing maelstrom of events and ideas in which they find themselves caught up. (p.254)

Such an understanding of the process of learning has implications for the conception of knowledge that one holds. According to Candy, constructivists refute the positivistic perspective of "knowledge as an accumulated body of empirically verifiable 'facts' derived directly from observation and experimentation" (p.262). Then, drawing on the work of another theorist, he asserts,

> While not denying the existence of an outside reality, it is fundamental to the constructivists' view that the environment can never be directly known, but that conception determines perception ... This means that knowledge is neither a copy nor a mirror of reality, but the forms and content of knowledge are constructed by the one who experiences it. The active interaction between the individual and the environment is mediated by the cognitive structures of the individual. ... People do not merely respond to the environment, they construe it. (p.263)

Bringing the concept closer to the formal world of teaching and learning, Wilson, Teslow and Osman-Jouchoux (1995) draw on the earlier work of Merrill (1991) to offer some key principles of constructivism. Among these are,

- Knowledge is constructed from experience.
- Learning is a personal interpretation of the world.
- Learning is an active process of meaning-making based on experience.
- Learning is collaborative with meaning negotiated from multiple perspectives.
- Reflection is a key component of learning to become an expert.
- Learners should participate in establishing goals, tasks, and methods of instruction and assessment. (p.141)

The link between constructivism and collaboration is more clearly brought out by Jonassen, Davidson, Collins, Campbell and Haag (1995). Unlike Kaye who makes room for a conception that recognises learning at the individual level, Jonassen et al. are clearly leaning towards learning as a social phenomenon. In this regard, they make two further points. First they state that learning is context-dependent, with context being described as a real-world setting or a replication of it in the classroom. The second point is that learning is conversation. As a follow-up, they assert, "Knowledge and intelligence is (sic) not the privilege of an individual, but rather is shared by the community of practice" (p.9).

Building on that platform they go on to introduce the notion of learning from a constructivist perspective. They totally reject the objectivist paradigm, which holds in part that knowledge is external to the knower, and that it can be transferred from one person to another. Rather they propose that "knowledge is a function of how the individual creates meaning from his or her experience; it is not a function of what someone else says is true" (p.11). Consequently, the writers contend that the role of the constructivist educator is to

> ... strive to create environments where learners are required to examine thinking and learning processes; collect, record, and analyze data; formulate and test hypotheses; reflect on previous understandings; and construct their own meaning. (p.11)

Ultimately, it is meaning-making that is the goal of learning.

The final conception of learning that Jonassen et al. propose therefore, recognizes the integration and joint manipulation of four attributes, namely context (briefly described earlier), knowledge construction, collaboration among learners, and conversation to support negotiation of plans for solving problems.

To a greater or lesser extent, it is this multi-faceted notion of learning that has informed attempts to implement collaborative learning strategies into the higher education sector.

LEARNING IN A CARIBBEAN CONTEXT

As stated in the introduction, even as one acknowledges a movement towards the incorporation of CL strategies in higher education, the practice is far from being widespread, even in the developed world. Earlier we noted Kaye's (1992) assertion that much educational practice is based on a transmissive model. Hansen and Stephen (2000) express similar concerns in their own discussion of collaborative learning. They assert,

> Collaborative learning ... emphasizes the virtues of active involvement. It requires students to take the initiative in the classroom, to become active creators rather than passive recipients of knowledge, and to rely on each other as much as or more than on the teacher's authority. (Page number unavailable).[1]

The above remarks are as applicable to the formal education sector at an international level as they are to the Caribbean setting. Elsewhere, in commenting on the situation at the UWI, I remarked,

> With few exceptions, teaching at this (university) level is mainly about the transmission of content, with students more or less left to their own devices to figure out how, and probably if, to acquire that content. (Kuboni, 2002)

It should be noted though that, as elsewhere in the world, the Caribbean region has a strong tradition of learning as a collective activity outside of the formal sector.

Take for example the steelband. The learning that ultimately leads to the performance of a musical work, is significantly influenced by the fact that it takes place in a group setting. Two factors underscore the shared nature of this learning enterprise.

First, as is the case in any other type of orchestra, the goal to be achieved after long periods of practice, is not a collection of individual performances, but a single work to which all the pannists (steelband musicians) would have jointly contributed. The process of learning in an orchestral setting must, of necessity, involve high levels of social and intellectual interaction.

The second emerges from the first and brings into sharp focus characteristics that are unique to the steelband as a musical orchestra. Specifically, the steelband has its origins in and continues to thrive among that sector of the population that traditionally has not been exposed to formal musical training as defined by the advanced industrialized countries. Stated briefly, a large proportion of pannists cannot read music. While this situation is changing[2] , the reality is that much of the learning of a musical work takes place through oral exchanges between the musical arranger and members of the band, and very importantly among the members of the various sections of the band.

It cannot be ignored that how the music is originally learnt is primarily through rote. Nonetheless, as the work is taken through the various stages leading to its perfection, the oral exchange takes on new dimensions that can more be described as learning together. The various participants all contribute from their stored knowledge, not only of this new learning, but of previous learning experiences to support and enhance one another in moving towards the goal which all of them share and, which they are continuously re-shaping as they continue to work together.

It can be argued that, more than in other orchestral contexts, knowledge within the group features significantly in the learning that the oral exchange facilitates among the pannists. I would contend further that what takes place in a steelband context closely approximates the understandings that led Kaye (1992) to conclude that learning is simultaneously a private and a social phenomenon.

As stated earlier, the overall objective of this paper is to assess the prospects for collaborative learning among students in a Caribbean higher education context. The paper is therefore dealing with individuals who have considerable experience in a range of learning contexts outside of the formal education sector. That notwithstanding, it is the formal rather than the informal sector that provides the route for academic and professional advancement. However, it would appear that, with its almost total reliance on the transmissive model of instructional delivery, and, linked to that, its emphasis on learning as an individual activity, the formal sector may be undermining rather than enhancing the potential of its students to attain the goals to which they aspire.

It is against this background that this paper seeks to examine a conventional teaching-learning interaction with a view to identifying the factors in current practice that should be examined if the Caribbean higher education sector is to make optimum use of the new interactive technologies.

OVERVIEW OF RESEARCH STUDY

A research study conducted in a teaching-learning situation via audioconferencing forms the basis for the examination cited above. In drawing on these data, it is acknowledged that, while audioconferencing belongs to the set of technologies collectively referred to as the ICTs, it is not normally associated with the practice of CL. However, the purpose here is not to treat with the practice of CL itself, but rather to examine existing practice in light of emerging trends towards more participatory teaching-learning strategies in higher education.

The study was undertaken in 1995 to analyse the processes of interaction in teacher education programmes offered by the University of the West Indies Distance Teaching Enterprise (UWIDITE) with a view to understanding how these interactions impacted on the learning that was taking place (Kuboni, 1997).

UWIDITE was an audioconferencing facility established in 1983 within the University of the West Indies (UWI) to deliver select programmes to students across the English-speaking Caribbean.[3] Students accessed these programmes through sites located on the three campuses of the University, as well as those in remote locations in both the campus countries and the non-campus countries.

One of the programmes that is still offered via this mode is the Certificate of Education, comprising five specializations and targeted mainly to practicing primary school teachers. It is coordinated out of the School of Education of the Mona, Jamaica campus. While most of the courses are delivered from that location, there have been instances when lecturers have been located either at the Cave Hill, Barbados campus or at St. Augustine, Trinidad.

The study was conducted at the site located at the St. Augustine campus in Trinidad with the students at that site being identified as the main participants for the purpose of the research. In one course the lecturer was located at the Mona campus site and in the other that person was at the St. Augustine campus. Observation and interviews were the two methods used for data collection. Videotaping was used to record the proceedings of the audioconference session at the site of interest. In this way, I was able to capture both the video and audio data of persons located at St. Augustine as well as audio recordings of the oral communication of students and the lecturer at the other sites.

Interviews were conducted with the students at the St. Augustine site as well as with the lone student at the off-campus site in San Fernando, Trinidad. Interviews were not conducted with the lecturers partly because of the difficulty of successfully negotiating this aspect of the study with the Jamaica-based lecturer, whom I had never met face-to-face, and partly because of my own interest to maintain the focus on the learners. Nonetheless, oral presentations by both lecturers during the sessions were included as part of the data analysed.

Data analysis drew on selected aspects of discourse analysis. Potter and Wetherell's (1987) perspective on discourse provided partial support for the approach used. These writers take the view that language is action-oriented and that people use it to do things. It is this interpretation of language that they refer to as 'discourse'. They explain further that the term 'discourse' covers "all forms of spoken interaction, formal and informal, and written texts of all kinds" (p.7). It is with this understanding of discourse that they propose an approach to discourse analysis that involves the analysis of three interrelated components within the discourse, namely *function, variation* and *construction.*[4]

Teacher-learner interaction in an audioconferencing environment

MacDonald (1998), in discussing the audioconference technologies, makes the claim that providing a means for real-time interaction is one of its main advantages. Through this real-time interaction, instructors and learners are able "to get feedback on progress, ask questions, debate ideas and be part of a learning community" (p.11). He also describes the technology as "a cost-effective way to allow [learners] to have a direct conversation with an instructor" adding that "it also brings them into contact with other learners…Learners are able to have the all-important group experience" (p.15).

Notwithstanding the claims made by MacDonald, the reality of the UWIDITE experience was that the technology was primarily used for delivering lectures. Thus the nature of the interaction that took place in this environment was essentially the same as that practiced in the conventional classroom setting.

Birk (1997) distinguishes between two types of lecture presentations – the traditional lecture, with the teacher doing most of the talking and the 'interactive' lecture, "where the teacher still does most of the talking, but engages students with questioning and storytelling". Kaye (1992), you will recall, remarked that the transmissive model of current educational practice would very likely work against constructive discussion. The question that arises therefore is:

- To what extent does the lecture presentation, of whatever type, facilitate and/or inhibit the emergence of learner behaviours consistent with collaborative learning practices?

Data associated with the delivery of both types of lecture will be used to address this question.

FEATURES OF TEACHER TALK IN A TRADITIONAL LECTURE

The episode below was extracted from a longer teacher presentation aimed at getting students to adopt new modes of evaluation in their classroom practice.

Lecturer:

The goal of genuine evaluation is to make the learner self-monitoring, self-regulating and independent. You know what we've said several times before. We want to set the children free so that they can do things on their own and not rely on us all the time. Evaluation involves observation of process and product and collecting data. Now we've talked about these things before haven't we? We are observing what goes on in the classroom, how the learning goes on, the process, as well as what is actually produced. We are not evaluating the product alone. That's the whole basis of the writing process. And then we saw, out of the writing process, the reading process. We have to be aware how it goes on. And that is where the teaching takes place and when the teaching takes place. It's not just the final product that we carry home in a notebook and mark. So it involves recording observations and data. We have to put these things down some place, and not just a quantitative mark but moreso narrative, prose statements about what the children are doing ...

On the surface, this episode can be described as being very conversational. The first person plural is used throughout, suggesting an intention on the part of the lecturer that her talk should be viewed as a communication among equals who share a common experience as classroom practitioners. This notion of a shared experience is brought out in the reference to past exchanges, ("Now we've talked about these things before, haven't we?). The use of colloquialism also adds to this conversational tone. For example, the expression "We have to put these things down some place", would be readily recognized by these practicing teachers as the everyday talk they themselves sometimes use to refer to the activity of entering grades in notebooks, or on official record cards held by the school administration, or in report books through which parents are informed of their children's progress.

At one level therefore, this discourse does not communicate as the talk of a dominant knowledgeable voice, handing out information to recipients considered less knowledgeable about the topic being addressed. When one examines closer however, another picture emerges from beneath the surface, one that strongly suggests a didactic dimension to the communication.

Among the features that define this piece of communication as essentially information-transmission, is its heavy reliance on generalizations. "The goal of genuine evaluation is to make the learner self-monitoring" and "Evaluation involves observation of process and product and collecting data". Moreover, since the ultimate purpose of this talk is to influence practice, inherent in the generalizations is an element of exhortation, no doubt intended to persuade the listener to adopt the new approaches to evaluation and assessment in the classroom.

Also reinforcing the didactic top-down quality of the communication is the subtle appeal to the listener's sense of professional ethics and commitment to a higher good. Underpinning the statement, "We want to set the children free" is very likely a gentle coercion, since no student would want to compromise their reputation in the professional community by being numbered among those who keep students dependent on the teacher.

The overall effect of this interweaving of generalizations, exhortations and subtle appeal to some professional ideal is that the entire episode conveys the impression that the knowledge claims being transmitted, are beyond question. The episode does not contain any language that invites reflection or analysis. Rather it is direct, assertive and authoritative. Notwithstanding apparent attempts to foster the notion of a community of professionals, the underlying reality is that within the interaction, the lecturer occupies the position of dominance. She is further able to maintain that position not only through her greater familiarity with the official subject matter content, but also through her shaping of the language to influence the thinking of the students. In the final analysis, the lecturer's word is to be accepted without challenge.

HOW THE STUDENT RESPONDS

Subsequent interviews with two of the students in the group revealed that, to a greater or lesser extent, this was the way in which the lecturer's talk was received.

Student A's response was one of complete acceptance and endorsement of the lecturer's viewpoint. (The initials 'OK' in the extract below and in subsequent episodes refer to me in the role of interviewer).

OK:

Now, I believe that when you went into that session, you would have been focusing on the things you already know about evaluation, assessment and so on. What I would like you to do now is to focus on all that you know about evaluation and assessment, and tell me what are your current thoughts, your views on the principles I will be mentioning. Okay. The current thinking is that pupils must develop their own self-assessment skills. Right? And some of the new approaches provide the opportunity for pupils to develop the ability and the know-how to evaluate and assess their own performance. I want to hear from you now, how do you feel about that? Do you feel comfortable with that kind of thinking?

Stud. A:

Yes, I agree that students should be able to develop (incomplete) *Teachers tend to just get these techniques (on essay writing) down and not really allow the child to go through the process of writing. Those types of techniques that we as teachers are using, the traditional techniques are really keeping back the growth of our children and I will really prefer to see teachers using the process approach where children move from one stage to the other and they can view what they are doing and see their development.*

OK:

What about that aspect of the new approach that says that they must develop skills to assess themselves, children assessing themselves.

Stud. A:

Yes, I agree that with time and practice children can start deciding, well this piece of work, you know, isn't as good as the piece that I would have done. Okay, he might be able to look at pieces of work that he has done during a certain period of time and look back at his portfolio and see where he has come from to where he is now. So he himself can start assessing his work, you know, given certain guidelines from the teacher in the classroom.

One interesting thing about this interview is what can be described as a mismatch between the question framed and the type of response generated. To a question that asks, "Do you feel comfortable…", the student responds "Yes, I agree…". In fact, she repeats the phrase in her second response. Thus, notwithstanding my attempt to induce reflection and to get the student to look at the new ideas in light of her own previous experience, she did not accept my question as an opportunity to engage in analysis. For her, the knowledge claims that I was articulating were not to be explored; on the contrary, they were to be taken as objectively true.

Her stance was clear. She had accepted the authority of the new knowledge and her only function was to defend it. Consequently, she could not let herself be seen as still subscribing to the old knowledge claims. Rather than viewing them as prior experience to be examined in relation to the new, her immediate response was to distance herself from the practices associated with those claims. It can be argued therefore that for this student, learning was not meaning-making, but rather the acquisition of new information.

While the second student also appears to give strong support to the claims presented by the lecturer, she gives voice to her own reservations.

Stud. B:

> *Well, of course all these things that (the lecturer) is telling us, I mean, we are hearing it for the first time because we didn't read it anywhere before. But it fits very nicely with my psyche and how I think about things. It presupposes, however, that the child is able to express himself in the language, because if the child is not able to do that, then you really would not be able to get what you call a qualitative assessment. Right? But I like the idea, you know, to say, well, okay 'Last two weeks I didn't know this and now I know it', as opposed to 15 out of 25 as the case may be.*

Unlike her colleague, Student B reserves the right to question the ideas that she is supporting. Her language is less prescriptive than that of Student A and there is a discernible attempt to be reflective as she seeks to examine the appropriateness of the new way of thinking in the context of her knowledge of current practice. Consequently the child's competence in language use is a factor that is to be considered when advocating more qualitative approaches to assessment.

Nonetheless one detects some tentativeness in her questioning. She therefore ensures that she ends the response by giving her unqualified support. It is possible that she is anxious not to convey the impression that she is rejecting the accepted wisdom of the professional community. Thus her intuitive urge to question is set aside as she hastens to restate her agreement with what, she too, in spite of herself, must be viewing as the authoritative position.

FEATURES OF TEACHER-LEARNER EXCHANGE IN AN INTERACTIVE LECTURE

As indicated earlier, there were two types of lecture presentations observed. In this more interactive type, the lecturer is attempting to get students to articulate how they would use checklists as a record-keeping tool as they undertake their Practicum. This episode includes input from students both at the site being observed as well as from two other sites (Site A and Site B) on the network.

Lecturer:

Checklists have been highlighted here (in articles students should have read). *Two questions. Do you think that you could use checklists in your specific classes effectively? And if you can, what do you need to do? How can you use it? What should you do in your own situation? What is the most appropriate content of those checklists if you think you can use it as a part of the evaluation process? Both articles focus on healthcare and* (unclear) *skills. I don't think you are concerned with healthcare at this point, but is it an appropriate tool? Is it an appropriate method to use, and if so what specifically can you use it for, given your own situation?*

Student X:

(keeps searching for her article.)

Student Y:

(already has hers and is silently browsing through it as the lecturer continues to talk)

Lecturer:

In the article, checklists were used as a means of evaluation and record-keeping. I would like you to think of your own situation and tell me whether or not checklists would be appropriate for you and if so, how you would use it, the specific things you would use it for.

Site A:

I don't have my notes here with me but I think it could be used in academic areas. You can make a list of (unclear) *topics that each child should be able or each child should have a chance of doing and as the child progresses from one to the other that can be, well, ticked off or something. It can also be used in a behaviour modification programme. If you have a behaviour in your classroom that you want to change, you can use this to check* (unclear). *Eventually that behaviour will be shaped so that each, with each day or week, some new part of the behaviour will be worked on.*

Lecturer:

(does not respond; calls on another site for a response; there is none from site called).

Lecturer:

Any additional points? (Calls on another site, but again there is no response from the site called).

Lecturer:

(as if now responding to Site A without actually directing the remarks to that site) Don't leave it at the theoretical level. Think whether or not you could use the checklist in your own teaching practice — in your own evaluation, or an evaluation of the unit, or evaluation of what the children would be doing (pause) [Also] what are the things you have to do, you have to put in place before you can formulate an appropriate checklist.

Student Y:

(Identifies self to lecturer on the network, as if intending to respond to lecturer's question, but fails to follow through).

***Lecturer*:**

I need to see whether or not you can use it ...if it is appropriate... If you decide to use it, what kind of background, what purpose, what do you need before you can formulate an appropriate checklist.

Student X:

(Continues to spend a lot of time flipping through own stack of reading materials).

Site B:

(Begins tentatively) I suppose you have to determine where the children are at, in terms of behaviour or whatever you are going to check, on the checklist. Right? And then you have to determine also some sort of goal. (Voice gaining in confidence) And what strategy you would use to achieve that goal...

Whether consciously or unconsciously, the teacher is making certain important assumptions as she conducts this interactive session. The first assumption is that students would be entering the interaction with a body of relevant knowledge to support their participation in the discussion. This body of knowledge would be a combination of the information gleaned from the articles they should have read, examples of teaching/learning situations drawn from their own classroom practice, and more specifically, some awareness of what they were planning to do for the proposed Practicum.

A second and related assumption is that, given these separate chunks of information, and given too the questions posed, the students would have the capability to identify and select elements from any or all of them, then synthesize and construct their own responses.

It can be argued therefore that attainment of the goal of the interaction would have been dependent on the depth of meaning students were able to derive from all the relevant information in order to construct their own unique knowledge claims.

It is evident that even though there were a series of questions from the teacher, and, for the purpose of this episode, two responses from the students, the goal of the teaching-learning transaction remained largely unattained.

Several reasons can be identified for this. In the first instance, it is likely that some students both at the site being observed and across the region did not read the article, as the lecturer was expecting. The problem of required reading not being done prior to the session may be more complex than is generally accepted among educational practitioners. It seems to me that not finding the time, forgetting the documents at home and reasons of that type, do not necessarily tell the whole story. This issue was not studied specifically as part of this research project, hence no possible reasons can be made here. Nonetheless, it is an area that needs more in-depth investigation.

In the meantime, it was interesting that Student Y still seemed unable to respond even after spending time browsing through the article, and even though it appeared that she wanted to contribute to the discussion.

The second is that, notwithstanding the fact that they were practicing teachers, the students seemed unable to identify any area of practice that they could have drawn on to formulate an appropriate response. In this regard, it should be noted that the first response offered (from the student at Site A) remained at the level of generalizations and may have been a regurgitation of her own class notes, which she said that she did not have at the time, but which, it seems, she remembered very well. It is likely that her reference to 'behaviour modification programmes' may not have been well received by the lecturer who may have recognized it as information previously communicated to the students. The lecturer therefore considered it necessary to advise students to go beyond the theoretical and think about their own practice.

The third reason is that the students had probably not yet started to plan for their Practicum and so could not use that context to address the question posed by the lecturer.

Whatever the reason, it is evident that the exchange was not progressing smoothly and the lecturer herself seemed dissatisfied both with the responses given and, it could be argued, with the long periods of silence and non-response.

HOW THE STUDENTS RESPOND

Based on subsequent interviews it seemed clear that the students themselves were sensitive to the tension in the interaction between themselves and the lecturer. The remarks of two of the students in the session discussed above are pertinent in this regard. One of the students was Student X at the site of observation, the other was located at Site A, the other Trinidad site. In the respective interviews, each of the remarks came as a follow-up to a discussion on note taking. When asked whether there was any input that was particularly hers in the notes she made, Student X not only responded to that particularly question but extended with a comment on the lecturer's approach to lecturing.

Student X:

> *There isn't any input from me [in my note-taking]. That is one of the things I know is a problem with me. That's why, when I go to classes and lecturers don't give information, I find they are not good because they are not giving me anything to write. I don't like lecturers who come and ask you to think. And they will ask probing questions, and the whole session will just be questions, questions, questions. The lecture goes*

on only if you answer and if you don't answer, it doesn't go anywhere. I hate that.

The student at Site A was less condemning and more analytical in her assessment. She observed,

SiteA stu.:

(Another lecturer) may give us notes at times if we don't have the reading material but (this lecturer) usually tries to get us to talk, so she would ask questions and have us talk, or she would try to get us to talk for most of the class. It does not always work

OK:

I was just going to ask you that, because I realize that she asks questions all the time.

SiteA stu:

But it does not always work.

OK:

Why, from your point of view?

SiteA stu:

People do not want to express their opinions. I don't know if they think it is wrong or what. They just would rather have another site go first. So, if she asks, everybody shuts up. Nobody would volunteer an answer.

OK:

I realize that that happens. You feel people don't know?

SiteA stu:

No. They just don't want to go first. That's all. If another site offers an answer, usually someone would say, 'Well, I don't agree or I agree with this or that'. By that time, people would

have time to think and they would come up with other points. But people don't like to go first.

OK:

You think it is something that (the lecturer) does or you think the fault is on your side?

SiteA stu:

No. I don't see (the lecturer) doing anything particularly wrong. I think sometimes people may read the material long in advance so that when they come and a question is presented off the bat, they know they saw it somewhere but they don't know exactly where. They have to look back now, see what they have there. So you need a little time to think and come up with the response.

Unlike her counterpart from the main research site, the student from Site A demonstrated a willingness to interrogate the learner role in the teaching/learning exchange. Indeed she can very well be described as someone with an inclination to be an active participant in the process, whereas Student X appears to feel justified in maintaining her position as a passive recipient. The insistence of the Site A student that the only reason for the lack of responses is that students "don't want to go first" suggests that she sees the issue of self-confidence as being a key factor impacting on students' capability and/or willingness to participate in the exchange. Overall what is significant in her response is her recognition and acceptance of the position that students must take responsibility for their learning.

An important factor emerging from this attempt at an interactive lecture, is that the students appeared to lack the requisite resources to play their part in the interaction. Both their responses and lack of responses seemed to indicate that they were unable to draw on their experience of classroom practice. What this seems to suggest is, not that they did not have this knowledge, but that they were unable to access and manipulate the appropriate aspects of it within the context of the discussion initiated by the lecturer. As a result, the necessary activities of knowledge construction and meaning-making were not taking place.

On the other hand, the strategies that the lecturer was using were not successful in getting the students to engage meaningfully in the discussion. The technique of "questions, questions, questions" was not working. It is my view that the problem could not have been resolved in the current interaction.

This chapter was developed out of research conducted in a teacher education programme. As stated earlier, this does not restrict its applicability to that discipline. Nonetheless, I would suggest that the issues raised here hold important implications for the professional development of teachers.

COLLABORATIVE LEARNING IN THE FORMAL SECTOR – THE CHALLENGES

There are several aspects of the teaching-learning interaction analysed above that can militate against the emergence of CL strategies. The dominant teacher voice and the techniques used to maintain that dominance, the unquestioning acceptance by the students of the teacher's knowledge claims, the apparent unwillingness and/or incapability to critique, can effectively suppress the emergence of behaviours and attitudes consistent with collaborative learning. On the other hand, the data also reveal a capacity on the part of some learners to engage in reflection and analysis and to be self- evaluative, however tentative the attempt may have been. Also evident is an intention on the part of one teacher to step back to facilitate the emergence of the learner voice.

While no claims can be made for representativeness, these data strongly suggest that, even while there are pockets of teaching-learning practices that can provide a platform on which to build a more participatory type of teaching-learning interaction, there are obstacles to be overcome.

Earlier, I noted that the Caribbean region, as other parts of the world, has a strong tradition of learning as a collective activity outside of the formal sector. With specific reference to the Caribbean, I drew attention to the conventional approach to the learning and playing of steelband music as an example of that tradition.

One Caribbean political commentator, in expressing his own concerns about the output of the formal education sector, makes an interesting contrast between the formal and the informal. While his arguments are not made with specific reference to teaching-learning strategies, they warrant consideration in that context. Best (2000) asserts,

> Formal schooling in the West Indies is a process by which graduates, from primary to tertiary, are systematically robbed of the capacity to describe what is on the ground … Our self-esteem is propped up less by education, knowledge and mastery, (and) more by certification and form.
>
> Every year, we're graduating larger numbers from the university but nowhere in sight (is) a cadre confident enough to take the responsibility of confronting the colonial regime with politics as distinct from insurrection. The elite system of the imperial school is mostly selecting the wrong people or the right people on the wrong terms. This is clearly the source of our crisis.
>
> The entrepreneurs and creators lie among the great multitude of the failures, compelled to take up art, craft, music and sport. Or to engage (in) activities where the authorized version does not block creativity and invention … Over the years, we've therefore operated two worlds.

> The theoretical one is dictated by formal schooling. The real world is the one in which people live. I find the confusion diabolical to the point of pathology. (Saturday Express, December 30, 2000, p.17).[5]

Whether or not one accepts Best's assessment of the Caribbean education system, a pertinent issue arising from his remarks is, to what extent can the formal sector draw on the ways of knowing and learning of the entrepreneurs and creators outside the sector? More specifically, given the interactive learning environments provided by the new ICTs, can the strategies employed by this 'great multitude of failures' be usefully transferred into these environments?

A Caribbean higher education administrator also raises some issues of relevance. His focus of interest is not so much the nature of the teaching-learning transaction (although that is implied), but the capabilities that university teachers possess. He is concerned about the extent to which university teachers are themselves capable of team learning. Thus, he contends

> The irony of higher education is that universities are not effective learning organizations because they have not learned to practise the things that they teach ... The way that courses are developed and taught – particularly the practice of individual teaching – lends itself to individual learning rather that team learning on the part of the faculty ... Conferences do offer opportunities for team learning, but they are generally too narrowly focused and punctuated to qualify as meaningful opportunities for faculty, staff and administrators to learn (how) to learn together as teams. (Kean, 2000, p.51)

The course team approach, which the Distance Education Centre (DEC) of UWI currently employs in the development of distance course materials and the building of on-line course sites, entails some degree of team learning on the part of all those involved. Nonetheless, the changes that Kean is advocating in organizational culture and professional self-definition can be expected to enhance the capability of the institution to incorporate collaborative learning strategies into its overall delivery mode.

Turning specifically to issues pertaining to student use of the interactive learning environments, the following observation from a participant in an on-line conference offers much food for thought. Responding to a preceding message posted in the conference on *Distance learning in the small island states in the Commonwealth*, the participant made the following comment, with particular reference to the islands of the South Pacific.

> Sala is correct in that often who says what is more important than what is said, at least for many island cultures. What some of my more knowledgeable colleagues call traditional learning styles (group-based, oral, elder to younger, watch-and-do etc.) are sometimes at odds with the learning demands of distance learning (solo activity, largely written language, largely in a foreign language etc.). We have learned a few things since we inaugurated our interactive video service two years ago.
>
> Culturally our island students are quiet. They prefer group situations where no one individual tends to stand out, Initially they are hesitant to interact with the technology, or even speak during a formal tutorial or class session. I've been told that is because many of our tutors and lecturers are expats (expatriates) from developed countries and older people. Perhaps true, because when younger lecturers or tutors from island backgrounds enter the video studio, the students respond differently. When the sessions are student-to-student in a local language, the sessions can be boisterous and playful. (Pre Pan-Commonwealth Forum Virtual Conference: Linda Austin, May 2002)

The higher education experience of the islands of the South Pacific has much in common with that of the English-speaking Caribbean, the primary aspect of that experience being that, in both regions, there is one higher education institution with responsibility for educational delivery to all the islands collectively. In both cases, the ICTs must meet the needs of a student population that is not only geographically dispersed but also socially and culturally different from the societies from which the ICTs came.

It is beyond the scope of this chapter to examine the conference posting more closely to determine the extent to which it may or may not apply in a Caribbean context. That notwithstanding, it brings to the fore two areas of inquiry that should be of concern to those interested in collaborative learning in a Caribbean higher education context. First, how important is oral communication in the contemporary Caribbean cultural experience? Secondly, in what ways do the features of oral communication in the wider society manifest themselves in the teaching-learning interaction within the formal education sector?

CONCLUSION

It is evident that the introduction of the ICTS and the related new modes of learning into Caribbean higher education must be accompanied by an appropriate research agenda to support the innovations.

ENDNOTES

[1] HTML version of paper accessed from restricted on-line site.

[2] In Trinidad and Tobago, there are several initiatives to enhance the approach to the learning and playing of steelband music. For example, the study of the pan (the single instrument) is a key component of subdegree and degree programmes in music offered by the Faculty of Humanities and Education at the St. Augustine campus of the University of the West Indies.

[3] In 1996, UWIDITE gave way to UWIDEC, the University of the West Indies Distance Education Centre. While audioconferencing is still a feature of UWIDEC's delivery mode, it is no longer the main technology for the degree programmes that were recently introduced . Nonetheless, it continues to be the principal technology for the sub-degree certificate programmes.

[4] For further details of the data analysis procedures used in this study, see Kuboni, 1997, pp. 172-192.

[5] The Daily Express is published in Trinidad and Tobago.

REFERENCES

Best, L. (2000). *Stalemate at short intervals.* Daily Express, December 30, 2000, p.17.

Birk, L. (1997). What's so bad about the lecture? *Education Digest. 62* (9), 58-61.

Candy, P.C. (1991). *Self-direction for lifelong learning: a comprehensive guide to theory and practice.* California: Jossey-Bass Inc.

Garrison, D.R. (1990). An analysis and evaluation of audioconferencing to facilitate education at a distance. *The American Journal of Distance Education. 4* (3), 13-24.

Gunawardena, C. (1991). Collaborative learning and group dynamics in computer-mediated communication networks. *Second American Symposium on research in distance education: Selected Papers No. 3*. Pennsylvania: Pennsylvania State University, American Center for the Study of Distance Education.

Hansen, E.J. and Stephens, J.A. (2000). The ethics of learner-centered education. *Change. 33* (5), 40-47.

Harasim, L., Hiltz, S., Teles, L., Turoff, M. (1995). *Learning Networks.* Massachusetts; The MIT Press.

Jonassen, D., Davidson, M., Collins, M., Campbell, J. and Haag, B., (1995). Constructivism and computer-mediated communication in distance education. *The American Journal of Distance Education. 9* (2), 7-26.

Kaye, A. (1992). Learning together, apart. In A. Kaye (Ed.), *Collaborative learning through computer conferencing: the Najadeen papers* (pp. 1-24). Berlin: Springer-Verlag.

Kean, O. (2000). Higher education and Caribbean identity. In G.D. Howe (Ed.), *Higher Education in the Caribbean: past, present and future directions.* Kingston, Jamaica: The University of the West Indies Press, Chap. 3, pp. 45-58.

Kuboni, O. (1997). Redefining interaction in open and distance learning with reference to teacher education programmes in the University of the West Indies. *Unpublished Ph.D. dissertation.* Milton Keynes, United Kingdom: Institute of Educational Technology, the Open University.

Kuboni, O. (2002). Distance education at the University of the West Indies: fashioning the new within the old. In NIHERST (Ed.), *Papers of the Information Technology Conference, 2000.* Port of Spain, Trinidad and Tobago: National Institute of Higher Education, pp. 172-185.

MacDonald, D. (1998). *Audio and Audiographic learning: The cornerstone of the information highway.* Montreal, Canada: Cheneliere/McGraw-Hill.

Merrill,M.D. (1991). Constructivism and instructional design. *Educational Technology, 31* (5), 45-53.

Nipper, S. (1989). Third generation distance learning and computer conferencing. In R.Mason and A. Kaye (Eds.), *Mindweave: communication, computers and distance education.* (pp. 63-73). Oxford: Pergamon Press.

Pre Pan-Commonwealth Forum on Open Learning, Virtual Conference, (2002). *4th conference: Distance learning in the small and island states of the Commonwealth – posting by Linda Austin, May 9, 2002. www.col.org/virtualconferences*

Volery, T. and Lord, D. (2000). Critical success factors in online education. *The International Journal of Educational Management, 14* (5), 216-223.

Potter, J. and Wetherell, M. (1987). *Discourse and social psychology: beyond attitudes and behaviour.* London: Sage Publications.

Wilson, B., Teslow, J. and Osman-Jouchoux, R. (1995). The impact of constructivism (and postmodernism) on ID fundamentals. In B. Seels (Ed.) *Instructional design fundamentals: a reconsideration.* (pp. 137-157). New jersey: Educational Technology Publications.

SECTION 3
ADMINISTRATION

A FOR AVERAGE, B FOR BAD AND P FOR PAID: GRADE INFLATION PROSPECTS FOR THE CARIBBEAN

Tony Bastick
University of the West Indies
Jamaica

Chapter 8

THIS PAPER describes the American system of Grade Point Averages (GPAs) that universities in the English speaking Caribbean are soon to adopt. It draws attention to possible problems of equivalence due to differing standards on which GPAs are calculated. It also explains the problem of rampant grade inflation associated with GPAs in North American Universities and identifies customer-oriented expectations of university teaching as a major cause of this problem that could spread to assessment in Caribbean universities. The paper shows how the institutional use of student evaluations of teaching, as used in both the US and in the Caribbean, significantly contributes to this problem in North American universities and warns that if Caribbean Universities move to the US GPA system and continue this practice of student evaluations of teaching, then Caribbean degree qualifications are very likely to be equated with the devalued grades awarded by many North American universities.

GPA CALCULATIONS

Tertiary institutions in the English speaking Caribbean are now moving to Grade Point Average (GPA) calculations of student attainment so as to articulate more closely with the assessment systems used in American Universities. GPAs are commonly calculated using a conversion table consisting of Grades Percentages and Quality Points (QPs) similar to that shown in Table 1.

Table 1: Typical Grades, Percentages and Quality Points Conversion Table for Calculating Grade Point Averages in the Caribbean

Grade	**Percentages**	Quality Points
A+	**86 - 100**	4.3
A	**70 85**	4.0
A-	**67 69**	3.7
B+	**63 66**	3.3
B	**60 62**	3.0
B-	**57 59**	2.7
C+	**53 56**	2.3
C	**50 52**	2.0
C-	**47 49**	1.7
D+	**43 46**	1.3
D	**40 42**	1.0
F	**0 - 39**	0.0

In US universities, it is common for percentage-grade equivalents to vary from syllabus to syllabus within a university, reflecting the difficulty of the work. In the Caribbean, one conversion table is expected to be utilised throughout an institution. The table is used to give the QPs that correspond to the percentage range that contains a student's raw percentage mark for each course. For example, 72% for a course is in the 70-85 percentage range, which gives an A for the course and 4.0 Quality Points. Universities also allot Credit

Units to each course. This is an indication of the quality of each course and is often based on the number of hours of teaching that each course requires; for example, one semester-hour being worth one credit unit. Some US universities actually use the hours as Quality Hours in place of Credit Units. A typical one semester course may be worth three credit units and a two semester course may be worth six credit units ('credits' for short). To calculate a current GPA for the present semester a student would multiply the QPs for each course by the Credit Units (CU) for that course. This multiplication 'weights' the course result according to the CU importance of the course. This is done for all courses taken by a student. The total of the QP x CU products is then divided by the Total Credit Units (TCU).

For example, suppose a student taking 4 courses received the results shown on the left of Table 2

Table 2: Calculation of current GPA

Course Number	Percentage result	Credits	Quality Points	QP x CU
1	70	3	4.0	12.0
2	62	3	3.3	9.9
3	54	4	2.3	9.2
4	50	3	2.0	6.0
		Totals	11.6	37.1
			GPA =	3.2
				B+

The Credit Units for each course are also noted in Table 2. The Percentage result for each course is converted to Quality Points using conversation Table 1 so that the QP x CU product can be calculated for each course and totalled to give 37.1. This can be divided by the Total of the Quality Points to give GPA= Total of (QP x CU) / Total of QP = 37.1/11.6 = 3.2. The numbers have been rounded to one decimal place.

A student's previous GPA can be combined with his or her current semester GPA to calculate a 'running average' or Cumulative GPA. To illustrate this calculation we will assume that a student already has a GPA from a previous semester, of say 22.3/10.2=2.2. These numbers are 'made-up' just to illustrate the calculation. The 'running average' or Cumulative GPA can be calculated by dividing the Total (QP x CU) so far by the Total QP so far. In this example it will be (37.1+22.3)/(11.6+10.2)= 59.4/21.8=2.7

The calculations may seem unnecessarily convoluted and you may wonder why the Table 1 uses such awkward numbers as 1.3 and 2.7 rather than simply starting at F=0 and counting each grade as one more quality point so the 12 grades simply go from F=0 to A+=11. The reason seems to be that originally this was the case when there were only five grades on a four-point scale starting with F=0, i.e. F=0, D=1, C=2, B=3 and A=4. However, when pluses and minuses were added by some universities to give more precision, they preferred to mark the new grades at a third above and below the old numbers so as to keep comparability of GPAs with universities that had not yet introduced the new grades. The thirds were rounded to the numbers in Table 1. Also, we cannot simply average the GPAs to get the Cumulative GPA and this contributes a little to the complexity of the calculations. We have to revert back to the cumulative totals and recalculate the division. The reason for this is that we cannot average numbers that are already averages in the normal way - we would have to use a harmonic mean - average the reciprocals of each GPA (one over each GPA) and then take the reciprocal of the result.

The GPA is not actually a Grade but the average of Quality Points each weighted by their Credit Units. It can be approximated back to a grade using the nearest number in Table 1. For example, in the four course GPA calculation in Table 2, the resulting GPA=3.2 corresponds to B+ in Table 1, as 3.2 is closer to 3.3=B+ than to 3.0=B. Actually the Grades, the Quality points and percentage ranges in Table 1 are not essential to this calculation. The Grades are convenient for communication and the percentage ranges and quality points only introduce rounding errors. The calculation would be more accurate if based only on the raw percentages the student received and the Credits for each course. This would give an average of percentages weighted by their Credit Units as shown in Table 3. The resulting Percentage Point Average could be converted to a grade, if necessary, using the same Table 1. You will notice that the same percentage marks result in different GPAs in Table 2 and Table 3, namely B+ versus B-. This is because, by not using the QPs and Percent Ranges in the calculation of %PA we get a more accurate result by eliminating the rounding errors they introduce.

Table 3: Calculation of percentage point average %PA - showing fewer rounding errors than GPA

Course Number	Percentage result	Credits	% x CU
1	70	3	210
2	62	3	186
3	54	4	216
4	50	3	150
	Totals	13	762
		%PA =	58.6
			B-

The current GPA system evolved like the dinosaurs. Each generation had to adapt what it had inherited to the new requirements of changing environments. They could not re-start with a better design for their current environment. Similarly, even if the %PA calculation is simpler and more accurate it is unlikely that it will ever replace the established GPA system.

DIFFERENT STANDARDS FOR THE SAME GPA

DIFFERENT COURSE DIFFICULTIES AND VALUES FOR COURSE CREDIT UNITS

The GPA system is intended to allow comparisons within and between universities. This assumes that the attainments represented by the same GPAs are equivalent within and across universities. For example, it assumes that a student with GPA of B+ in one course has the same attainment as any other student with a GPA of B+ on any other course in any other university. This assumption is far from justified, simply because the two foundations on which GPA are calculated - received percentages and credit units - are not equivalent across courses within or between universities. Some courses are more difficult than others, in that the average percentage gained by students varies greatly from course to course. The average percentage mark for undergraduate courses of ten or more students in the University of the West Indies in 2001/02 ranged from 28% to 82%. Generall, fewer students achieve 'A's in the sciences than in the humanities (Shea, 1994; Becker, 1997). In aggreement with this, Johnson (2002) states, "The Duke study confirmed the common belief that natural science and math classes are graded the hardest and humanities the easiest." This appears to be common, despite the higher entry qualifications usually found among science students. Similarly, course credits are usually derived from the number and type of contact hours a course requires. However, it is not unusual to find courses with equivalent credits and different hours for the same type of contact. The contact hours for a course may even be changed, perhaps for economic reasons, without changing its credit units. Some Caribbean university regulations state that attendance is not compulsory, so lecture hours attended cannot be verified. Both difficulty and credit units need to be equitable for GPA to be meaningful.

DIFFERENT STANDARDS OF MARKING

A major problem with the GPAs in North American universities is rampant grade inflation. For example, Brown University graduates 59% of its students with 'A' grades (Muresiano, 2002). In 2001, 41% of grades at Yale were 'A' grades (Steinberg, 2001). At the University of Illinois in 1999 more than 40 percent of grades were A's (Westfall, 2000). At Princeton 40% of all grades are A's (Margolick, 1994). More than 45 percent of Duke undergraduate grades are A's. These percentages are typical. Considering B's as well, eighty percent of grades at Yale are A's and B's (Johnson, 2002). Almost 90% of grades at Stanford are A's and B's (Margolick, 1994). The percentage of students receiving honours at Harvard has increased from 31% in 1942 to 91% today. Universities like Yale and Princeton have now put an upper limit such that no more than 60% of their students receive honours. Some research has found 80 to 90 percent of college students receive grades of either A or B (Sonner, 2000). Within this grade inflation system of GPAs, students complain if they receive a B and consider it as a failed grade. Currently, a B is considered a good pass in the Caribbean. However, although examination marking in the Caribbean is likely to stay as stringent as it now is for many years to come, our students with B grades will be judged by the common GPA system to be equivalent to US students with B grades. The American university accreditation system has been unable to contain grade inflation. Although US university courses are often accredited by more than one accreditation agency, these agencies turn a 'blind-eye' to the problem (Leef & Burris, 2002).

CUSTOMER-ORIENTED TEACHING AND GRADE INFLATION

One of the major causes of grade inflation is the customer orientation that universities expect lecturers to take to their teaching. One of the most cost-effective methods of mitigating customer complaints from students is to lighten course assessment requirements. So, for example, if expected resources have been unavailable or some other administrative problem leaves students aggrieved, then some allowance can be made in the assessment of the course - an assignment submission date can be extended or examinations can be more 'sensitively' marked to take into account the 'difficulties' of the students.

> "Students are paying a fortune for their educations, and it's like any other consumer good: If you're paying for it, you should get what you're paying for," Kramnick said. "And what you're paying for is not a lousy grade." (Kline, 2001)

Yet students who report doing average work expect to be awarded A's and B's (Landrum, 1999).

The customer evaluation model can effectively be applied to many services offered by a university. However, it is questionable, in its responsibility for quality teaching, how much a university should take the role of academic leadership or be managed as a business subservient to the student customer where 'the customer is always right'.

DIRECT INFLUENCE OF CUSTOMER-REACTION FORMS ON OVER-GRADING

By far the greatest contribution to grade inflation is the causal link between student expectation of high grades and staff career promotion made by formal institutional use of student feedback forms in promotion, tenure and contract renewal decisions. These are equivalent to customer-reaction forms for evaluating at Level 1, the reaction level, of consumer-oriented education (Kirkpatrick, 1959, 1994). This is one of the most cited causes of grade inflation (Foster & Foster 1998; Savitt 1994). Edwards (2000) reports that faculty are of the opinion that giving low grades results in low student ratings, small class enrolments and eventual loss of their jobs. These student opinionnaires have been criticised as popularity contests, where staff reduce the standards of their courses and lead students to expect high grades in order to 'win their vote' (Greenwald, 1997; Greenwald & Gillmore, 1997; Howard & Maxwell, 1982; Marsh & Dunkin, 1997; Marsh & Roche, 1997, 1998).

> "Our research has confirmed what critics of student ratings have long suspected, that grading leniency affects ratings. All other things being equal, a professor can get higher ratings by giving higher grades," adds Gillmore, director of the UW's office of educational assessment. (University of Washington Office of News and Information, 1997)

Often these customer-reaction forms are anonymous because it is believed that students would fear retribution for 'failing' their teachers or that they might be thought to be soliciting favourable grades for favourable assessments of their teachers. Consequently, aspects of their validity are questionable (Marks, 2000; Haskell, 1997).

The use of student feedback forms for assessing the quality of teaching are variously known in the literature as Student Opinion Surveys (SOS), Student Evaluations of Teaching (SET), Student Evaluation of Faculty (SOF), and Student Perceptions of Teaching (SPOT). Their influence on grade inflation is pervasive because their use is so wide spread, with 100% of US research universities now using them. These universities are considerable larger than those in the Caribbean. Indiana University, for example, processed 133,000 student ratings sheets in 1994 (Jacobs, 2002).

One may wonder why their use is so ubiquitous. Robert Haskell, Professor of Psychology at the University of New England, reporting on Student Evaluation of Faculty (SEF) in American universities, states:

> "SEF provides a mechanism of control in a system otherwise lacking direct control over faculty, and are a powerful tool in assuring classroom changes that lead to the retention of student tuition dollars by assenting to student consumer demands and of parents who foot the tuition bill. ... From a purely psychological/behavioral learning theory perspective, when a faculty's livelihood is at stake, it is understandable why many will adjust their grading and course content level in order to receive a good evaluation. It is also predictable: behaviors that are rewarded tend to increase the probability of their recurrence." (Haskell, 1997).

The influence of giving high grades on student feedback of teaching has been demonstrated by research comparing correlations between SETs and Grades both before and after students know their grades. Correlation increases from 0.38 to 0.85 have been found (Cohen 1981, D' Appolonia & Abrami, 1997). Valen Johnson, a professor of Biostatistics at Duke University, clearly showed the causal link between grading and SETs. He did this in a large-scale study (n= 11,521) named DUET (Duke Undergraduates Evaluate Teaching). Students completed a 38 item SET form both before and after they knew their course grades. The first time, they were asked to note the grade they expected to get. The second time, using the same form, they noted the grade they actually got. Johnson (2003) found that students who received less than they expected reduced their ratings on all 38 items, those who received more than they expected increased their ratings on all 38 items and those who were awarded what they expected showed no significant difference in their ratings. These items were rated 1 to 6 or 7 - for example (1) Very bad (2) Bad (3) Fair (4) Good (5) Very Good (6) Excellent (7) Not Applicable

The following examples of the items that students rated show that they were typical of items to be found on SETs

- How effective was the instructor in encouraging students to ask questions and express their viewpoints?
- How would you rate this instructor's enthusiasm in teaching this course?
- How easy was it to meet with the instructor outside of class?
- How does this instructor(s) compare to all instructors that you have had at Duke?
- How good was the instructor(s) at communicating course material?
- To what extent did this instructor demand critical or original thinking?
- How valuable was feedback on examinations and graded materials?
- How good was the instructor at relating course material to current research in the field?

Overviews of the grade inflation research consistently point to the institutional use of SETs for faculty career decisions as the causal link between grade inflation and teaching. According to Moore and Trahan (1998):

> " .. 'The effects of tenure and promotion decisions are directly related to students' evaluation of courses and professors, thereby creating disincentives to assign grades that more accurately reflect students' scholarly achievements or lack thereof". Given the strong incentive for better course evaluations, professors are also likely to reduce educational standards in the classroom and teach to a lower common denominator. Similarly, because student complaints may reflect poor teaching ability and adversely affect tenure and merit decisions, such conflicts

over grades are minimized by improving grade point averages (Moore and Trahan 1998; Redding 1998)." (Hesseln & Jackson. 2000).

Because of their effect on grade inflation, some current US university reports recommend phasing out SETs. Consider for example the following 2002 recommendation of the Executive Faculty Merit Evaluation Review Committee of Georgetown University in Washington:

> "Recommendation 9: Other methods of evaluating teaching quality and accomplishment should be developed, tested, and phased in so that eventually student evaluation scores would account for no more than 50% of the teaching component of a faculty member's merit evaluation." (Executive Faculty Merit Evaluation Review Committee, 2002, p. 52).

The University of Washington itself makes statistical adjustments to faculty ratings to compensate for these over-grading practices (Gillmore & Greenwald, 1997).

Some university reports recommend suspending the use of student opinion surveys (SOS) on teaching altogether. A 2002 report from the Faculty Center for Academic Excellence at Central Michigan University states:

> "... MOST important recommendation is that we consider a moratorium on the use of the SOS. If we're serious about changing the culture at CMU, we need time to review grade inflation, and faculty need time to develop and implement new strategies to increase the level of rigor in classes without fear of retaliation from students or low SOS scores, which hurt faculty in personnel decisions. This may mean a 3-4 year moratorium, but before we could begin that, an important problem would need to be solved: we would need to find [an] alternative mode of evaluation of teaching to use during that moratorium that is demonstrably valid..." (Zakrajsek, 2002).

CARIBBEAN ARTICULATION WITH THE US GPAS COMPARED WITH THE EUROPEAN CREDIT TRANSFER SYSTEM (ECTS)

When students in the US move between tertiary institutions, it tends to be after finishing an accredited programme at one institution to register for another programme at the receiving institution. However, in Europe it is much more common for students to transfer between institutions as part of their degree programmes, taking courses at different institutions. These exchanges are facilitated by European exchange programmes such as SOCRATES and ERASMUS. An essential part of these exchange programmes is the European Credit Transfer System (ECTS). This is a standardised grading system enabling students' credits from the sending institution to be accepted as equivalent to those in the receiving institution. Currently, more than 1500 tertiary institutions use this system (Bradley, 2001). The ECTS does not replace local institutions' grading systems but supplements them. What is of importance for this paper is that (i) the ECTS serves a similar and more demanding function than the GPA system in the States, (ii) it defines set proportions for each grade as seen in Table 4, and (iii) these proportions are maintained against possible grade inflation by departmental and institutional coordinators who help to align standards. This last point, in particular, contrasts with the inability of the US accreditation system to combat grade inflation and suggests that, universities in the Caribbean could protect their grade standards by also using the ECTS.

Table 4: European Credit Transfer System

ECTS Grade	% of Students normally achieving the grade	Definition
A	10	EXCELLENT - Outstanding performance with only minor errors
B	25	VERY GOOD - Above average standard but with some errors
C	30	GOOD - Generally sound work but with a number of notable errors
D	25	SATISFACTORY - Fair but with significant shortcomings
E	10	SUFFICIENT - Performance meets the minimum criteria

COMPARING CURRENT GRADE INFLATION IN US AND CARIBBEAN UNIVERSITIES

It was mentioned above that prestigious American universities are suffering grade inflation at unprecedented levels. Some recent figures (cited above) are displayed in Table 5. With the figure for The University of the West Indies, which is the average percentage of first class degrees awarded for the last 13 years (1990-2002).

Table 5: Percentage of students receiving 'A' grades at The University of the West Indies and at a sample of US Universities

Awarding University	Percentage receiving 'A' grades
Illinois	40%
Princeton	40%
Yale	41%
Duke	45%
Brown	59%
West Indies	5%

The University of the West Indies (UWI) is the largest regional university in the Caribbean. The UWI grading system is derived from the British system which denotes four classes of degree which would correspond to the ECTS and the four point US grade system nomenclature shown in Table 6.

Table 6: Nomenclature of notional equivalents for Degree Class, Grade and Point systems

Awarding University	Percentage receiving 'A' grades
Illinois	40%
Princeton	40%
Yale	41%
Duke	45%
Brown	59%
West Indies	5%

Using this common nomenclature of notional equivalents for comparing the systems it can be seen for Figure 1 that the University of the West Indies has maintained the standard of its first class degrees (Grade A's) well within the 10% ECTS expectation over the last 13 years. During this time the number of first class degrees awarded by UWI has naturally increased in line with the massification of tertiary education in the US, Britain and the rest of Europe - actually a massive 594% increase from 1990 to 2002.

Figure 1: Percentages of First Class Degrees (Grade A) awarded by UWI over a 13-year period.

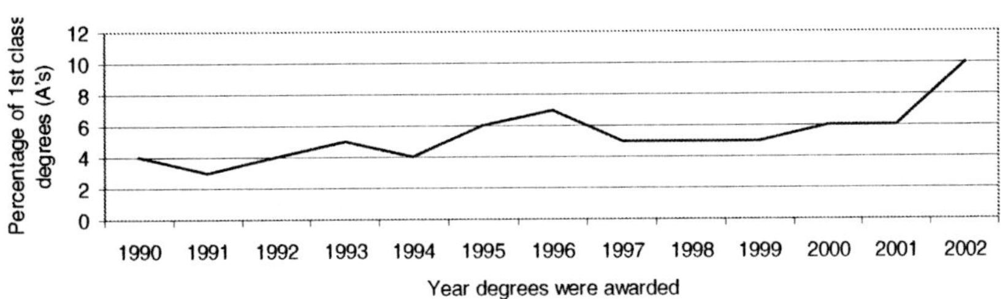

Although the proportion of A's has been well maintained over this time it is interesting to note the recent unprecedented rise to 10%, which we will consider in more detail below.

It was noted above, that internationally there is a tendency for degrees in the humanities to be awarded at a higher grade than those in the sciences. In UWI the difference is not so marked at the first class level (A grade). It is more apparent in the differences between the number of upper and lower 2nd class (Grade B and C) degrees that have been awarded. Figure 2 compares the average percentage of each class of B.Ed and B.Sc degrees awarded at UWI by Social Science and Education over the last 13 years. This pattern is quite stable over successive years.

Figure 2: Comparasion of B.Ed. and B.Sc. degress by percentages of class of degree - 13 year averages.

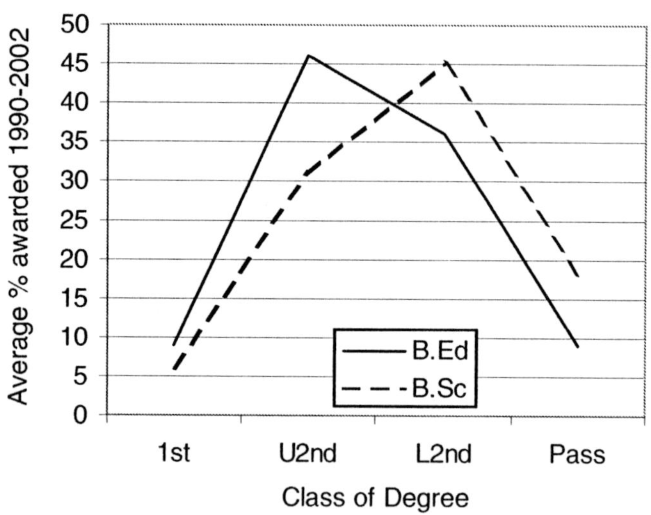

Using the US notional conversion equivalents from Table 6, we can measure this difference in terms of GPAs and percentage higher marking. The calculations for this are shown in Table 7.

Table 7: B.Ed degrees awarded at 13% higher GPAs than B.Sc. degrees - averages over 13 year period

	Percentage of degrees awarded by class of degree with equivalent Grade points						
	Grades	A	B	C	D		
	Grade points	4	3	2	1		Percent
1990-2002	Degree	1st	U2nd	L2nd	Pass	GPAs	difference
Soc.Sc	B.Sc	6	31	45	18	2.25	0%
Ed.	B.Ed	9	46	36	9	2.55	+13%

The GPAs have been calculated by weighting each percentage by its grade point value. For example the GPA for the B.Ed. = (4x9) + (3x46) + (2x36) + (1x9) = 255% = 2.55. This shows that the B.Ed. is awarded at a GPA of 2.55 compared to a GPA for the B.Sc. of 2.25, or 13% higher.

WARNING OF GRADE INFLATION IN THE CARIBBEAN

Figure 1 showed an uncharacteristic increase in the percentage of first class degrees awarded by UWI in the last few years. We now examine this in relation to the complete grading trends more closely for the last six years - from 1997 to 2002. Table 8 shows exactly the same weighted percentage calculations as in Table 7, but for classes of all degrees awarded from 1997 to 2002.

Table 8: GPAs equivalents of UWI degrees 1997-2002 evidencing a year-to-year grade inflation doubling

Percentage of degrees awarded by class of degree with equivalent Grade points

Grades	A	B	C	D		
Grade points	4	3	2	1		Percent
Year	1st	U2nd	L2nd	Pass	GPAs	difference
1997	5	30	41	24	2.16	0%
1998	5	31	40	24	2.17	+0.5%
1999	5	31	41	23	2.18	+0.9%
2000	6	33	39	22	2.23	+3.2%
2001	6	35	40	19	2.28	+5.6%
2002	10	40	34	16	2.44	+13.0%
2003					2.70	25.0%
2004					3.24	50.0%
2005					4.32	100.0%

This shows an alarming recent trend in grade inflation which is illustrated in Figure 3.

Figure 3: Year-to-year doubling of grade inflation of UWI degrees 1997-2002

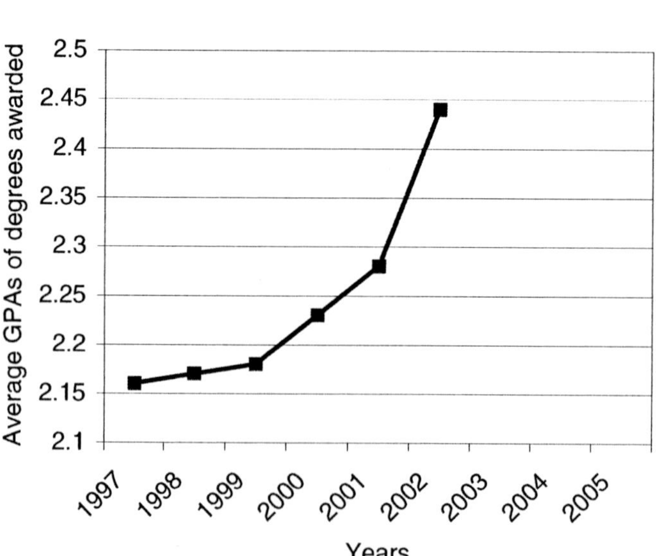

Over the last six years, grade inflation at UWI has at least doubled every year. To illustrate the grave importance of this, it can be seen from the extrapolations on Table 8, that if grade inflation continues at the same rate as in the last six years then in less than three years (by 2005) every degree awarded by UWI will be a first class degree: 'A' for Absolutely everything.

Why did this grade inflaton begin in 1997 and why is it so extreme? In 1996, UWI went through major management restructuring, part of which was a commitment to customer-oriented student support. However, no distinction was made between the appropriateness of applying customer-orientation to administrative services and to faculty teaching. In recent years, customer-orientation to faculty teaching has been increasingly institutionalised by administrative uses of student evaluations of teaching. New machine-marked forms were introduced in 2002 and students' anonymous ratings of named lecturers were available in the library. Although other factors, such as co-curricular credits, are recognised contributors to grade inflation, this administrative use of SETs is seen in the literature cited above as one of the major causes of grade inflation.

CONCLUSION

This paper has explained some of the rationale for using Grade Point Averages and some of the standardisation problems that hinder their use as an intended comparative standard within and across universities. It has shown how the institutional use of student evaluations of teaching (SETs) for faculty career decisions directly causes grade inflation by formally linking higher teaching evaluations to the awarding of higher student grades.

As universities in the Caribbean change to GPAs for greater articulation with the North American GPA system and increasingly promote customer-orientated teaching through the institutional uses of student evaluations of teaching for faculty career decisions, it is very likely that the grades of Caribbean degrees will be equated with the decreasing value of their North American Grade Point equivalents. Commonly, in US universities 40-60% of students are awarded 'A' grades. The US system for accrediting universities has been unable to contain this rampant grade inflation. However, the University of the West Indies, which is the largest regional university in the Caribbean, has maintained its first class degree standards well within 10% over the last 13 years. This is in keeping with expectations of the British system from which the UWI grading is derived. It is also in line with the expectations of the European Credit Transfer System (ECTS) set at a 10% proportion of 'A' grades and maintained by EU support to participating universities.

Although the UWI has previously maintained its standards while considerably increasing its student enrolment, it has, over the last six years, experienced a year-to-year doubling of grade inflation. This is so extreme that if continued for just three more years every degree awarded at UWI will be a first class degree! To constrain this looming catastrophe as we move towards the US GPA system, the problem of SETs and grade control needs to be addressed immediately.

First, in parallel with their change to the US GPA system, Caribbean universities could participate in the ECTS or similar more far-reaching transfer systems now being developed in Germany and the Netherlands, e.g., **Cu**rriculum **B**uild**er** for a Federated Virtual University for the Europe of Regions CUBER, The Netherlands Organisation for International Co-operation in Higher Education NUFFIC and/or The European Association of Distance Teaching Universities - EADTU. Secondly, it is unlikely that universities in the Caribbean or in the US will discontinue the use of student evaluations of teaching, not because they improve teaching or that they are valid, both of which are doubtful, but because for the administration (i) they exercise control over faculty, (ii) conveniently contain student consumer demands for influence and, (iii) as the students assume much of the time-cost burden, they cost-effectively satisfy university quality assurance requirements.

Hence, an alternative method of using student evaluations of teaching is needed that can still be used for faculty career decisions but which uncouples the causal link between students evaluating faculty and faculty evaluating students. One possible solution to this difficult situation is Alignment Assessment (Bastick, 2002, 2003), which is discussed, in the next chapter.

REFERENCES

Bastick, T. (2002). Research Watch: An Alignment Model for Evaluating Teaching. *The National Teaching and Learning Forum, (11)*3 Retrieved on December 15, 2002, from The National Teaching and Learning Forum Web site http://www.ctl.mnscu.edu/ntlf/research.htm

Bastick, T. (2003). Alignment assessment: Battling grade inflation in the English speaking Caribbean. In T. Bastick & A. Ezenne (Eds.), *Researching change in Caribbean Education (pp.xxx-xxx).* UWI, Jamaica: DES.

Becker, W. E. (1997). Teaching economics to undergraduates. *Journal of Economic Literature 35,* 1347–1373.

Cohen, P. A. (1981). Student ratings of instruction and student achievement. *Review of Educational Research, 51*, 281-309.

D'Apollonia, S., & Abrami, P. C. (1997). Navigating student ratings of instruction. *American Psychologist, 52*, 1198-1208.

Edwards, C.H. (2000). Grade inflation: The effects on educational quality and personal well being. *Education, 120*(3), 538 – 546.

Executive Faculty Merit Evaluation Review Committee. (2002, September). *Assessment of the merit evaluation procedures currently in use among Main Campus units* (Report). Washington, DC: Georgetown University.

Foster, D., & Foster, E. (1998). It's a Buyer's Market: "Disposable Professors," Grade Inflation and Other Problems. *Academe, 84*(1), 28-35.

Greenwald, A. G. (1997). Validity concerns & Usefulness of Student Ratings of Instruction. *American Psychologist 52*, 1182-1186.

Greenwald A. G. & Gillmore, G. M. (1997). Grading leniency is a removable contaminant of student ratings. *American Psychologist 52*, 1209-1217.

Haskell, R. E. (1997). Academic Freedom, Tenure, and Student Evaluation of Faculty: Galloping Polls In The 21st Century. *Education Policy Analysis Archives, 5*(6), 33 p. Retrieved on December 15, 2002, from http://olam.ed.asu.edu/epaa/v5n6.html

Hesseln, H., & Jackson, D. (2000). Academic inflation: the devaluation of a university degree. In M. R. Ryan & W. B. Kurtz (Eds.), *Proceedings of the Third Biennial Conference on University Education in Natural Resources* (pp. 112-127). Columbia, Missouri: The School of Natural Resources University of Missouri-Columbia.

Howard, G. S., & Maxwell, S. E. (1982). Do grades contaminate student evaluations of instruction? *Research in Higher Education 16*, 175-188.

Jacobs, L. C. (2002). *Student ratings of college teaching: What research has to say*. Retrieved on December 15, 2002, from http://www.indiana.edu/~best/

Johnson, V. (2002, April 14). " An A Is an A Is an A ... And That's the Problem" invited viewpoint for edition of the *New York Times*.

Johnson, V. E.. (2003). *College Grading: A National Crisis in Undergraduate Education*. New York: Springer-Verlag.

Kirkpatrick, D.L. (1959). Techniques for evaluating training programs. A four-part series beginning with the 1959 issue of *Training Director's Journal*, USA.

Kirkpatrick, D. L. (1994). Evaluating Training Programs: The Four Levels. San Francisco: Berret-Koehler.

Kline, H. (2001, November 21). Eyebrows are raised as grades soar in Ivy League. *The Yale Herald*. Retrieved December 15, 2002, from http://www.uwire.com/content/topnews112101001.html

Landrum, R. E. (1999). Student Expectations of Grade Inflation. *Journal of Research and Development in Education, 32* (2), 124 –128.

Leef, G. C., & Burris, R D. (2002). *Can College Accreditation Live Up to its Promise?* Washington, DC: American Council of Trustees and Alumni.

Margolick, D. (1994, June 4). Stanford U. decides to make courses harder to drop but easier to fail. *New York Times,* 1-7.

Marks, R. B. (2000). *Determinants of student evaluations of global measures of instructor and course value. Journal of Marketing Education, Boulder, 22*(2), 108-120.

Marsh, H. W. & Dunkin, M. (1997). Students' evaluations of university teaching: A multidimensional perspective. In R. P. Perry & J. C. Smart (Eds.) *Effective Teaching in Higher education: Research and Practice* (pp. 241-320). New York: Agathon.

Marsh, H. W., & Roche, L. A. (1997). Making students' evaluations of teaching effectiveness effective. *American Psychologist 52*, 1187-1197.

Marsh, H. W., & Roche, L. A. (1998). Effects of Grading Leniency and Low Workloads on Students' Evaluations of Teaching: Popular Myth, Bias, Validity or Innocent Bystanders? Manuscript in review.

Moore, M., & Trahan, R. (1998). Tenure status and grading practices. *Sociological Perspectives, 41*(4), 775-782.

Muresiano, A. (2002, September 12). Brown needs pluses and minuses in grading policy. *The Brown Daily Herald*. Retrieved from http://www.browndailyherald.com/stories.cfm?ID=7168

Redding, R. D. (1998). Students' evaluations of teaching fuel grade inflation. *American Psychologist, 53*(11), 1227-1228.

Savitt, R. (1994, February 9). The causes and consequences of grade inflation [Letter to the editor]. *The Chronicle of Higher Education, 40*, B3.

Shea, C. (1994). Grade inflation's consequences. *Chronicle of Higher Education 40*(18), A45–46.

Sonner, B. S. (2000). A Is for 'Adjunct': Examining Grade Inflation in Higher Education. *Journal of Education for Business, 76*(1), 5-9.

Steinberg, J. (2001, December 5). Debate at Harvard Asks if Its A's Are Too Cheap. *The New York Times*, A16.

University of Washington Office of News and Information. (1997, December). *Student evaluations don't get a passing grade: Easy-grading professors get too-high marks, new UW study shows*. Retrieved December 15, 2002, from the University of Washington Web site: http://www.washington.edu/newsroom/news/k120497.html

Westfall, J. (2000, December 6), "The Rate of (Grade) Inflation." *The Daily Illini Online*. Retrieved December 15, 2002, from http://www.daily illini.com/dec00/dec06/news/printer/news01.shtml.

Wilson, B. P. (1999). The Phenomenon of Grade Inflation in Higher Education. *National Forum, 79*(4), 38.

Zakrajsek, T. (2002). *Evaluation of Teaching Effectiveness* (White Paper). Michigan, USA: Michigan Central University, Faculty Center for Academic Excellence.

ALIGNMENT ASSESSMENT: BATTLING GRADE INFLATION IN THE ENGLISH SPEAKING CARIBBEAN.

Tony Bastick
University of the West Indies
Jamaica

Chapter 9

THIS PAPER acknowledges the impact of traditional student evaluations of teaching on the devaluation of grade standards in North American Universities and warns that, as the English speaking Caribbean adopts the US grading system, the same devaluation of standards is set to happen in the Caribbean, unless among other precautions, an alternative system for evaluating university teaching can be put in place. The paper then suggests an alignment method of using student evaluations of teaching that has been tested in the Caribbean, as a way of avoiding a similar devaluation of Caribbean degrees in universities that will use the common US GPA system. The paper describes how the Alignment Method (i) decouples the assessment of teaching from the grading of students (ii) protects the lecturer from unrealistic student and institutional expectations and (iii) maintains high standards of teaching and learning whilst protecting the institution from grade inflation.

One of the major causes of grade inflation is the institutional use of student evaluation of teaching (SETs) for faculty promotion, retention and tenure decisions (Eiszler, 2002). This institutionalises the causal link between the student assessment of faculty and faculty grading of students that results in grade inflation (Bastick, 2003).

In order to fight grade inflation some researchers have proposed that we "...eliminate student evaluations of faculty. Proposal 7" (Edwards, 2000). Others recommend that we "...radically revise student evaluations of faculty to guard against the inflationary effect they may have on grades" (Wilson, 1999). Because student evaluations are a cost-effective method of satisfying university quality assurance requirements - by passing most time-costs on to students - it is unlikely that universities will follow the first recommendation. Hence, this paper more realistically takes up the second recommendation of introducing a radically revised method of utilising student evaluation. I call it Alignment Assessment.

ALIGNMENT ASSESSMENT

SETs are anonymous student evaluations solicited towards the end of a course. They cannot feedback for the benefit of the students and the course to which they apply precisely because they are post-mortem evaluations. However, they are used by the institutions for promotion and tenure decisions. This separation of context and purpose results in lecturers employing techniques of managing their teaching that increase SET results but contribute to grade inflation. For example, one technique of ensuring high student evaluations is to over-grade continuous in-course assessments and block-teach model examination answers. Block teaching uses extensive practice on a small homogeneous set of low-level skills that can be objectively tested.

Such objective assessments tend to emphasize Bloom's lowest cognitive level of rote learning. For example, "McKeachie (1987) has recently reminded educational researchers and practitioners that achievement tests assessing student learning in the sorts of studies reviewed here typically measure lower-level educational objectives such as memory of facts and definitions rather than higher-level outcomes such as critical thinking and problem-solving that are usually taken as important in higher education" Feldman (1989). Students learn not to criticize the views of faculty but to unquestionable do as they are told and to parrot what they believe Faculty expects them to regurgitate in examinations.

Students who have adopted a successful learning style for such courses are over-confident in their ability to transfer their learning to other courses. Although this over-confidence boosts SET ratings for the lecturer, it results in diminished self-directed learning skills. The ripple effect is that lecturers on dependent courses must employ similar techniques. Hence, dumbing down courses to increase popularity rating results propagates grade inflation on successive courses. One resulting problem is the difficulty these students then have in completing research theses and assignments. In American universities, research courses and research course components, which of necessity are dependent on transfer of learning, critical and evaluative thinking and self-directed learning, are being replaced by taught courses.

This paper presents an alternative means of monitoring teaching quality that can be used by lecturers and administrators. It is designed to break the causal link between students assessing teaching and lecturers grading of students. This alternative method of assessment was derived from in-depth faculty and student interviews. Its criterion of quality has been validated on empirical data by computer sensitivity analysis and the assessment process successfully tested in clinical teaching trials in the Caribbean and elsewhere.

This assessment method explicitly promotes students' understanding and professional attitudes, as well as their traditional skills, by operationally defining the assessment of skills, understanding and attitudes. It respects professional freedom and the inherent culture of each subject area by giving lecturers the responsibility of promoting the culture of their subjects through their teaching and assessment of its skills, understandings and attitudes. It allows faculty to adjust their in-course teaching and assessment schemes to the changing needs of the student body and to students in their classes who are more or less prepared. The method results in a single administrative decision-point number that is a measure of quality teaching as it applies to (i) a particular individual, or (ii) a minority group or (iii) the whole class.

ASSESSMENT MOTIVATED TEACHING AND LEARNING

There is a business maxim that states, "What gets measured gets done and what gets rewarded gets repeated" (Friend, 1972). In educational institutions, what gets rewarded is (i) the assessment of faculty teaching and (ii) the assessment of student learning. However, it is how the assessment of how teaching is done and how the assessment of learning is done that has a great influence on the learning and teaching culture of the institution (Beichner, 1994; Hake, 1998; Halloun & Hestenes, 1985; Halloun, Hake, Mosca & Hestenes, 1997; Hestenes, Wells & Swackhamer 1992; Hestenes & Wells, 1992; Sokoloff & Thornton, 1997). These three aspects (i) teaching (ii) learning and (iii) the assessment of both, are so inter-related that they should be considered together. Unfortunately, traditional forms of assessment lack integration and problems caused by these traditional forms of assessment negatively influence the learning and teaching culture of institutions. The process and format of traditional SETs has not allowed for the fact that assessment of teaching and assessment of learning are so integrated.

It is also important to separate evaluations of attainment from evaluations of enjoyment, so that student evaluations of course quality are not simply 'smile sheets' misused as assessments of academic attainment (Kirkpatrick, 1994). Smile sheets only measure the first level of Kirkpatrick's training evaluation hierarchy: reaction, learning, application, and results (Kirkpatrick, 1959, 1994). Hence, the two separated and distinct criteria of effective teaching used by this alternate method of assessment are to maximise (i) the academic attainment of the students and (ii) the students' and the lecturer's enjoyment of the course. The measurable indicator of effective teaching used is that the students and the lecturer are working towards the same expectations. The construct validity that this measurable indicator assesses the criteria is $p<0.01$ for both (i) and (ii) (Bastick, 1995).

Interviews with faculty on professional courses have indicated that their implicit expectations can be described and assessed in terms of three process objectives (i) skills - assessed by the accuracy of reproduction (ii) understanding - appropriate transfer of skills to a novel situation, assessed by the justification of appropriateness and (iii) attitudes - the integration of one's life and work by one's values and beliefs, assessed by demonstration (Bastick, 1995). Faculty can be assisted in making these expectations explicit and in designing coursework and examinations that offer opportunities for assessing these three process objectives. It should be their professional prerogative to decide, and their professional responsibility to justify to their peers and their students; the emphasis they judge should be given to each of the three process objectives on their courses. These judgements will depend on the subject, its level and the professional inclination of the lecturer. For example, lecturers on three-year B.Ed courses expect an emphasis on technical skills in the first year, moving to an emphasis on professional competence through understanding in the second year and a greater emphasis on professional attitudes in the third year.

MEASURING ALIGNMENT

Alignment Assessment is a complete alternative to traditional post-mortem student opinionnaires and their attendant problems. It uses the proxy measure of student/lecturer alignment to uncouple the assessment of teaching from the assessment of learning. Figure 1 shows part of the Alignment Assessment form used to collect student feedback for measuring alignment. The alignment feedback form has only eight necessary ratings that take less than 5 minutes to complete. Hence, the form can conveniently be used many times by the lecturer during the course for in-course tracking of teaching quality. At the end of the course it can be used by the administration to give a single decision point number representing the quality of teaching. This is also fairer and less threatening to faculty who, by previous uses of the form, have had opportunities to respond to the feedback and so improve the course for their students and for themselves. Previous research has connected teaching and assessment problems on professional courses with staff/student mis-matched expectations of these three process objectives (Bastick, 1995). Alignment assessment uses the alignment of staff/student expectations of changes of emphases on these three objectives as the proxy measure of teaching effectiveness.

The alignment form asks for two ratings of each of these objectives; ratings of how it is emphasised now on the course and ratings of how the student would want it to be emphasised. This is shown in Figure 1. The form takes longer to complete when additional information is requested, such as age, sex, etc., used for targeting results to student subgroups.

Skills refer to the traditional speed and accuracy of reproducing facts and processes and are assessed by timed accuracy of reproduction. Understanding refers to the ability to use the skills in a novel situation or extend these skills in a novel way. The assessment is by justification of the appropriateness of what is done. Attitudes refer to values that are appropriate to the subject. They are assessed by demonstration in practical situations.

Figure 1: Alignment feedback form asking for two ratings of each of the three process objectives

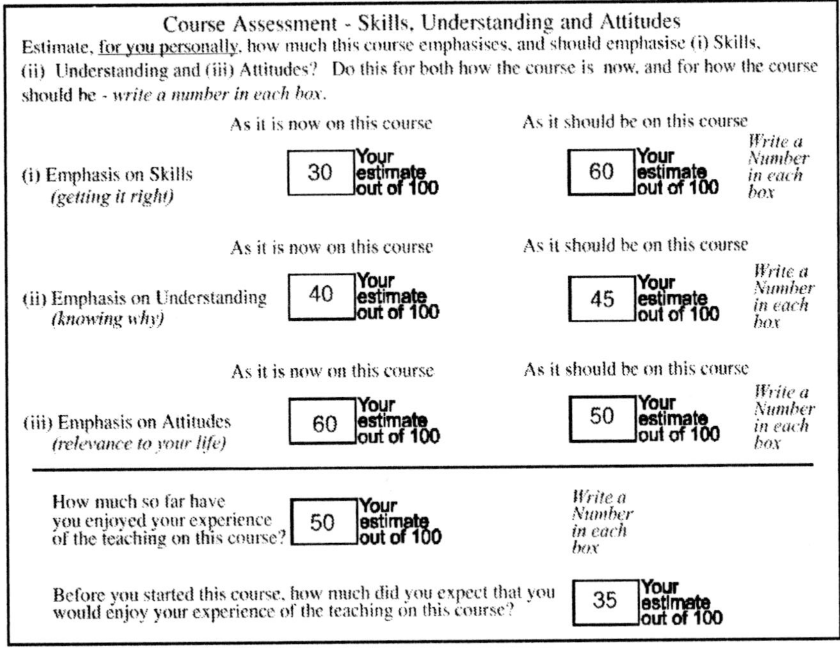

Course Assessment - Skills, Understanding and Attitudes

Estimate, for you personally, how much this course emphasises, and should emphasise (i) Skills, (ii) Understanding and (iii) Attitudes? Do this for both how the course is now, and for how the course should be - *write a number in each box*.

	As it is now on this course	As it should be on this course	
(i) Emphasis on Skills *(getting it right)*	30 Your estimate out of 100	60 Your estimate out of 100	*Write a Number in each box*
(ii) Emphasis on Understanding *(knowing why)*	40 Your estimate out of 100	45 Your estimate out of 100	*Write a Number in each box*
(iii) Emphasis on Attitudes *(relevance to your life)*	60 Your estimate out of 100	50 Your estimate out of 100	*Write a Number in each box*

How much so far have you enjoyed your experience of the teaching on this course? 50 Your estimate out of 100 *Write a Number in each box*

Before you started this course, how much did you expect that you would enjoy your experience of the teaching on this course? 35 Your estimate out of 100

The forms are confidential rather than anonymous so that, using the difference in each pair of ratings, it is possible to calculate each student's expectation for change in emphasis on that objective. The lecturer completes the same ratings at the same time and from the lecturer's form it is possible to also calculate, in the same way, the lecturer's expectations for change in emphases on each of the three objectives. Previous research in the Caribbean has shown that when the students' expectations are aligned with those of their lecturer, that is both students and lecturer are working towards the same degree of change (indicator of effectiveness), then students get high grades and both the lecturer and the students enjoy the course (criteria of effectiveness). The correlations between the in-course indicators and the post-course criteria are significant at $p<0.01$ (Bastick, 2002).

MEASURING QUALITY OF TEACHING (QT)

The alignment method involves more than using the feedback form and calculating the results. There are four steps in the complete application of the method. In steps 1 and 2, faculty are supported as part of their institutional staff and course development programme.

1. Pre-course peer justification of ratings

In the design stage, before the course teaching starts, the lecturer needs to use his/her professional expertise to decide on what should be the emphasis on the course for each of the three objectives. A rationale should justify this decision, and it needs to be ratified by the institution through peer agreement. The lecturer can then build his/her expectations of the three objectives into the teaching and the design of course assignments that give students the opportunities to demonstrate the required level of each objective.

2. Explain and justify three objectives to students

During orientation, students are briefed on the alignment method and take a simple test that qualifies them as course assessors. Soon after the beginning of the course the lecturer needs to make sure the students understand the three objectives and how they will be taught and assessed through the content of his or her particular course.

3. Monitor 'as-is' and 'should-be' for students and lecturer

Students and the lecturer complete the alignment feedback form when the lecturer is ready to monitor the course, or the administration is ready to assess the teaching.

4. Calculating the quality of teaching

This is done in the following two stages (a) and (b).

a) Calculate expected change for each student and lecturer:

Change=|'should-be'-'as-is'|/'as-is'

b) Calculate alignment:

Alignment=| student change - lecturer change|

Zero is the perfect score

The alignment is the Quality Teaching (QT) score - there is an adjustment for student intransigence that is explained later. The QT score can be calculated for each student or as a mean for any group of students. Hence, the quality of teaching can be monitored for any target group of interest, e.g., older students, students taking special electives, minority groups, gender balance, etc. Adjustments can be made to in-course teaching as necessary.

SAFEGUARDS FROM VARIATION IN STUDENTS' SET EXPECTATIONS

Students' expectations vary across faculties and subjects, by years of education, previous experience and even by whether the course is compulsory or optional (Goldman, 1993). This creates an 'unlevel playing field' when traditional opinionnaires are used to assess faculty teaching. From the alignment feedback form the variation in students' expectations can be calculated and the result used as a safeguard to protect the lecturer from inappropriate student expectations. It will be realized that all course evaluations depend on matching student expectations to the expectations of the lecturer for course. The quality of teaching is a function of the complex relationship between the student, the course and the lecturer. All three contribute to the responsibility for quality teaching as assessed by the alignment of expectations. Some aspects of the course can be presented in different ways to match different student expectations. For example, so called 'learning styles' can be matched by adopting different 'teaching styles'. However, some aspects of the course may not be open to change to match student expectations, e.g., externally accredited content standards or the institutionally ratified peer agreed emphases of the three objectives.

Just as students' expectations vary so does the flexibility of their expectations. If students' expectations of these unchangeables cannot be altered so they can accept them, then teaching ratings will go down through no fault of the lecturer. Traditional opinionnaires penalize the lecturer because they make no allowance for large variations in unchangeable student expectations. However, the alignment method allows the lecturer to show evidence that the original peer agreed emphases may not be appropriate for some groups on the course. The minimum possible alignment can be calculated for the whole class or for any sub-group of students on the course. This evidence can be used to either change the course expectations or change the student selection criteria. The QT score is adjusted for this minimum possible student alignment. This allows for the institution to control grade inflation and protects the lecturer from individual or group student feedback that may unjustly penalise him or her.

INSTITUTIONAL COMMITMENT TO STAFF DEVELOPMENT

The full Alignment Framework is more than collecting and analysing student feedback. It includes the commitment of the institution to develop faculty's ability to use their subject specialisation as a vehicle for explaining, teaching and assessing the three objectives. Institutional staff development support includes promoting academic freedom and professional responsibility, assisting faculty in making expectations explicit, in designing assessment opportunities for the three objectives and developing the ability of faculty to teach the three objectives using the content of their subject areas. As was mentioned above, there is a saying in business that "what gets measured gets done and what gets rewarded gets repeated" (Friend, 1972). Quality teaching and quality learning get measured and get rewarded by alignment assessment.

SUMMARY OF ALIGNMENT ASSESSMENT AND HOW IT COMBATS GPA GRADE INFLATION

To use alignment assessment in practice, lecturers explain to their students the three process objectives and how these will be taught and assessed. When they wish to monitor the effectiveness of their teaching they ask the students to rate how they see the current emphasis of these three objectives and to rate how they would prefer the emphasis to be. The lecturer makes the same ratings for the course. A proxy measure is then calculated that disconnects the assessment of teaching from the assessment of learning.

The proxy measure of effective teaching is that the students and the lecturer are working towards the same changes. This is measured by 'the change expected by the lecturer' subtracted from 'the change expected by the students'. Zero is the perfect score on the total of the three objectives, and indicates perfect alignment. The alignment score is the measure of effective teaching and can be calculated for individual students, and the mean calculated for minority groups or for special comparisons, e.g., to measure if the teaching more effective for males than for females and how effective teaching is for students with different degrees of preparedness. However, the alignment is unlikely to be perfect for all students because some students and courses are more difficult to teach than others. A minimum possible alignment can be calculated to protect the lecturer from unrealistic institutional expectations or unrealistic student expectations. Similarly, goal expectations can be agreed before the course to protect the institution from lecturers possibly dumbing down their courses and contributing to grade inflation.

The method promotes a positive teaching and learning culture both directly and indirectly. It promotes a positive teaching and learning culture indirectly by encouraging forms of teaching and learning that faculty and students use to increase their valued assessment results, i.e., assessment driven teaching and learning. Namely, this method encourages teaching and learning that promotes students' critical and evaluative thinking, high standards in skills and attitudes because this is what is assessed in faculty teaching and in students learning.

The assessment method also promotes a positive teaching and learning culture directly through student and faculty assessment support processes, as follows:

1. The institution promotes academic freedom and professional responsibility by confirming the lecturers' professional prerogative to decide, and justify to their peers and their students, the emphasis they judge should be given to each of the three objectives on their courses. This is reinforced by recognising an assessment process that lecturers control and guards the institution against lecturers dumbing down courses.

2. The institution promotes professional development by assisting faculty in making their professional expectations explicit in terms of the three process objectives in their subject area and in assisting them to design coursework and examinations that offer opportunities for assessing these three objectives in their subject areas.

3. Faculty encourage students' critical and evaluative thinking to the extent that faculty can justify this as desirable, by not assessing the correctness of professional competence, but by assessing the students' justifications of why the novel aspects of their applications are appropriate.

4. Faculty also explicitly encourage professional attitudes, to the extent that they can justify these as desirable, by assessing demonstrations of professional attitudes on course assignments.

Generally, the development of skills is already well served by traditional methods of assessment. Now staff development programmes need to be brought on-line to share successful methods of teaching and assessing understanding and attitudes. Processes 3 and 4 directly promote the research culture of the university by raising faculty and student awareness of the importance of critical and evaluative thinking, rewarding faculty for enhancing these objectives for their students and explicitly rewarding faculty and students for demonstrating these objectives. The proxy measure of alignment asks students and lecturers to focus on expectations for change in the three process objectives, rather than asking for more threatening and less valid ungrounded ratings of the lecturer.

This alignment measure correlates with higher student achievement and enjoyment of learning, which are traditional criteria of quality teaching. In this way the alignment assessment uncouples the students' assessment of teaching from lecturers' assessment of learning that drives grade inflation. However, it still results in a single decision point number that can be used to compare quality teaching within and across universities. By measuring the minimum possible alignment it protects lecturers from unrealistic student and institutional expectations of teaching. It guards against grade inflation by agreeing negotiated goals which protect the institution from lecturers who may want to lower those goals and it promotes higher standards of learning and teaching through assessment that rewards lecturers for quality teaching and rewards students for quality learning.

REFERENCES

Abrami, P.C. (1989). How Should We Use Student Ratings to Evaluate Teaching? *Research in Higher Education, 30*(2), 221-227.

Abrami, P.C., d'Apollonia, S., & Cohen P.A. (1990). Validity of Student Ratings of Instruction: What We Know and What We Do

Not Know. *Journal of Educational Psychology 82*(2), 219-231.

Arreola, R.A. (1983). Establishing Successful Faculty Evaluation and Development Programs. *New Directions for Community Colleges 11*(1), 83-93. New Directions for Community Colleges.

Askew, M., Brown, M. L., Rhodes, V., Wiliam, D. & Johnson, D.C. (1997). The contribution of professional development to effectiveness in the teaching of numeracy. *Teacher Development 1*(3), 335-355.

Bastick, T. (1995, July). Alignment: The three ability framework for assessment in tertiary education. Paper presented at The 8th International Conference on *Assessing Quality in Higher Education*, Finland.

Bastick (2002). Research Watch: An Alignment Model for Evaluating Teaching. *The National Teaching and Learning Forum, (11)*3 Retrieved on December 15, 2002, from The National Teaching and Learning Forum Web site http://www.ctl.mnscu.edu/ntlf/research.htm

Bastick, T. (2003). A for Average, B for Bad and P for Paid - Grade inflation prospects for the Caribbean. In T. Bastick & A. Ezenne (Eds.), *Researching change in Caribbean Education (pp. xxx-xxx).* UWI, Jamaica: DES.

Becker, W. E. (1997). Teaching economics to undergraduates. *Journal of Economic Literature 35,* 1347–1373.

Beichner, R. J. (1994). Testing student interpretation of kinematics graphs. *Am. J. Phys. 62*, 750.

Cashin, W. E. (1983). Concerns about Using Student Ratings in Community Colleges. *New Directions for Community Colleges 11*(1), 57-65.

Cherry, R. L. Grant, P. H. Kalinos, K. D. (1988). Evaluating Full-Time Faculty Members. In Richard I. Miller (Ed.). *Evaluating Major Components of Two-Year Colleges.*

Cohen, P. A. (1981). Student ratings of instruction and student achievement. *Review of Educational Research, 51*, 281-309.

Crumbley, L. (1995). On the dysfunctional atmosphere of higher education: games professors play. *Accounting Perspectives, 1*.

D'Apollonia, S., & Abrami, P. C. (1997). Navigating student ratings of instruction. *American Psychologist, 52*, 1198-1208.

Edwards, C.H. (2000). Grade inflation: The effects on educational quality and personal well being. *Education 120*(3), 538 –546.

Eiszler, C. F. (2002). College Students' Evaluations of Teaching and Grade Inflation. *Research in Higher Education, 43*(4) 483-501.

Executive Faculty Merit Evaluation Review Committee. (2002, September). *Assessment of the merit evaluation procedures currently in use among Main Campus units* (Report). Washington, DC: Georgetown University.

Feldman, K. A. (1989). The Association Between Student Ratings of Specific Instructional Dimensions and Student Achievement: Refining and Extending the Synthesis of Data from Multisection Validity Studies. *Research on Higher Education 30*, 583.

Foster, D., & Foster, E. (1998). It's a Buyer's Market: "Disposable Professors," Grade Inflation and Other Problems. *Academe, 84*(1), 28-35.

Friend, G. (1972). Assessing environmental performance: What gets measured gets done. *The new bottom line: strategic perspectives on business and environment 1*(2).

Goldman, L. (1993). On the erosion of education and the eroding foundations of teacher education. *Teacher Education Quarterly, 20*, 57-64.

Greenwald A. G. & Gillmore, G. M. (1997). Grading leniency is a removable contaminant of student ratings. *American Psychologist 52*, 1209-1217.

Greenwald, A. G. (1997). Validity concerns & Usefulness of Student Ratings of Instruction. *American Psychologist 52*, 1182-1186.

Hake, R. R. (1998). Interactive-engagement vs. traditional methods: A six-thousand-student survey of mechanics test data for introductory physics courses. *Am. J. Phys. 66*, 64.

Halloun, I. & Hestenes, D. (1985) The initial knowledge state of college physics students, *Am. J. Phys. 53*, 1043.

Halloun, I., Hake, R. R., Mosca, E. P.& Hestenes, D. (1997). *Peer Instruction: A User's Manual.* New York: Prentice Hall.

Haskell, R. E. (1997). Academic Freedom, Tenure, and Student Evaluation of Faculty: Galloping Polls In The 21st Century. *Education Policy Analysis Archives, 5*(6), 33 p. Retrieved on December 15, 2002, from http://olam.ed.asu.edu/epaa/v5n6.html

Hesseln, H., & Jackson, D. (2000). Academic inflation: the devaluation of a university degree. In M. R. Ryan & W. B. Kurtz (Eds.), *Proceedings of the Third Biennial Conference on University Education in Natural Resources* (pp. 112-127). Columbia, Missouri: The School of Natural Resources University of Missouri-Columbia.

Hestenes, D., & Wells, M. (1992). A Mechanics Baseline Test. *Phys. Teach. 30*, 159.

Hestenes, D., Wells, M., & Swackhamer, G. (1992). Force Concept Inventory. *Phys. Teach. 30*, 141

Howard, G. S., and Maxwell, S. E. (1982). Do grades contaminate student evaluations of instruction? *Research in Higher Education 16*, 175-188.

Jacobs, L. C. (2002). *Student ratings of college teaching: What research has to say.* Retrieved on December 15, 2002, from http://www.indiana.edu/~best/

Johnson, V. (2002, April 14). " An A Is an A Is an A ... And That's the Problem" invited viewpoint for edition of the *New York Times*.

Johnson, V. E.. (2003). *College Grading: A National Crisis in Undergraduate Education.* New York: Springer-Verlag.

Kirkpatrick, D.L. (1959). Techniques for evaluating training programs. A four part series beginning with the 1959 issue of *Training Director's Journal*, USA.

Kirkpatrick, D. L. (1994). Evaluating Training Programs: The Four Levels. San Francisco: Berret-Koehler.

Kline, H. (2001, November 21). Eyebrows are raised as grades soar in Ivy League. *The Yale Herald.* Retrieved December 15, 2002, from http://www.uwire.com/content/topnews112101001.html

Landrum, R. E. (1999). Student Expectations of Grade Inflation. *Journal of Research and Development in Education, 32* (2), 124 –128.

Leef, G. C., & Burris, R D. (2002). *Can College Accreditation Live Up to its Promise?* Washington, DC: American Council of Trustees and Alumni.

Mark, S. F. (1982). Faculty Evaluation in Community College. *Community Junior College Research Quarterly 6*(2), 167-78.

Marsh, H. W. & Dunkin, M. (1997). Students' evaluations of university teaching: A multidimensional perspective. In R. P. Perry & J. C. Smart (Eds.) *Effective Teaching in Higher education: Research and Practice* (pp. 241-320). New York: Agathon.

Marsh, H. W., & Roche, L. A. (1997). Making students' evaluations of teaching effectiveness effective. *American Psychologist 52*, 1187-1197.

Marsh, H. W., & Roche, L. A. (1998). Effects of Grading Leniency and Low Workloads on Students' Evaluations of Teaching: Popular Myth, Bias, Validity or Innocent Bystanders? Manuscript in review.

McKeachie, W. J. (1987). Instructional Evaluation: Current Issues and possible improvements. *J. of Higher Education 58*(3), 344.

Miller, R. I. (1986). A Ten Year Perspective on Faculty Evaluation. *International Journal of Institutional Management in Higher Education 10*(2), 162-68.

Moore, M., & Trahan, R. (1998). Tenure status and grading practices. *Sociological Perspectives, 41*(4), 775-782.

Moses, I. (1996). Assessment and Appraisal of Academic Staff. *Higher Education Management* 8(2), 79-86.

Muresiano, A. (2002, September 12). Brown needs pluses and minuses in grading policy. *The Brown Daily Herald.* Retrieved from http://www.browndailyherald.com/stories.cfm?ID=7168

Pederson, D. (1997, March 3). When an **A** is average. Duke takes on grade inflation. Easy A's. The gentleman's C is fast becoming a relic at today's universities. *Newsweek,* 64, pp. 3-4.

Redding, R. D. (1998). Students' evaluations of teaching fuel grade inflation. *American Psychologist, 53*(11), 1227-1228.

Savitt, R. (1994, February 9). The causes and consequences of grade inflation [Letter to the editor]. *The Chronicle of Higher Education, 4*0, B3.

Scriven, M. (1994). Using Student Ratings in Teacher Evaluation. *Evaluation Perspectives: Newsletter of The Center for Research on Educational Accountability and Teacher Evaluation 4*(1), 1-4.

Scriven, M. (1995). A Unified Theory Approach to Teacher Evaluation. *Studies in Educational Evaluation 21*(2), 111-29

Seldin, P. (1984). Faculty Evaluation: Surveying Policy and Practices. *CHANGE 16*(3), 28-33.

Shea, C. (1994). Grade inflation's consequences. *Chronicle of Higher Education 40*(18), A45–46.

Sokoloff, D. R., & Thornton, R. K. (1997). Using Interactive Lecture Demonstrations to Create an Active Learning Environment. *Phys. Teach. 35*, 340.

Sonner, B. S. (2000). A Is for 'Adjunct': Examining Grade Inflation in Higher Education. *Journal of Education for Business, 76*(1), 5-9.

Steinberg, J. (2001, December 5). Debate at Harvard Asks if Its A's Are Too Cheap. *The New York Times*, A16.

University of Washington Office of News and Information. (1997, December). *Student evaluations don't get a passing grade: Easy-grading professors get too-high marks, new UW study shows.* Retrieved December 15, 2002, from the University of Washington Web site: http://www.washington.edu/newsroom/news/k120497.html

Westfall, J. (2000, December 6), "The Rate of (Grade) Inflation." *The Daily Illini Online*. Retrieved December 15, 2002, from http://www.daily illini.com/dec00/dec06/news/printer/news01.shtml.

Wilson, B. P. (1999). The Phenomenon of Grade Inflation in Higher Education. *National Forum, 79*(4), 38.

FOSTERING SCHOOL AND COMMUNITY PARTNERSHIP IN EDUCATION IN JAMAICA: PROBLEMS AND PROSPECTS.

Austin Ezenne
University of the West Indies
Jamaica

Chapter 10

THE SCHOOL is a formal organization which exists in a community. The school and the community are social systems, which interact with their environments. Education is a process that involves the training and education of the young people and the citizens and there should be co-operation and harmony between the school and its communities.

A positive school-community relationship can stimulate students' interest in schools and also motivate them to learn. An active Parent-Teacher's Association is vital because through this, parents and guardians are made aware of the needs of their children in the school. The principal, who is the school community leader and manager, has important roles to play in fostering good school-community relationship through ensuring efficient communication and effective public relations between the school and its communities.

There are many areas of co-operation between the school and its communities. Thus, the school should initiate a good relationship with its communities and make allowance for community use of its facilities. This relationship should urge the community to provide land, money and equipment for the development of the school and also help to keep a watchful eye on school property at all times. Parents should strive to work more closely with teachers and the school for the benefit of their children. Since the school exists in a community, both school and community should work together as partners in the education of future citizens for their own benefit and for the benefit of the Jamaican society at large.

INTRODUCTION

Education in Jamaica is a complex enterprise, which is accomplished through a number of institutions and agencies. The organised public school system is one important agency that must collaborate with other agencies of society to realise the desirable objectives and outcomes of education. The public school system had its origin in the home and the community many centuries ago, and since then, a partnership was created between the home, the community and the school. In recent times, government policies in education in Jamaica, like in many other nations have been emphasizing the importance of active participation by the home and the community in the affairs of the school. This partnership is safeguarded by community control through the formation of boards, parent- teacher's associations and other school community unions. Parents and other prominent members of the community usually maintain formal and informal relationships with the school.

The school exists in the community and it greatly affects the community's most precious possession, the children. The school does not exist in a vacuum. It, and the community are involved in educational processes and therefore, a healthy school-community relationship is vital for the achievement of the goals of both the school and the school community. Drake and Roe (1999), and Cunningham and Cordeiro (2000), in support of this view stated that education is an activity that involves the co-operation of teachers, parents, children and the community as a whole. Within the community, the school is a formal organization established to educate the people so that they will become useful citizens for their own benefit and for the benefit of the society at large. Thus, many tasks are set out for the school by the society. These tasks according to James-Reid (1983) include:

- Preserving and transmitting the cultural heritage of the people from one generation to another
- Providing a means of social direction and encouraging loyalty and respect for the home, the community and the state.
- Providing for the social needs of the people through family life and health education and continuous improvements of the society's education, growth and well-being.

The community implies people, relationships, shared interests and values. Drake and Roe (1991) posited that a community can be defined in a number of ways and can be studied from the point of view of space, population groupings, shared institutions and values, interactions between local people and power structure, ethnic structure or social systems. The community consists of groups of people living or working together in a locality with a collective identity through common physical, cognitive and affective educational relationships. The community is a social system just like the school and, therefore, it has component parts, definite geographical boundaries, and receives inputs and releases outputs to its environment into other systems.

The wider school community consists of several communities around the school and so a school may have many communities. In a community, there may be a school, an industry, a church or churches and other organisations and these are small communities inside one large community and these small communities also form the school's communities.

There may be many schools in one large community as well. In Jamaica, each individual school may form a part of a larger school community in one region or zone or school district. Each neighbourhood school and its neighbours or community exist in a broader school community or district or region. Individual school communities may be determined by the geographical boundaries or school attendance area boundaries, but with the advent of school choice and distance and online learning, boundary crossings intended to achieve equity of opportunities are now common and the community may be extended and scattered according to Drake and Roe (1999). These situations make it difficult to determine who makes up the school community although they do not eliminate the important idea that the school is a community of its own. It should be noted that all persons living in the school attendance areas and all persons employed by the school, including citizens without children in the school, parents of children in the school, children in the school or teachers and other employees of the school are parts of that school community.

The phrase 'sense of community' is usually used to describe people and organisations. In this sense, the community has the same meaning as the family. The community or family relationships are that of trust, openness and honesty. Though challenging but supportive there should be a bond among members. Etzioni (1991), observed that the individual and the community compliment one another and individuals are not able to function effectively without deep links to others in the community. Sergiovanni (1996) sees community members responding to the substance of ideas. This implies that leadership builds a shared followership not on who to follow, but on what to follow. A school community is, therefore, a group of people who share common ideas and aspirations about schooling and learning.

School community relationship can be referred to as the quality of interaction between the school and the community. School-community relationship suggests that a high level of harmony should exist between the school and its communities. Sometimes, however, there is a breakdown in the harmonious relationship between the school and its communities and this breakdown often leads to disputes between them.

THE SCHOOL COMMUNITY AS SOCIAL ORGANISATIONS

An organisation is a social unit purposely constructed to achieve specific goals. It consists of groups of people and individuals who work together to achieve certain objectives. Therefore, an organisation is a social system consisting of people who perform distinct but interrelated and coordinated functions for accomplishing specific tasks. The school and community are social organisations because they consist of people who are working together to achieve specific goals.

The school and the community are social systems. Lunenburg and Ornstein (1996), stated that a social system refers to activities and interactions of group members brought together for a common purpose. This means that a community, school district, school and even the classroom can be viewed as a social system. A useful framework for understanding the administrative process within the social systems is the Getzels and Guba (1951) model, which conceived of a social system as involving two dimensions that are independent and interactive. The first dimension consists of institutions with certain roles and expectations that will fulfil the goals of the system while the second dimension consists of individuals with certain personalities and need-dispositions inhabiting the system, whose interactions comprise observed behaviour. In the school setting for example, the school organisation is designed to serve one of society's needs, that of educating the citizens. In the school organisation also there are positions or roles such as the roles of the student, teacher, principal, education officer and so on. For each role, there are certain expectations and these expectations represent the duties and actions expected of the role player. The individuals who play roles have personalities and personal needs, which must be satisfied if the system is to work well.

THE IMPORTANCE OF GOOD SCHOOL-COMMUNITY RELATIONSHIP

A good relationship is vital for the survival of both the school and the community and this cannot be overemphasized. James-Reid (1983), stated that the school is an integral force in the community of which it is a part. Both the school and the community receive inputs such as students' money and materials from their environments. They also make outputs of trained and skilled graduates. Therefore, a healthy input-output relationship is important for the two systems, which exist together in the society. Drake and Roe (1999), argued that the educational process extends beyond the walls of the school and the influence of the outside forces are so important that close co-operation with other community agencies, organisations and institutions is essential to the development of a sound educational programme in the school for members of the community.

In Jamaica. The government has always argued that too much money is spent in the provision of education, especially at this time when public resources are severely constrained by debt burden. Thus, the cost-sharing scheme in the financing of secondary education was introduced by the government through the Ministry of Education, Youth and Culture in the 1994/5 school year. Cost-sharing resulted from the wide gap between government subventions and the actual costs of managing secondary schools. Government therefore expects the private sector, parents, students, families and the communities to be more actively involved in the financing of education. Consequently, a good school-community relationship is vital to the survival of the schools. Many private organisations, including business enterprises, support the school by assisting them in various school projects by donating materials, cash and human resources. The Schools Community Outreach Project in Education (S.C.O.P.E) is a good example of community assistance to the schools, in Jamaica. Many studies done on school-community relationship indicate that vandalization of school properties is reduced where good school-community relationship exists, especially where members of the school communities are cooperative and are willing to keep a watchful eye on the school and its properties, particularly during vacations and when the school is not in use.

A positive school-community relationship can also stimulate students and motivate them to learn. An active and vibrant Parent-Teachers' Association is important because through this union, parents are made aware of the needs of their children at home and in the school. Many research studies have found that where parents are involved in their children's education, the students achieve the set objectives. The Parent-Teachers' Association as a community group is most influential in terms of its vast potential and its significant contributions to the school.

Where a good school-community relationship exists, parents are aware of the school policies and programmes and they lend their support to them. The Parent-Teachers' Association usually gives approval to the disciplinary measures adopted by the school and urges the children to conform to such rules and regulations of the school. This can make the task of the teachers less stressful, and the student also achieve more as teachers and can then spend less time on disciplinary problems, and more time on tasks.

The existence of a good school-community relationship also gives the principal and the teachers the opportunity to become actively involved in the life of the community, which is likely to have a positive impact on the student's behaviour, and on the school and community. Many studies conducted on various communities indicated a strong relationship between the quality of the school and the level of public understanding of its policies and that good schools are found in communities where the public has an interest in schools and a reasonable concept of what they can do. Both the school and the community benefit when there is good school-community relationship for school facilities can be used freely for community and supporting activities. These facilities include sports fields, auditoriums and classrooms. This shared use of facilities is endorsed in the philosophy of modern education. Teachers and students can integrate learning activities with community assistance. Community involvement in the affairs of the school can help to create a healthy partnership in the enterprise of educating the young people. A good school-community relationship provides the school with rich resources of expertise, experience and opportunities for service. School authorities should realise the importance of community involvement in the affairs of the school because this relationship helps to enhance the development of both the school and its community.

AREAS OF COOPERATION BETWEEN SCHOOLS AND THEIR COMMUNITIES

The school can assist the community by encouraging shared use of the facilities: Some suggestions follow

1. The school should allow the community to use school facilities when students are not using them.
2. The community can use the school's sporting field such as football fields, netball courts for matches and events including cultural festivals.
3. The community can use school classrooms and halls for ceremonies, festivals and other functions.
4. Schools provide employment for teachers, students, skilled and unskilled local personnels.
5. School buildings and facilities can be used by the public for social, political and religious meetings.

6. Schools can invite community members for fundraising activities for the improvement of school facilities and programmes.
7. The school can be used by the community as polling station for national elections
8. School libraries can be used by members of the community for local research and to search for information.
9. Members of the community can use classroom in schools for adult education classes.
10. The school can serve as a local museum and for recording local events.
11. The school can be used for extra-mural studies, conferences, workshops, seminars and correspondence courses for members of the community.
12. The school can be used for meetings relating to health education, hygiene and public awareness programme on public health.

The community can assist the school in the following ways:-

1. The community can provide residential accommodations for teachers and students, who do not reside in the school communities.
2. The community can provide the school with lands for farming and agricultural studies.
3. The community can provide land for the building of a new school including land for school buildings, compounds, sporting field and access roads to the school.
4. The community can provide human resources for the school such as teachers, students, secretaries, security workers and drivers and ancillary workers.
5. The community can provide free and voluntary labour and services to the school from time to time.

6. Well-to-do and rich members of the community can donate money for the repair and maintenance of school buildings and facilities.
7. The members of the school community can provide school equipment and materials.
8. Community members can provide security for the school by acting as watchdogs for the security of school properties and facilities.
9. The community can provide sites for field trips, excursions, zoos, parks, botanical gardens and other centres of interest for the students.
10. Community members can participate in school committees for sports, games and festivals.

THE PRINCIPAL AS A SCHOOL-COMMUNITY LEADER AND MANAGER

In recent years, there have been many disputes between the schools and their communities in Jamaica. Such disputes may arise in the areas of security for school properties, school boundaries, student's behaviour in their communities, and members of the school community may have disputes with school management and teachers. Parents and teachers can disagree on matters relating to the students progress and performance in the school, and reporting of the student's progress to parents. Another area of disagreement between the school and the community is the issue of school discipline and students disruptive behaviours in the school. Very often parents accuse teachers of not doing enough to control students' behaviour in schools and teachers usually respond by accusing parents of not bring up their children well at home. Teachers also accuse parents of supporting their children when they violate school rules in the school. Parents also take action against teachers when students are punished for disobeying school rules.

One of the major roles of the school principal is the management of the school-community relationship. This is a very important task for the principal because the community has a strategic position in the life of the school. Both teachers and students come from the community, and the school itself is located in the community. A good school-community relationship is established when parents, guardians and members of the school community have a good understanding of the mission, goals and objectives of the schools. Principals and teachers must use their initiative to develop and nurture a vibrant Parent-Teachers' Association so that every school can form worthwhile linkages with their community.

In order to achieve school goals all the stakeholders and other members of the community must work together as partners in education. The school action plan should include community interest and the school should strive to set out strategies that would help the school and community to work together in a partnership. This is important because in recent times many schools in Jamaica are facing social and economic problems, which parents and members of the community should work together to overcome.

The school communities also have problems and needs and this call for the introduction of programmes which the school can implement to assist the communities to work toward reasonable solutions. The school is an agent of change in the community and, therefore, should introduce programmes in areas such as adult education and current affairs in order to assist community members to cope with changes and the challenges of everyday life.

THE ROLE OF THE SCHOOL PRINCIPAL IN FOSTERING GOOD SCHOOL-COMMUNITY RELATIONSHIP

The principal as a school-community leader and manager can do several things to encourage schools and their communities to work together as partners in education and national development. The principal should create avenues for communicating with the school communities. S/he can do this through regular newsletters, circulars, telephone calls, e-mails, faxes, public announcements and through teachers and students. The principal should also familiarize himself or herself with the various influential bodies and persons in the school communities. Influential bodies include the church communities, social clubs, youth organisations, civic bodies, Parent- Teacher Associations, business groups and other similar associations in the school communities. The principal should try to create opportunities to address these bodies and make them aware of school programmes. This will help the principal to open communication channels between the school and the community. The principal should at all times encourage community members to discuss whatever they dislike about the school with him or her.

For example, community members can report any problem regarding students and teachers to the principal, and this is likely to help the principal in explaining the mission and goals of the school to the members of the school community.

On the other hand, the principal should always identify with the community by attending important functions organised by the school communities. By attending these functions, the principal helps to foster good school-community relationship. Parents and other community members can also be invited to visit the school to witness teaching /learning processes in the school. Parents can also assist their children with their homework.

Both the school principal and the members of the school communities should understand that the school-community relationship is a two way process. There should be a joint search for knowledge, skills and positive attitudes by the school and its communities for young people. Effective participation of the school in community activities will enrich the lives of not only the staff and students but also the members of the school communities. On the other hand, parents and members of the school communities should strive to perform their roles in the education of their children and this will help to increase student achievement in the school. The task of developing and maintaining good school-community relationship is a difficult one, but principals should strive to achieve this since it has serious implications for students' achievements and school effectiveness.

WHY MANY TEACHERS AND PARENTS FIND IT DIFFICULT TO WORK TOGETHER AS PARTNERS IN EDUCATION

Some teachers do not want to work with some parents in dealing with students problems in school because these teachers believe that parents are uncooperative. Because of this, some teachers are less enthusiastic about including parents in their classroom management plans. Froyen and Iverson (1999), argued that teachers couldn't be sure that parents will understand their point of view or appreciate the circumstances that often restrict their options when dealing with disciplinary problems of students. Teachers in general often feel that parents sit in judgement of them and this situation is complicated by the fact that there is always little support that is received from colleagues and school administrators. Because of these problems that usually arise, many teachers are reluctant to work with many parents in certain areas of school-community partnership. Many parents have problems with their children at home before the student arrives at school, but some parents as a matter of principle, do not want teachers to intrude on their private lives. These parents, believe that the home and school are two separate aspects of living and thus it is best to keep it that way.

On the other hand, some parents do want teachers to intrude on problems arising between them and their children at home. About fifty years ago, many parents reported their children's misbehaviour to teachers and the school authorities as they wanted school authorities to assist them in solving their problems. In recent times, their approach has changed because they have little trust in the school and the teacher. Every parent wants his or her child to succeed in school and, therefore, he or she fears that any hint that their child is not doing so well in school could be an impediment. As a result, parents quickly blame teachers and school authorities for poor performance of their children in their schoolwork and in their behaviours. Also many parents feel that their children's poor performance in school reflect negatively on them and some parents object to being judged by teachers and school authorities.

Many parents do not want to cooperate with teachers because they are suspicious of teachers. These parents may not like how teachers do their work in the school and how the school programmes are organised. Parents, in general, believe that teachers and school administrators are not doing all that they are supposed to do to enable their children to perform well in school. Parental views of teachers and schools are sustained by the arrogant manner in which some of the teachers conduct themselves in the schools and by the way in which the schools deal with their communities. Negatives views of teachers and the school help to sustain parental suspicions, fear, and lack of trust in the teacher and the school.

CONCLUSION

Schools should strive to face parental apathy and resistance to participate fully in their children's education by laying the foundations for parental support. This can be done by identifying the expectations about their children's performance in school and by having frequent dialogue with teachers and the school management about how to assist their children to do better in school. Rotter, Robinson and Fey (1988), and Wolf and Stephens (1989), pointed out that parent - teacher conferences have been the main stay in programmes of parental cooperation. Learning to work with parents can make a profound difference in the quality of the student's performance in the classroom and in the school. This is because parents can play a vital role in the school's preventive disciplinary plans and can constitute a key influence in their children's motivation to learn. Many disciplinary problems may arise due to the teacher's inability to fulfil some of the demanding tasks of teaching and learning. Many of the problems facing students in schools can be resolved by parents and teachers working together in a partnership. Students, then are more likely to live up to their expectation when they realise that both teachers and parents are working together for their progress and success in the home and school.

Collaboration and networking between teachers, parents and other members of the community to improve student learning are vital for the survival of the school and its communities. Students should take an active part in community activities such as giving services in health centres, nursing homes and participating in the community clean-up projects. These activities can enhance concept of communities in the minds of students. Schools should work with parents in helping preschool children to get ready for formal schooling. School personnel should be sensitive in making parents and guardians feel safe by using adequate language to communicate to them and other members of the school communities. In recent times, schools are facing difficult problems in relation to student's disruptive behaviours and lack of adequate resources, and they need the cooperation of all stakeholders to find solutions to these difficult problems.

Since the school exists in the community, it should work in partnership with the community in the education of students, who originate from the community and will ultimately serve their communities and the society at large after their education in the school. School personnel and members of the community, consequently, must strive to foster good school-community relationship at all times for the benefit of both children and society.

REFERENCES

Cunningham, W.G. and Cordeiro, P.A. (2000) *Educational Administration. A Problem- Based Approach*, Boston, London: Allyn and Bacon

Drake, T.L. and Roe, W.H. (1999) *The Prinicipalship (5th edition)* New Jersey: Merrill & Prentice Hall

Etzioni, A. (1991) *A Responsive Society* San Francisco: Jossey-Bass Publishers

Froyen, L.A. and Iverson A. M. (1999) *School wide and Classroom Management. The Reflective Educator-Leader (3rd Edition)* New Jersey: Merrill & Prentice Hall

Getzels, J. W. and Guba, E. G. (1957*) Social Behaviour and the Administrative Process. School Review* 65, pg 423 – 441.

Lunenburg, F.C. and Ornstein, A.C. (2000) *Educational Administration. Concepts and Practices (3rd Edition)* Belmont: Wadsworth Publishers

James-Reid, Olga (1983) *Teaching: Its Management and Function:* Kingston Publishers Limited

Rotter, J., Robinson, E. and Fey, M. (1988) *Parent-Teacher Conferences (2nd Edition)* Washington: National Education Association

Sergiovanni, T. J. (1996) *Leadership for the Schoolhouse*s San Francisco: Jossey-Bass Publishers

Wolf, J. S. and Stephens, T.M. (1989) *Parent/Teacher Conferences*: Finding Common Ground *Educational Leadership Journal* 47 (2), pg 28 - 31.

THE DOUBLE-SHIFT SYSTEM OF SCHOOLING IN JAMAICA

Austin Ezenne
University of the West Indies
Jamaica

Chapter 11

IN A DOUBLE-SHIFT system of schooling, schools cater for two entirely separate groups of pupils during a school day. The first group of pupils usually attends school from early morning until midday, and the second from midday to late afternoon. Each group uses the same buildings, equipment and other facilities. In Jamaica, the two groups are taught by two different sets of teachers.

The main purpose of double-shift schooling is to increase the provision of school places while avoiding serious strain on the education budget. The double-shift system allows a single set of buildings and facilities to serve more pupils and this may be especially important in urban areas where land is scarce and buildings are expensive. This system of schooling has helped many countries to move towards universal education.

Double shift system of schooling helps in increasing access to education. It helps school authorities to make better use of scarce human and material resources, and reduces costs and overcrowding in schools. However the double shift school can create educational and social problems such as reduced teaching time, a tense school atmosphere and cut-backs on extra curricular activities. Double-shift schooling is a movement towards mass education which is a national objective in Jamaica, and this outweighs the disadvantages of this system.

INTRODUCTION

Education has played a major role in national development in Jamaica from the colonial era to the post-independence period. Government, religious, community and private organizations established schools in different parts of the country and functional literacy has been on a steady increase especially during the first half of the twentieth century. The National Population Survey of 1987 showed that functional literacy rate among the population aged 15 years and over was 86.9 percent, according the Statistical Institute of Jamaica (1997). The current structure of the educational system was established by 1980 Education Act, which identified four levels in the formal education system, early childhood, primary, secondary and tertiary. Since the introduction of the 1980 Education Act, private sector participation is minute as the government is the primary provider of education throughout the country. With the expansion of education programmes financed by the government at the primary, secondary and tertiary levels, the educational attainment of the population has risen over time and the educational system has shown an impressive growth in the last thirty years.

Children of three to five years of age, attend early childhood education in infant, basic, nursery and kindergarten schools. Primary education is provided to children aged six to 11 years in a six-year programme in primary, all-age, primary and junior high schools and private preparatory schools. Secondary education consists of two sections in the first section are Grades 7, 8, and 9 and in the second section are grades 10 and 11. The secondary and comprehensive high schools are five years duration for Grades 7 to 11 and some of these schools offer Grades 12 and 13, that is sixth form, and prepare students for the General Certificate of Education (GCE) Advanced Level. The Caribbean Examinations Council (CXC) offers a terminal examination for secondary school students. This serves as an entrance examination for post secondary education, which is offered by tertiary institution. Six teachers' colleges offer pre-university, courses in different academic disciplines. The Universities of the West Indies, University of Technology, The Northern Caribbean University and a number of off-shore universities, offer a variety of undergraduate and graduate courses in various fields of human endeavours.

Since independence in 1962 and the implementation of the 1980 Education Act, education has been brought more and more under the financing of the central government, with increasing control by the Ministry of Education, Youth and Culture (MOEYC) according to Tsang (1998). The recent white paper on Education, Education: The Way Upward published in February (2001) sets out a path for Jamaica's education at the start of the new millennium. This paper highlights a commitment of the Government of Jamaica to engage the people in a partnership in the development of human resources as a primary tool for personal, social and economic development. The Ministry of Education, Youth and Culture has a mission to provide an education system which secures quality education and training for all persons in Jamaica. It hopes to achieve effective integration of educational and cultural resources in order to optimize individual and national development. Some of the strategic objectives of the Ministry in the 2001 White Paper in Education are as follows:

1. to devise and support initiatives striving towards literacy for all in order to extend personal opportunities and contribute national development.

2. to secure teaching and learning opportunities that will optimize access, equity and relevance throughout the education system.
3. to support student achievement and improve institutional performance in order to ensure that national targets are met.
4. to enhance student learning by the greater use of information and communication technology as preparation for life in the national and global communities.

One of the strategic objectives of the Ministry of Education, Youth and Culture stated in the 2001 White Paper in Education is to secure teaching and learning opportunities that will optimize access and equity in the educational system. The objective is directly related to the provision of the shift system of schooling in Jamaica.

MODELS OF SHIFT SCHOOLING IN INTERNATIONAL PERSPECTIVE

An international survey carried out by Bray (2000) under the auspices of the International Institute for Educational Planning (I.I.E.P) and the United Nations Educational, Scientific and Cultural Organization (UNESCO) published by the Commonwealth Secretariat reveals many different models for double-shift schooling in many developing countries. The outlines of the most common models of double-shift schooling are presented here, in order to provide a framework for this paper.

In many double shift systems, one group of pupils leaves the school before the next group arrives. In Malaysia for example, the first group of pupils in a double shift arrives early in the morning but leaves at midday and the second group arrives at midday and leaves late in afternoon. Structures of the double shifts in Malaysia are as follows:

First Shift	:	7:40 am	to	12:40 pm
Second Shift	:	1:00 pm	to	6:00 pm

In Jamaica, the first shift is known as the AM shift while the second shift is called the PM shift. The first group of pupils arrives early in the morning and leaves at midday; the second group arrives at midday and leaves in the late afternoon as follows:

First (AM) Shift	:	7:30 am	to	12:30 pm
Second (PM) Shift	:	12:30 pm	to	5:30 pm

The Zambian model is a triple-shift system and there, three groups of pupils share one set of buildings and facilities. The pattern in some Zambian schools is as follows:

First Shift:	7:00 am	to	10:45 am
Second Shift:	11:00 am	to	2:45 pm
Third Shift	3:00 pm	to	6:45 pm

These schools operate with a very short school day and the authorities in Zambia use it as an emergency measure to accommodate the upsurge of school enrolments in those localities.

One common feature of the Malaysian, Jamaican and Zambian models is that there is no overlapping of the shifts because the first shift ends before the second shift starts. Provision of 'Holding Areas" is not necessary except where pupils arrive very early for the afternoon shift because of this arrangement.

The Indonesian model is an example of an overlapping shift system. The operation of the shifts is as follows:

Shift A: 9 periods per day,	8:15 am	to	3:10 pm
Shift B: 9 periods per day,	9:35 am	to	4:30 pm

Both shifts have the same lunch hour, from 12:10 to 1:10 pm. This helps student of each shift to meet each other and to feel a part of a single institution. The system requires efficient timetabling, but does not cause major problems. Space for the students when the two shifts are in the compound together is found by using laboratories, workshops, the library and sports fields for physical education. The schools that use this model in Indonesia increased their enrolment by 25 percent while still maintaining the status of a full-day school, (Bray, 2000).

A more complex system of overlapping shifts has been used in Malawi to tackle the problem of insufficient classrooms in many schools. In some schools, pupils in standards (grades) Three, Four, and Five can only arrive at school after pupils in standards one and two have left, but pupils in standards six, seven and eight overlap with both groups. Some schools in the Philippine model manage even a more complex timetable with quadruple overlapping shifts. The model shows that classrooms can be used non-stop from 7:00 in the morning to 7:40 in the evening. This situation contributes to the efficiency of the schools and the school system.

DIFFERENT OR SHARED TEACHERS FOR THE SHIFTS

Hong Kong primary schools have different teachers for the morning and afternoon sessions. Government prohibits staff from working in both sessions because it is afraid that teachers will be tired and that quality will suffer. A similar policy is followed in Singapore, Jamaica, South Korea and parts of Nigeria. The situation in Senegal is different. There is shortage of qualified teachers and the authorities are keen for these limited human resources to be utilized as fully as possible. Some of these qualified teachers welcome the opportunity of teaching in more than one session as this helps them to increase their earnings through extra work.

ONE SET OF SCHOOL BUILDING FOR TWO LEVELS OF EDUCATION

One set of school buildings may be used for students in two levels of education. In Bangladesh, for example many double shift primary schools teach Grade One and two in the morning and Grades Three, Four and Five in the afternoon. In Puerto Rico, Palestine and India some institutions accommodate elementary children in the morning and high school students in the afternoon shift, Bray (2000).

DOUBLE-SHIFT SYSTEMS IN URBAN AND RURAL COMMUNITIES

Double shift systems are common in urban than in rural areas, Bray (2000). This is because land and buildings are more expensive in towns than in the rural areas and urban areas have high population densities and, therefore, have enough pupils to run extra shifts. In rural areas, double shift is used to minimize costs. Rural schools often suffer from teacher shortages and this can be alleviated by teachers teaching more than one set of students.

In countries such as Botswana, the Philippines, Pakistan and Tanzania, private and community schools borrow or rent the premises of public schools when the public school is closed for the day. This is a kind of double shift system, for the buildings are used twice by two sets of students. It also promotes shared use of facilities.

In some countries, school authorities are permitted to decide which model to use, while in other countries, central authorities decide on the best system for each school. The main purpose of the shift system is to reduce costs.

THE DOUBLE SHIFT SYSTEM OF SCHOOL IN JAMAICA

The Double-shift system as practiced in Jamaica caters to two entirely separate groups of students during a school day. The first group of students usually attends school from early morning until midday, and the second group usually attends from midday to late afternoon, using the same buildings, equipment and other facilities. The two shifts are taught by different teachers. Double shift schools may also be called: double session, bi-sessional and half day schools.

In Jamaica, the main purposes of the Double Shift System are to increase access by providing more school places and also to reduce the strain on the annual budget for the education sector of the national economy. Leo-Rhynie (1981) reported that the double shift system was first proposed in 1953 by Harold Haughton who was the then Director of Education in the Ministry of Education. The then Minister of Education, the Honourable Edwin Allen, favoured the proposal, but was of the view that the advantages inherent in the implementation such as loss of teaching time, truancy and delinquency would far outweigh any advantages that would accrue. Leo-Rhynie (1981) also stated that the double shift system was eventually introduced on a trial basis in 1972 in the Jones Town Primary School and Tarrant Secondary School respectively. Each shift operated as a separate school at that time and the afternoon shift was administered by a vice principal who received additional pay.

In the double shift system in Jamaica, the schools cater to two entirely separate groups of students during a school day. The same set of school buildings and faculties are used by the two sets of students in a school day. During the early days of the double shift system in Jamaica, one day in the school week was extended with the additional four and half hours for each shift to provide for extra-curricular and other school enrichment activities, Leo-Rhynie (1981). This arrangement has since been discontinued and extra curricular activities are now provided in both the morning and the afternoon shifts. The double shift system of schooling which was started in 1972 as an interim measure to deal with the rising demand for school places by young people is now a permanent feature of the Jamaican school system. This experiment started with two schools in 1972 and by the 1999/2000 school year there were 106 double shift schools in Jamaica (School Profiles 1999/2000). The spread of this system of schooling in the Parishes is shown in Table 1. The Table also shows school types in the various parishes

Table 1: Number of Public Educational Institution with double shift in Parishes by School type by 1999/2000 school year in Jamaica

Parish	Primary	All-Age	Primary & Junior High	Secondary High School	Comprehensive High School	Technical High School	Total
Kingston					3		3
St. Andrew	3		4		6		13
St. Thomas				1			1
Portland	1				1		2
St. Mary			2		1		3
St. Ann	2	2	2		1	1	9
Trelawny		2			2		5
St. James			5		3		8
Hanover			2		1		3
Westmoreland	3	1	1		3		8
St.			2	2	2		6
Elizabeth	1	1	4		2		8
Manchester	3	1	6		2		12
Clarendon	10	2	9	2	2		25
St. Catherine							
Total	23	9	37	7	29	1	106

Source: MOEYC School Profiles 2000/2001

Table 1, shows that St. Catherine has the highest number of double shift schools, 25. This is followed by St. Andrew with 13, Clarendon with 12, and then St. Ann with nine schools. On the other hand St. Thomas has only one shift school, followed by Portland with two schools and Kingston, St. Mary and Hanover having three shift schools each. Primary and Junior high schools have the highest number of double shift schools of 37. This is followed by comprehensive high schools with 29 and the Primary level with 23 schools. Among Technical High schools there is only one shift school; secondary high have seven and All Age have nine schools. The table indicates that the double shift system is popular at the primary and secondary levels of education, and in rural and urban areas of the country.

THE ECONOMIC ADVANTAGES OF DOUBLE- SHIFT SYSTEM OF SCHOOLING

It has now been established that the double-shift system of schooling can help to achieve important economic goals by helping to reduce the unit cost of education in the double-shift system and also both pupils and teachers can be released for productive work elsewhere in the economy. Although the double shift system has economic costs such as parents employing people to care for children who would otherwise be in school, the benefits certainly exceed the cost in Jamaica and in many other countries.

1.SCHOOL FACILITIES

The double shift system of schooling permits major savings in land, buildings, equipment, facilities and libraries because it allows two groups of pupils to use one set of school facilities every school day. The economic savings from multiple shift systems are usually considerable. For example, in Zambia where extensive use of double and triple shifts are made, cost estimates are reduced by about 46 percent, Bray (2000). The Government of Jamaica and Zambia are keen to achieve universal primary education but have financial constraints and they are using the shift system of schooling as an alternative route to achieve universal primary education for their citizens. The increase in the population of primary school children and the pressure on the annual education budgets have strengthened the need for the use of shift systems of education in these countries.

2.STAFF SALARIES

In Jamaica there are two sets of teachers for the double shift and some teachers may be allowed to teach in both shifts in some subject areas where there are acute shortages of trained teachers. If teachers are paid double salary for double work, then there is no saving in salaries. Alternatively, teachers may receive extra pay for extra work, but at a lower rate. In Senegal, teachers who work in both shifts are paid an additional 25 percent of their basic salaries, Bray (2000). This is because the double shift schools provide only 20 hours of classroom teaching each week instead of 28 hours and the increase in salary is a smaller proportion than the increase in work. This gives the government some amount of saving in the teachers salaries.

The double shift schools in Jamaica, Singapore and Puerto Rico have two teams of teachers but have only one team of clerks, cleaners, labourers, messengers and security personnel. This arrangement allows the authorities to make salary savings. The use of a single team of clerks and ancillary staff to serve double session schools does require careful planning and management in order to ensure that the staff members are on duty throughout the school day.

3. SAVINGS IN TIMEAND LABOUR

Double shift schools have a shorter day than single shift schools and therefore, can serve the time and labour of teachers and pupils. For example, if teachers work in one shift, they are free to go for other economic activities such as studying, taking on part-time job and even performing domestic activities. Pupils may use their time for studying at home or in the libraries, take part-time jobs, look after younger brothers and sisters at home or do domestic work, when their parents are at work.

EDUCATIONAL AND SOCIAL COSTS AND DISADVANTAGES OF THE DOUBLE-SHIFT SYSTEM OF SCHOOLING

Many educators agree that the general atmosphere of double shift schools is inferior to that of single-shift schools. This belief is based on the following factors:

1. The shift school is always under pressure and everybody seems to be in a hurry since both the teaching and the breaks are shortened.

2. Teachers and students of the different shifts feel like they are in two different schools and they do not easily identify with students and teachers from the other shift.

3. Teachers and students often miss their breakfast and later become hungry and find it difficult to concentrate on lessons, especially when they arrive very early for the morning shift.

4. Children find it hard to study in the afternoons in Jamaica and in other tropical countries. These adverse weather conditions affect students' performance in the schools. Teachers that work in two shifts usually are tired in the second shift and may have less time to prepare for classes and to correct students' assignments.

5. If afternoon shift pupils arrive at school early they may be noisy and may disturb the last lessons of the morning shift if there is no "holding area" for the students to wait until it is time for their lesson. Similar problems arise if the morning shift pupils stay late instead of going home as soon as their classes are dismissed. The transition period between the morning and afternoon shifts should be managed carefully. Otherwise, the meeting of the two

groups could be chaotic, and teaching time may be lost in attempting to control the situation.

6. Classroom facilities such as wall space and even the chalkboard may not be adequate for both shifts. For example, morning shift pupils, may tamper with the wall pictures of the afternoon shift and vice versa. Likewise, teachers may not leave any work overnight on the chalkboard or it will be cleaned off by teachers and pupils of the next shift.

7. Excessive use of the facilities in shift schools increases wear and tear, thereby creating high maintenance costs. Double shift schools should have extra facilities such as cupboards, storerooms, offices and "holding areas" for the afternoon pupils who arrive early and morning pupils who stay late.

8. When the length of a school day is seriously reduced in a double shift school parents are often worried about the extent to which their children are able to cover the school curriculum. Some of these parents may send their children for private lessons to make up for what is lost in the school and this increases the cost of their children's education.

9. The double shift system of schooling can release young people for productive employment. It is however, hard for young school children to find good jobs and because of this some of these children will be exposed to gangs which may cause social problems in the society. The government may save money through a double shift system but it may have to spend money to deal with social problems caused by young people who are out of the shift schools.

10. Extra curricular activities provide one of the major ways of achieving the goals of education in all nations. Through sporting activities, children learn about cooperation and competition and how to grow physically strong and healthy. They also develop their talents in subject areas such as music, drama, debates and scouting and so on. Many educators believe that shift schooling helps to cut back on

the time available for these subjects and extra curricular activities, because the school day is shortened and the campus may be too congested to allow simultaneous activity by children of both shifts.

CONCLUSION

Double shift schools may suffer educational disadvantages when compared with single shift schools. For example, teaching time for each shift may be reduced, and the need to compress a lot of school activity into a short time may make the school day rather tense. Also, both teachers and children may be tired, particularly during afternoon shifts in tropical countries with hot climate such as Jamaica. This may affect not only academic aspects of the school life but also the social and extra curricular activities. Some researchers have indicated that academic achievement in double shift schools may be just as high as in single shifts schools and trained school administrators with planning skills may find ways to get over the problems of shorter school days and of congested school compounds in the double shift system.

Double shift systems can provide major economic benefits such as more efficient use of buildings and other facilities, and more efficient use of trained teachers. There may be savings in teacher training if the shift system allows reduction in the total number of teachers. The system can be cost-effective and can permit substantial savings in money, materials and human resources. Even when there is a loss in quality of education offered, the benefits of reduced unit costs and of larger enrolments outweigh the costs implied by loss of quality.

Since 1972, the shift system of schooling has been a prominent feature of the education system in Jamaica. The shift system was introduced in 1972 as a temporary measure to solve the problem of overpopulated schools, resulting from high student enrolments. The shift system started with two schools in 1972 and rose to 106 by the

2000/2001school year, as shown in Table I, in this paper, and this rapid growth in the number of double shift schools has helped to make the shift system a permanent feature of the Jamaican educational system today.

The double shift system may have reduced teaching time, compressed activity, tense school days, tired children and tired teachers. Nevertheless, we have the national objective of mass education to educate all the nation's children, and this national objective outweighs the disadvantages of the double shift system. Educational administrators and planners must strive to identify strategies that will help to minimize and solve the problems created by the shift system of schooling in Jamaica.

REFERENCES

Bray, Mark. (2000) *Double-Shift Schooling: Design and Operation for Cost Effectiveness*, London: Commonwealth Secretariat

Darlington, Norma. (1993) *The Administration of the Double Shift System in Jamaican Schools* Unpublished M.Ed. Thesis, University of the West Indies, Mona

Edgar, Arthur. (1980) *The Shift System in Calabar High School.* Caribbean Journal of Education Vol. 7, No.1, 1980

Education: *The Way Upward* (2001) A path for Jamaica's Education at the start of the new Millennium. Kingston: Ministry of Education, Youth and Culture.

Government of Jamaica. The Education Act 1980. Kingston: Ministry of Education, Youth and Culture.

Jamaica School Profiles (1999/2000 and 2000/2001) Kingston: Ministry of Education, Youth and Culture.

Leo-Rhynie, Elsa (1981) *Report of the Shift System in Jamaican Schools.* Kingston: School of Education, University of the West Indies, Mona.

Linden, Toby. (2001) *Double-Shift Secondary Schools: Possibilities and Issues.* Washington: World Bank Development Network

Statistical Institute of Jamaica (1997) The Labour Force Survey 1996, Kingston, Jamaica.

Tsang, Mun C. (1998) The Financing of Education in Jamaica, Issues and Strategies. Kingston: Inter-American Development Bank.

ACCESS TO SECONDARY EDUCATION IN ANGLOPHONE CARIBBEAN COUNTRIES: BARRIERS TO EQUALITY OF OPPORTUNITY

Lindsey T. Allard
Harvard Graduate School of Education
USA

Chapter 12

Many Anglophone Caribbean countries have increased access to secondary education by large percentages, and the region holds a place near the world mean for enrollment at this level (Wolff and Castro, 2000). However, the region still faces many challenges in the provision of secondary education, and economically marginalized groups, especially those inhabiting rural areas, remain at a disadvantage in acquiring upper levels of education in these countries. As stated by Caribbean education expert Errol Miller, "Notwithstanding the impressive gains, the goals of equity and equality of opportunity remain distant for the majority of Caribbean people" (1996, p.6).

This report will explore briefly the historical and contextual factors of education within the region. Next, an examination of the barriers to equality of opportunity in relation to secondary education that currently stand in place will be conducted. These barriers include physical space, including material and human resources, the quality of teaching and learning at secondary and each of the previous stages of education, testing mechanisms in place that limit and control admittance to traditional secondary schools, the various social factors that impede effective participation and progression. The report will then compare options through analysis of empirical evidence, and make recommendations based on the current economic, political and societal situation of the Anglophone Caribbean.

HISTORICAL AND CONTEXTUAL STATE OF EDUCATION

There are many factors which characterize education in this region. Recent independence from the British colonial system has given way to a multitude of new nations, which must quickly adapt the systems, put in place to maintain control over the laboring class, to more equitably suit the populations that they serve. The Caribbean region is made up of small island nations who presently undergo the economic challenges of adapting primarily agricultural societies to be mobile enough to function in a global economy, as well as the daunting task of steady economic stability and growth (Atchoarena, 1989).

Errol Miller preludes any discussion of education in this region by positing, "Secondary education in the Caribbean cannot be discussed in isolation from the rest of the educational system or the general society or be understood without reference to its immediate past in the post-independence period" (1996, p.3). This period, thought of as the years 1950-1985, saw major changes and reforms of secondary education as well as throughout the education system in general. A major marker of this period was attention to development of secondary education, and the provision of mass secondary was achieved in at least ten countries in the region, up from only ten percent regional enrollment in 1949. This period was a time of economic growth, political will, and strong social demand, and the achievements made greatly strengthened education, especially at the secondary level.

Secondary education in the English-speaking Caribbean, as well as other formerly colonized developing countries, was formed within an elitist system that aimed to serve only the university-bound upper class. Since the widespread expansion of primary education, there has been an overwhelming increase in primary graduates, who seek higher education opportunities.

The ways in which the history of education in the region manifests itself in secondary education currently are through the barriers of access and quality. These barriers are most commonly applicable to the lives of low-income and rural populations, who do not gain access to important educational opportunities that could help to change their social and economic status. An estimated 25% of the population in the Anglophone Caribbean are living in poverty, according to a cross-country study of poverty reduction in the region (Baker, 1997). This evidence shows the importance of developing better education and related services for economically marginalized persons, as one in four persons is affected by poverty, the highest incidences being in children and youth (UNDP, 2001). This phenomenon, affecting most developing countries, also has much to do with the education ladder, as described by Reimers. "The two [access and quality] become inextricably linked... access to secondary education is only possible upon completion of primary education, which is possible only upon a strong foundation of early learning, all which require quality teaching" (Reimers, 2001, p.450). This is a relationship that must be explored when attempting to identify the major barriers to access and equality of opportunity.

There are several other mitigating factors which hamper children's opportunities to move successfully through the education system. Educational success is tied closely with family income, level of education of parents, health, nutrition and rural or urban residence. Donald Winkler, in Unequal Schools Unequal Chances, maintains that these factors have a direct influence on children's performance at school (p.113, 2001). The external factors listed above can be roughly translated into economic and social disadvantages, and children who experience these disadvantages are more likely to be excluded from the educational process. Existing information reveals limited access for low-income groups, as "Miller (1990) found that only 15% of high school children in Jamaica had parents who were unemployed, unskilled or semi-skilled, despite the fact that 50% of the population could be so classified" (Miller referenced by World Bank, 1993).

Economic and social disadvantages play a very important role in secondary education because this is the time in young people's lives where many must start earning wages, especially young men. "The poor, especially those in rural areas, are grossly underrepresented in secondary education; and secondary education programs rarely, if ever, take into account the needs of working students and potential students living in rural areas" (Wolff and Castro). Children who must contribute to the family income incur a tremendously high opportunity cost when attempting to complete the secondary cycle of education. This is a time when youth, especially young men, could be entering the labor force, and beginning to contribute to the family earnings, a more urgent matter when a family is living in poverty. Secondary school has been shown to be in high demand in the region, as Caribbean people recognize education as a vehicle for social mobility. The dropout rate for traditional secondary students in Dominica is less than 2%, showing the incredible importance that students and families place on education (World Bank, 1995). To this end, Cavichionni concludes that "Socioeconomic disparities are among the most important factors underlying access to smooth progression in education" (2001, p.228)

The issue of access is particularly exacerbated in rural areas, where youths will have to travel as much as two hours each way to reach their secondary school. Henry (1994) suggests that the lack of access to a secondary education may be a factor of geographic proximity to these schools, since there may be tremendous costs involved and time required to attend some schools due to their geographic location. Students, especially those in rural areas, are required to pay up to $400 US on transportation per academic year. This accompanies textbook and material costs of up to $370 US (World Bank, 1995). Some countries do have some form of assistance in place, including textbook assistance programs, but students, especially at the secondary level, are expected in most cases to cover the bulk of this expense, especially with regard to transportation.

Access to education can be viewed, especially in developing countries, as the lone opportunity for social mobility. Therefore, it is critical that in countries where inequality has been a historical trend, education is made available and accessible to those who will benefit the most from it, namely the disadvantaged. In countries where much of the population is poor, education becomes a crucial aspect of economic, political and social success for the masses. The role of schools is one of responsibility as a public service, as the authors of a study detailing efficiency and equity in education inform us, "Society should be responsible-at least, partially, for inequalities in professional success because school is seen as carrying out a democratic mission: that of diminishing gaps and avoiding the reproduction and increase of differences from one generation to another." (Bourdieu & Passeron, cited by Demeuse et al., p.72)

BARRIERS TO ACCESS AND EQUALITY OF OPPORTUNITY

After examination of the historical and current factors influencing education systems in this region, it is imperative to examine the factors that impede the equitable and universal provision of secondary education across the Caribbean region. The first and most obvious of barriers to secondary education is that of access, not only to space but access to high-quality education and social circumstances throughout the student's pre-academic and academic life. In the case of poor children, access to social factors, such as proper nutrition, healthcare, families whom are both educated and able to advocate for their children, socioeconomic status, and rural or urban residence play a major role in their ability to engage in and benefit from an education.

Also to be examined is the system of education, which is organized as a progression through stages where graduation to each stage is impingent on the successful completion of stage before it. Evidence from St. Lucia and Trinidad and Tobago show that half as many poor children receive access to pre-primary programs in comparison to their wealthy counterparts (Baker, 1997). Inequities are born then, at both the pre-primary and the primary level, and are "as much a result of the inadequacies of primary education as that of secondary education" (Wolff and Castro).

Although each country has a different system of cost retrieval in place, there is most certainly some form of private cost at every level of education. This cost might not be in the form of traditional fees, but rather on uniforms, transportation or textbooks. Also included is an indication of space, as pre-primary, secondary, and tertiary admittance are reliant on the availability of places, and the shortfall in places at the secondary level is a considerable constraint to access (EFA, 2000).

In looking at secondary education, we can see that education at this level is broken down into two stages, upper and lower (also referred to as junior and senior). The argument for traditional secondary schooling for all derives from the evidence that junior or lower secondary schools are inferior in quality, and produce graduates who do not possess the education or skills to enter into an educated labor force. In Jamaica, almost 50% of students graduating from lower secondary (all-age schools) are considered to be functionally illiterate (Baker, 1997). This is an issue that is currently being addressed by Barbados, St. Kitts and Antigua, who have achieved near universal access to traditional secondary education. Other countries are also working on ways to increase access at the secondary level.

Common Entrance exam, which is administered by most countries (with the exception of St. Kitts, Jamaica, and Barbados, who have phased out the Common Entrance in favor of newly developed testing mechanisms, GSAT, BSSE). The Common Entrance determines students' placement at the next level of education. Those who score above the passing limit (determined by spaces available at traditional high schools), are granted a place in an academic track. The numbers of students who progress to some form of the secondary level averages 65.5% (USAID).[1] Those children who do not "pass" the CEE are streamed into various types of junior secondary or all-age schools (administered slightly differently in each country), which usually repeat much of the content from primary school. "Sharp differences in quality exist between secondary schools serving those who pass the CEE...and the junior secondary schools or all-age primary schools enrolling students who fail the CEE. (World Bank, 1993). For many students, especially poor performers, this test represents the terminal point in their formal education.

There is currently a shortage of qualified teachers in the Caribbean region. schools with disadvantaged populations with the least trained or untrained teachers. In Guyana, regions with high amounts of poor residents receive the lowest quality of inputs (teachers and materials). In the three sub-regions of Guyana with the highest incidence of poverty, approximately 70% of teachers are unqualified, much higher than the national average of 30%. The situation is similar in Belize (72% teachers untrained in poorest region, compared to 48% national average), Trinidad, Jamaica and Dominica (Baker, 1997).

The curriculum in many countries, while a high priority for all Anglophone nations in the region presently, must continue to be rationalized to raise the general level of education for all students and produce a generally educated and responsible cohort of graduates. Evidence shows that some students receive less material resources, while their counterparts have access to more textbooks and materials (Reimers and McGinn,). In Guyana, the percentage of students in poor districts who receive textbooks is only half the national average (Baker, 1997). Age-appropriate services provided at all levels by support staff will increase the success and learning of students with disadvantages. Outputs represent the actualization of successful graduation from the higher levels of the system, taking the form of graduates who are literate, generally educated, prepared to accommodate the current job market, and who are productive members of their society.

Education systems in the Caribbean, as in many other countries, vary greatly in what is delivered and to whom. While increasing overall quality is important, equally important is the recognition that schools within a system are segregated, and some schools are able to provide more resources and higher quality of teaching and learning. To summarize, there are five major barriers identified in order to achieve equality of access to secondary education in Anglophone Caribbean countries. The first is physical space, as buildings, materials, human resources and other shortages prevent most countries in the region from offering secondary education to all children. As of 1993, there were spaces for a reported 75% of primary graduates in some form of secondary education, more than half of which consist of all-age or junior secondary school places (World Bank, 1993). The second is the quality of teaching and learning at both secondary and at each of the previous stages, especially in relation to disadvantaged student populations. A third barrier is the testing mechanisms that are in place to limit and control admittance to traditional secondary schools, these tests serve to segregate students by academic level, which is really a representation of the quality of education received by different children. Another important barrier to examine is the existence of various social factors that impede effective participation and progression, including finances, health care, nutrition, rural or urban residence, and parental level of education.

In assessment of which youths these barriers serve to alienate from the educational process, I argue, based on the current literature, that economically disadvantaged, especially those children residing in rural areas, are repeatedly marginalized by the educational process. In an exploration of empirical research, the given policy options will evaluate and make recommendations to improve access to secondary education, embedded in the knowledge that secondary education cannot be separated from the educational system at large. Upon exploration of the literature, the following are potential ways to address and overcome the aforementioned barriers to equality of opportunity.

CURRENT RESEARCH AND POLICY OPTIONS

There are some options for reform that can be generalized to all levels, such as teacher preparation and variety of support services provided, while a few aspects focus particularly on the secondary level in this context, such as vocational options and the implications of entrance exams. In detailing the current body of research, highlighted are the six areas which the research shows to be of critical importance to the successful reform and improvement of secondary schooling in the Caribbean context, with special attention paid to options that will increase access and equity. These options will include the importance of setting goals for the system of education, teacher education and training, targeting and compensatory policies, curriculum reform, tracking and the Common Entrance Examination, and physical access or space. Each option is examined and assessed through a lens of equality of opportunity.

GOALS AND STRUCTURE

In order to elicit productive and long lasting reform, the Caribbean region must clearly define its vision of education and goals for its citizens. The goals of education, when undefined, present a challenge in regimenting a strong universal secondary program. The options for redefinition of goals are dependant on the vision that stakeholders have for Caribbean citizens, and what is identified as the purpose that secondary education is to serve.

Questions that must be asked are; do the purposes of secondary education fit the needs of the society, and are they congruent with the goals of each nation? This new definition might alter the structure of the secondary cycle, and could affect the system of provision of secondary education. Wolf and Castro identify the structure of secondary education and its relationship to the world of work as one of six critical areas of secondary reform (2000). With the onset of globalization and the desire of each country to compete globally in a knowledge-based economy, new skills are needed to accommodate the new job market, making now a prime time to rethink both the purpose and delivery of secondary education. In examining the relationship between education and the world of work, the figure of unemployment for the English-speaking sector of the region is 15%, considered high in comparison to the world mean of 4% for middle income countries (Baker, 1997). The importance of the relationship between education and work has strong implications for the poor, whose unemployment typically lasts twice as long as their non-poor counterparts (Baker, 1997). This evidence put pressure on the education system to better prepare its charges for the existing world of work by developing and delivering a curriculum that will prepare students for entry into and expansion of the existing labor market.

Errol Miller makes a case for rationalizing the institutional structure in his generation of the twelve most prominent issues facing Caribbean secondary education. "Equity remains a major issue in Caribbean education. No where is the issue more manifest than with respect to the institutional arrangement for secondary education" (p.13, 1996). The UNESCO-OREALC report of 1997, addressing objectives, expansion, demands and modalities in Caribbean secondary education, recommends the reformulation of secondary education towards a perspective of lifelong education.

TEACHER EDUCATION

A strong case can be made for the advancement of teacher education and preparation. The region experiences a lack of trained teachers, and teachers at the secondary level are more often untrained than trained. This trend varies however, among countries. Barbados boasts 100% of permanent teachers trained, while in Dominica, only 38% of teachers at the secondary level have some form of professional training, and only 28% possess a university degree (World Bank, 1995). The strength of teacher training programs must be analyzed, as Reimers and McGinn report that the teacher is the most important variable in learning, and Wolff and Castro assert that two of the most sensitive aspects of quality of education are those of teacher training and teachers' level of education. Again, evidence from Dominica shows the minimal effects of the current teacher-training arrangements. Performance of the bulk of trained teachers is "barely distinguishable from that of untrained teachers." This is attributed to irrelevant curriculum and insufficiency of supervised practice teaching while enrolled in the teacher training program (World Bank, 1995). This evidence shows the importance of well-educated and well-trained teachers, and brings to bear the importance of these elements in the discussion of reform and policy options.

With the receipt of these research results, ministries must pay great attention to the improvement of teacher preparation institutions. Wolff and Castro identify teaching and instruction as another of six critical areas of secondary reform (2000). Although teaching must be improved at the secondary level, better teachers throughout the system will also improve the system overall. From the perspective of equality, evidence is present to show that strides towards efficient instruction, as characterized by Bloom, reduces inequality, evens out achievement, and reduces achievement's correlation with poverty (Cited in Demeuse, 2000). Therefore, strengthening teacher education is vital to the progression of both secondary as well as other stages of education, as well as movement towards equality of opportunity for all children.

The EFA assessment of Dominica maintains that sixty percent of teachers are untrained (2000), and Wolff and Castro report that the result of this trend is that pedagogy is usually outdated, based on frontal lectures, lacking student participation and making little use of textbooks or teaching materials (2000). Ongoing in-service professional development is important in addressing the high numbers of untrained teachers already in the system. This option is vital to the progression of the secondary system, as Beeby warns us that teachers are products of the system in which they were taught. "Such teachers can, with the best will in the world, teach only what they have been taught." (p.44) Knowing this, ministries of education must aim to improve the efficiency and efficacy of teachers currently in the system, especially those who are untrained, to pave the way for future teachers to have the ability to first learn and then teach through a more progressive lens. Utilizing these options ensures that the trained teacher population will continue to grow, as evidence shows that the demand for teachers is consistently greater than the supply of trained teachers (World Bank, 1993), presenting an ongoing challenge for these small island nations.

TARGETING AND COMPENSATORY POLICIES

Targeting and compensatory policy options are crucial to equalizing the opportunities experienced by all social groups. Both identifying marginalized groups, and creating programs that would allow the education system to better serve them are critical to increasing access to all levels of education, particularly at secondary level. There is evidence to show that the result of targeting reform to the lowest-income groups is likely to increase access (Young). Additionally, Cavichionni informs us that widespread reforms [those who don't employ targeting] produce a queuing effect, in which poor children are proven to be at a disadvantage, being the last to benefit from expansion services (2001). This further shows the importance of targeting for the advancement of equality of opportunity for poor and marginalized children.

Wolff and Castro give a number of concrete program recommendations for targeting poor at the secondary level that address both the supply and demand aspects of access. Governments should undertake, construction [of schools in rural and impoverished areas], funding, both recurrent and initial, incentive for good teachers, distance education, and direct financial support (2001).An extensive examination of compensatory policies was undertaken by Don Winkler in Unequal Schools, Unequal Chances. Winkler alludes to the complexity of issues faced at the secondary level by suggesting that the combination of poor quality of primary education and lack of classroom space underlie low levels of coverage (Winkler, p.117). Winkler explores the differences between supply and demand driven reforms, and acknowledges that there comes a point when the two cannot be "disentangled" He does report though, that reforms and compensatory programs can combine both the supply and demand approach to generate a more comprehensive policy option (2000).

Reflection on the Reform of Secondary Education in Jamaica (ROSE), a supply-driven compensatory reform, currently in its second phase, brings to bear the importance of multi-level interventions, and the support of a variety of educational inputs. The ROSE program was generated after all stakeholders were involved in the definition of what purpose the program should serve, resulting in the decision to increase access at the upper secondary level, which currently hovers below seventy percent (Riemers and McGinn, 1997). Another goal of ROSE is to phase out all-age schools, the form of junior secondary that is frequently attended by students who fail the CEE, many of them poor and rural. ROSE serves seventy-nine percent of the poorest quintile of Jamaican students, through curriculum reform, textbook assistance and teacher training (World Bank, 1999). ROSE is a combination of quality and access objectives, and is quickly becoming a model program soon to be adapted and implemented by both by Trinidad and Dominica in the upcoming years.

While ROSE concentrates on improvement at the lower secondary level, compensatory programs must be implemented at all levels of the educational system, including indirect programs that target the social factors that impede successful progression through the educational system. Winkler offers evidence that these indirect interventions, addressing health and nutrition, appear to show improvements in achievement for disadvantaged children (2000). At the secondary level, compensatory policies become central in poor children's ability to access a secondary education. "There is empirical evidence which indicates that policies which impose financial burdens on the poor results in effectively denying their children access to educational opportunity" (Miller, 1996, p.16) The cost, both direct and opportunity, is tremendous for secondary-age students to attend school, especially boys.

Compensatory programs must accurately identify the populations who most need assistance, then structure policies and programs that will treat the educational process holistically. This undertaken with the understanding that removing one barrier might not solve the issue of access, but rather a mix of inputs that serve to cater specifically to the target group's needs would be effective. Wolff and Castro acknowledge that countries will need to implement proactive policies to serve the underserved and poor, creating more educational opportunities for historically disadvantaged groups (2001).

TRACKING AND COMMON ENTRANCE EXAMINATION

Two major barriers to accessing a secondary education are the existence of tracking and the provision of the Common Entrance Exam. As evidence shows, education systems with high disparity are mostly those where tracking happened early (Demeuse, 2001). Tracking is commonplace in Caribbean education. Students are grouped according to perceived ability level, and receive different teachers and even materials for learning. "Researchers have shown…that this kind of policy [tracking] results in different amounts of inputs to students in the different tracks" (Reimers and McGinn). In many cases, better teachers gravitate and are assigned to higher tracked students, as school reputation rests on the rates with which selected students pass the Common Entrance Exam. The Education for All report on Dominica states that, "students are streamed, pre-selected and coached for the exam [CEE] years before it is written" (2000). In many countries, passing rates for the CEE are less than 30%, highlighting the low numbers of children who are granted access to traditional secondary education (World Bank, 1995). This presents a major barrier to access, as the most advantaged students will be selected early in the primary cycle to undergo this preparatory process.

Tracking in itself limits exposure and reduces expectations for certain groups of students. However, tracking in this context, where entrance to higher levels of education is contingent on a high-stakes test, serves to segregate students who have been negatively evaluated, and offers them an inferior education with limited expectation for their success. The ramifications of this disparity is seen in the high numbers of primary leavers who are functionally illiterate (30% in Jamaica). Children respond to the educational path before them, and Reimers and McGinn found that students spend less time learning when the expectations of them are lower than that of their peers (1997). In order for children to pass the Common Entrance and gain entrance and success at the secondary level, children must have received a high quality of instruction that prepares them for future stages of education. This policy has major implications for equity and equality within an educational system. If education in the Caribbean is attempting to provide an equal education for every child, tracking has proven itself to be one practice that must be left behind. "In general, students from low-income families populate the slower tracks, and they receive the least prepared teachers and fewer materials" (Reimers and McGinn, p.7).

The discussion of tracking in this context makes an important segue into concerns about the Common Entrance Exam and its implications for poor and disadvantaged students. The Common Entrance serves as a major barrier to equality of opportunity with regard to secondary education. As previously mentioned, the CEE has been phased out of the system in some countries St. Kitts, (1996), Jamaica, (1998), and Barbados, and replaced by other tests which appear to serve the same purpose, which is to control the number of entrants into secondary or upper secondary education. This test is well known to cause a great deal of anxiety among children and families, as it is seen as the only way to further one's education. The limited amount of space at the secondary or upper secondary level is the reason why this test becomes "high-stakes" as passing rates are dictated each year by the availability of secondary places. "Which children go to which of the types of secondary education depends on the results of the examination at the end of primary school and on places available. Whether or not a child goes into vocational education is therefore governed more by constraint than by choice" (Atchoarena, 1989, p.9).

In upcoming policy discussion, it is important that there is recognition that the administration of the Common Entrance Exam and the preparation for writing of the exam, including tracking, are not equitable processes, and serve to marginalize groups of children who could potentially thrive at the secondary level. The CEE, used as a selection tool, should be phased out in an effort to universalize traditional secondary education. Comprehensive evaluations of student learning might be put into place in order to aid teachers and families to assess students' learning strengths as well as challenges and identify options that will help teachers be more effective in their strategies. Tracking is another policy that should be abandoned in the effort to increase equity and equality within the educations system. Children should receive equitable instruction, encouraged by interactions with other students and teachers within the school community, and should each be placed with the highest expectation for achievement, as all children are able to learn.

CURRICULUM

The quality of curriculum at the secondary level is extremely important in predicting the qualities of the graduates produced by the system and what their skills will be. "Quality [of curriculum] is best defined as the extent to which children learn the basic skills and knowledge necessary to function in a modern society and utilize these skills in their life" (Wolff and Castro). Caribbean systems must translate defined goals for graduates of the education system into a curriculum that increases the level of general education and perpetuates lifelong learning, preparing students for the world of work, and granting them entry into the evolving knowledge-based economy. Finally, education must engender citizens with the values that are consistent with the goals set by each nation or the region as a whole.

Currently, there are varying degrees of standardization in secondary curriculum. Jamaica's ROSE program, Barbados' Secondary Reform, and the Secondary Education Modernization Project in Trinidad, are working or have succeeded in establishing national standards at the secondary level. However many of the remaining countries in the region continue the provision of secondary education possessing no national secondary curriculum or guidelines (EFA, 2000). This method has grave implications for equality and equity among schools and even within schools, allowing institutions and individuals within institutions to set different standards and hold different expectations for different groups of children.

The increase of practical knowledge alongside higher levels of general and technological education would best serve all students, as it would leave them options for either direct transition into the world of work, or further schooling. This mixture is important for issues of equity, as we see the poorest performing children receiving an education that serves to dictate their future options with regard to education. In their report to the UNESCO commission, J. Delors and his colleagues argue that vocational schooling takes away the option for further schooling and that "Secondary education should be the time when the most varied talents are revealed and flourish" (2000, p.65).

Empirical evidence demonstrates the importance of a relationship between education and the world of work upon graduation from the formal system. In their study of secondary education in the Caribbean, Wolff and Castro purport that there needs to be major shifts in paradigm and pedagogy to prepare students for the work world. The authors offer suggestions that would further develop the importance of relationships between workplaces and pedagogies, illustrating both traditional and recommended arrangements. One important suggestion is the transformation from teachers as experts conveying knowledge to passive learners, to students' assumption of responsibility for learning, under teacher support and guidance, in the process developing knowing-how-to-learn skills. In most countries, "teaching tends to focus on basic facts with limited attention given to developing critical thinking skills or fostering student research and investigation" (World Bank, 1995). Scheerens also offers evidence in favor of this transformation, and argues for active learning in favor of vocational education (1998).

In order to increase the efficacy of curriculum, and to engender equality of opportunity within the educational system, curriculum standards must be set, and expectations for all children must be raised. Technology must be employed as a vehicle for learning for all student populations, as much of the work world of today relies on computer literacy and competence. Wolff, Castro, and Miller attest to the importance of technology in secondary education, identifying this as a top priority for reform, and hypothesizing that the impacts of a more computer literate population on economic growth in Caribbean societies could possibly be very high (2001). Not only would giving children more and better opportunities to learn improve their lives, but a more educated population serves the interest of nation building and economic growth, a challenge that Caribbean nations have faced throughout their history.

SPACES

In examining the physical availability of places at the secondary and especially upper secondary level, we are able to see this lack of provision as a major barrier to equality of opportunity within the education system of the Caribbean. In Dominica, only a portion of students, 35%, will be granted access to a traditional high school education (Samuels, 2001, World Bank, 1993). In St. Lucia, the number of children who succeed in passing the CEE, therefore gaining admittance to a coveted traditional secondary education, is 27%. This situation is one where the lack of equality of opportunity is seen most blatantly, with students being funneled into junior secondary programs or forced into the work world at a young age. Students who are most affected by the lack of physical availability are those living in rural areas where high schools are not available, and students in densely populated urban areas where competition is fierce because most schools are over-enrolled.

We see evidence that, "as secondary education enrollment ratios increase, the main new clientele will be those from the lower and middle classes" (Miller, 1996). This shows the importance of expansion of traditional high school places in policy dialogue, as an increase in spaces overall would provide opportunities for more disadvantaged youths to experience a full-cycle secondary education.

In considering the options presented, it appears that by taking a multi-faceted approach, with the goal of increasing equity and equality in the education system, and advances in the system in general, the Caribbean region has the ability to make great strides in the provision of education. Using the recommendations provided, ministries could begin to aggressively initiate reforms at every level, eliciting contribution from all stakeholders in defining and improving the education systems of the Anglophone Caribbean.

CONCLUSION

In conclusion, the barriers to access of secondary education in the Anglophone Caribbean are significantly more apparent for poor and disadvantaged children. In looking at the social, economic and political factors influencing education, the author has attempted to identify the most significant barriers to equality of opportunity within this context, namely those relating to the provision of secondary education. The barriers identified are those of space, quality of teaching and learning at each of the previous stages, testing mechanisms in place that limit and control admittance to traditional secondary schools, and the various social factors that impede effective participation and progression. Caviochionni, in her recommendations for monitoring disparities in less developed countries, concludes that "In almost every country, inequality in educational systems is progressive; the further one advances, the more selective access to certain learning opportunities becomes" (2001). This shows the importance of improvement at every level and the increase of equitable provision of education at the secondary level and beyond, as "It is not only a question of access per se, but of equal opportunity to a good education" (Caviochionni, p.218)

According to the World Bank framework for poverty alleviation, the single most important key to development and to poverty alleviation is education" (World Bank, 2001). With this in mind, the author recommends attention of policy makers towards the identified barriers, in order to further develop Caribbean societies socially and economically, and provide increased opportunity for each child to take advantage of a sound education.

Secondary education is, "A point in time when students must make the transition to adulthood, and define their professional future in the midst of a profoundly changing world" (UNESCO/OREALC). Caribbean countries must aim to support youth in this crucial time of development, and help to shape them into the citizens of tomorrow. Education is the vehicle with which to support all children and provide them with the opportunity to grow and flourish, creating an education system, and moreover a society, that manifests both equity and equality.

ENDNOTE

[1] This figure, however, might be somewhat misleading, as statistics rely on "inconsistent definitions of secondary students applied across the region" (World Bank, 1993). Some countries report enrollment by percentage of age group 12-15 enrolled, while others report by passing of common entrance examination. A finite number is difficult to assert, in light of the reported inconsistencies.

REFERENCES

1) Adams, D., G. Kee and L.Lin. 2001. Linking Research, Policy, and Strategic Planning to Education Development in Lao People's Democratic Republic. *Comparative Education Review. 45(2)*: 220-241.

2) Attchoarena, D. Educational Planning is Small-Area Countries: The Case of the Caribbean. Study made on behalf of Unesco. July, 1989 Paris, France.

3) Baker, J. (1997). Poverty Reduction and Human Development in the Caribbean: A cross-Country Study. Washington, D.C: World Bank.

4) Barbados (Ministry of Education). White Paper on Education Reform: Executive Summary . July, 1995. 10/22/01.
5) Beeby, C.E. 1966. The Quality of Education in Developing Countries. Cambridge, MA. Harvard University Press.
6) Cavichionni, V. and A. Motivans. 2001. Monitoring Educational Disparities in Less Developed Countries. In Hutmacher, W.D. Cochrane and N. Bottani (Eds.) In pursuit of equity in education. Dordrecht. Kluer Academic Press. Pp. 217-240.
7) Demeuese, M., M. Crahay and C. Monseur. 2001. Efficiency and Equity. In Hutmacher, W., D. Cochrane and N. Bottani (Eds.) In pursuit of equity in education. Dordrecht. Kluer Academic Press. Pp.65-91
8) Education For All: Country Report, Dominica (1999) UNESCO.
9) Heyneman, S. The World Bank and Human Capital: Distortion or Contribution? In Baker, D. and Gustafson, D. (Eds.) *International Perspectives on Education and Society.* Oxford. Elsevier Science.
10)The Logical Framework Approach (LFA). Handbook for Objectives-Oriented Planning. Norrad.
11) Miller, E. Secondary Education in the Caribbean. Achievement and Challenges Bulletin 39, April 1996/ The Major Project of Education. UNESCO-OREALC.
12) Miller, E. Education for All: Caribbean Perspectives. 1992. Washington, D.C. Inter-American Development Bank.
13) Pigozzi, M. and V. Cieutat. Education and human resources sector assessment manual. Florida State University. 1988.
14) Reimers, Fernando and McGinn, Noel. (1997). *Informed Dialogue. Using research to shape education policy around the world.* Praeguer.
15) Reimers, Fernando (Ed.) (2000). *Unequal Schools, Unequal Chances. The Challenges to Equal Opportunity in the Americas.*Cambridge, MA. Harvard University Press.
16) Samuel, W. personal communication, 10/4/2001

17) Scheerens, J. The school effectiveness knowledge base as a guide for school improvement. In Hargraves, A.A. Lieberman, M. Fullan and D. Hopkind (Eds.) *International Handbook of Educational Change*. Boston. Kluwer academic Publishers. 1998. Pp.1096-1115

18) The Republic of Trinidad and Tobago. Secondary Education Modernization Program: Executive Summary. Ministry of Education/IDB.

19) UNESCO/OREALC. Secondary Education in Latin America and the Caribbean: Objectives, Expansion, Demands, and Modalities. Bulletin 42, April 1997/The Major Project of Education.

20) UNESCO: *World Education Report 2000. the right to education. Towards Education for all throughout life*. Paris. Unesco Publishing.

21) Wolff, F. and C. Castro. Secondary Education In Latin America and the Caribbean: The Challenge of growth and Reform.

Washington D.C. Inter-American Development Bank, Sustainable Development Department Technical Series.

21) World Bank. Reform of Secondary Education Project: Jamaica. Project Appraisal Document. World Bank, Washington, D.C. 1999.

22) World Bank. Basic Education Reform Project: Commonwealth of Dominica. Staff Appraisal Report. World Bank, Washington D.C. 1995

23) World Bank. Caribbean Region: Access, Quality and Efficiency in Education. World Bank Country Study. Washington, D.C. 1993.

24) Young, M. Early Child Development: Investing in the Future. Washington, D.C. The World Bank.

APPENDIX A

Figure 1: Proportions of Various Age Groups in Secondary School, Most Recent Estimates, (World Bank, 1993)

Country	**12-15 Years**	**Country**	**12-16 Years**
Antigua	97	The Bahamas	75
Dominica	68	Barbados	95
Grenada	78	Guyana	60
St.Kitts and Nevis	95	Jamaica	75
St. Lucia	78	Trinidad and Tobago	76
St. Vincent	79	Suriname	61

Figure 2: Passing Rates for the Common Entrance Examination, (World Bank, 1993, World Bank, 1995)

Country	**Passing Rate**
Dominica	**35%**
Guyana	**33%**
Jamaica	**24%**
St. Vincent	**33%**
St. Lucia	**27%**
Grenada	**48%**

Figure 3: Education System in the Anglophone Caribbean

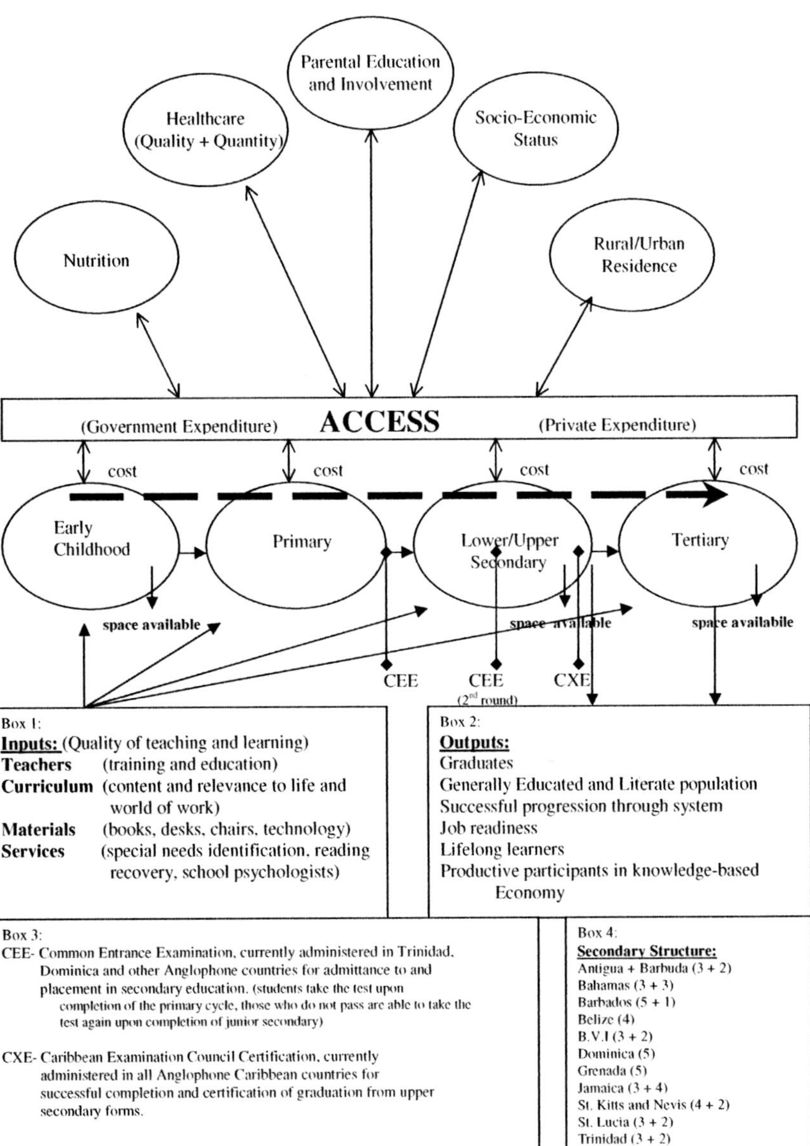

NOTES ON CONTRIBUTORS

LINDSEY T. ALLARD

Lindsey T. Allard presently holds her Master's of Education in International Education Policy from the Harvard Graduate School of Education. While at Harvard, Ms. Allard founded and coordinated a student organization called the Caribbean Education Forum, in which a space was created for the Harvard community to explore its role in the advancement of education for Caribbean people both at home and abroad. She also holds a Bachelor of Science in Human Development and Early Childhood Education. She is a former Head Start educator and is most interested in equality of opportunity in education for economically disadvantaged children, both in the Caribbean and the United States. She has most recently worked for the Unit for Social Development and Education at the Organization of American States, where she conducted policy analysis of the systems of education, labor and social policy in the Anglophone Caribbean.

LILLITH BARNABY

Lillith Barnaby received her first degree at the University of the West Indies. She did her 'maîtrise' at the Université de Besançon, France, and a D.E.A at the Université des Antilles-Guyane. She was seconded to the Department of Modern Languages and Literatures, University of the West Indies, for three years, and currently teaches at Kingston College, Jamaica.

TONY BASTICK

Tony Bastick has an abiding interest in developing, through his teaching and research, each individual's personal creative contributions to our appreciation and quality of life. He has been fortunate in living and working in many different cultures and universities around the world, having over the last thirty years held substantive positions in universities in the U.S., South Pacific, U.K., Australia, Asia and the Caribbean. It is these pan-national and inter-cultural experiences that help to enrich the original perspectives he brings to his research in assessment and evaluation and to his education consultancies in developing countries.

His first degree in Mathematics was awarded by the University of Exeter in England; his Ph.D. in Education and Psychology is from Brunel University of West London. Since October 1997 he has been with the Department of Educational Studies at the University of the West Indies in the Caribbean and can be contacted at their Jamaica campus through tbastick@uwimona.edu.jm.

LEGRACE BENSON

LeGrace Benson directs the Arts of Haiti Research project in Ithaca, New York. Her Ph.D. from Cornell University was an interdisciplinary study in art history, philosophy of education and the psychology of perception. She has done field studies in Haiti since 1981, primarily focused on the visual arts, more recently adding a study of educational practices. She taught in Haiti in 2000 and 2001. She is on the Board of the Haitian Studies Association and is an Associate Editor of the Journal of Haitian Studies.

She has published articles on pedagogy in higher education, with special attention to returning adults and distance methodologies. Professor Benson has produced textbooks for adult students,

'Understanding the Visual World', concerned with both art and environment; and 'Understanding Television', dealing with analysis of television programs as arising out of and influencing contemporary life. She also directed the design of adult, distance learning course materials in writing, communications, literature, and religions. Since 1992 she has been Professor Emerita at the State University of New York.

BÉATRICE BOUFOY-BASTICK

Béatrice Boufoy-Bastick is a linguist who holds a Master's Degree from the Sorbonne in France and a doctorate from the University of the West Indies in Jamaica. She is a post-graduate of London University, holds a Diploma from the Spanish Chamber of Commerce in Paris and has an award for poetry published in English.

Her main research interests are in the interaction of culture and second language education, in modern language teaching methodology and in anthropological research methods. She has a wide cross-cultural experience in teaching and researching in Europe, Australia, Asia, the South Pacific and the Caribbean. Her publications include journal articles in anthropological research methods and educational change.

AUSTIN EZENNE

Austin Ezenne received his Ph. D. degree in Educational Administration from the University of Wales, Cardiff, United Kingdom. He taught for over twenty-five years in Nigerian Universities before joining the University of the West Indies as a consultant in Educational Administration. He has published a number of books and has many articles in learned journals. His research interests are in Educational Administration and Planning, Educational Leadership, Financing of

Education, and Human Resource Development in Education. He is a member of the British Society for Research Into Higher Education (SRHE), British Educational Leadership, Management and Administration Society. (BELMAS), the Association for Supervision and Curriculum Development (ASCD, USA) and the Jamaica Association for Human Resource Development, (JATAD).

MAXINE HENRY WILSON

The Hon. Maxine Henry Wilson is Minister of Education, Youth and Culture for Jamaica and holds the firm belief that education is the tool for effective change. She has expressed the view that “a nation that is well learned is a nation with greater capacity to stand on its own”.

Prior to her appointment as Minister of Education, Mrs. Henry-Wilson served as Minister of Information as well as Minister Without Portfolio in the Office of the Prime Minister. A former Leader of Government Business in the Senate, Minister Henry-Wilson has had a long and successful sojourn as the General Secretary of the ruling People’s National Party (PNP).

The Education Minister was born in Manchester, Jamaica. She attended Vaz Preparatory School, St. Andrew High School, the University of the West Indies, Mona, and Rutgers State University, United States. Mrs. Henry-Wilson is the holder of two Masters degrees - one in Public Administration and the other in Public Policy.

She has taught at St. Hugh’s High School in Kingston and the University of the West Indies, Mona.

The Minister is married and has one child.

ZELLYNNE JENNINGS

Zellynne Jennings has Masters degrees from universities in the United Kingdom and a PhD from the University of the West Indies. She has served as Head of the Department of Educational Studies, UWI, Mona, and as a Professor of Education at the University of Guyana, she also served as Head of the Department of Foundations and Administration. She is a specialist in Curriculum Studies and her areas of research span curriculum innovation and change, programme evaluation, literacy, teacher education and the interface between education and the world of work. She has a number of publications in international journals, including the Journal of Curriculum Studies, Compare, Comparative Education and the International Journal of Educational Development. She is Executive Editor of the Journal of Education and Development in the Caribbean.

OLABISI KUBONI

Dr. Olabisi Kuboni is the Campus Coordinator of the University of the West Indies Distance Education Centre (UWIDEC) at the St. Augustine campus of the university. She also functions as Curriculum Development Specialist (CDS). In the latter capacity she heads the course materials development unit on this campus and works with academic staff to design and develop materials for delivery in the university's distance programme. Her work as CDS also involves assisting academic members of staff in the design and development of on-line teaching-learning environments. One of her current research interests is also in this latter area. Her other research interests relate to the design of organisational systems for the delivery of distance education in a multi-island context and the incorporation of open and flexible delivery modalities into a conventional higher education institution.

Prior to her appointment within the Distance Education Centre, she served as educational technologist in the School of Education, St. Augustine campus, with special responsibility for coordinating the School's programme for the training of teachers and other related personnel in the development and production of instructional materials. Dr. Kuboni holds a M.A. degree in Educational Technology from Concordia University, Montreal, Canada and the Ph.D from the Open University, UK. Her Ph.D thesis is titled Redefining interaction in open and distance learning with reference to teacher education programmes in the University of the West Indies.

JO-ANNE L. MANSWELL BUTTY

Dr. Jo-Anne Manswell Butty is currently the Project Director of Research and Evaluation for the Talent Development Secondary School Project (SSP) at the Center for Research on the Education of Students Placed At Risk (CRESPAR), Howard University, Washington, D.C. She is also an adjunct lecturer in the Department of Human Development and Psychoeducational Studies, School of Education, Howard University, Washington, D.C.

She has considerable experience in teaching, research, and evaluation gained from her current position, training, and consulting experiences. At present, she is responsible for developing and implementing data collection and statistical analyses related to SSP interventions at CRESPAR. She has consulted with organizations such as A Better Chance, Inc. and the National Alliance for Black School Educators.

JO-ANNE L. MANSWELL BUTTY

Dr. Manswell Butty holds membership in the American Educational Research Association (Division D – Measurement &

Research Methodology and Division H – School Evaluation & Program Development), Special Interest Groups (Research Focus on Black Education and the Talent Development of Students Placed At Risk), and the National Council on Measurement in Education.

Dr. Manswell Butty received her M.Ed. in International Development Education and Ph.D. in Educational Psychology from Howard University.

She has published journal articles, reports, and book reviews and also presented papers at professional meetings. Her research interests include educational reform issues, instructional practices, foreign teachers' perspectives, and minority student performance.

HUGUES PETERS

Hugues Peters received his "licence" in Romance Philology from the Université Libre de Bruxelles, Belgium and his Ph.D from the Pennsylvania State University. His research focuses mainly on the syntax of French. He is a lecturer at the Department of Modern Languages and Literatures, UWI, Mona, Jamaica.

GLENDA PRIME

Dr. Glenda Prime is a graduate of the University of the West Indies, having received her B.Sc in Biology, in 1970, her Dip. Ed in Science Education in 1975, her M.A Education in 1988 and her Ph.D in Education in 1994.

Dr. Prime has authored a number of research articles in technology education and has made numerous presentations at international conferences on science and technology education, many of these have been invited presentations. She has also served on the editorial board of the International Journal of Design and Technology Education.

From 1989 to 1999 Dr. Prime taught Science education at the School Of Education, UWI St. Augustine. Currently she is Associate professor in Science education and Coordinator of Graduate programs in mathematics and science education at Morgan State University in Baltimore, Maryland.

ALDRIN E. SWEENEY

Aldrin E. Sweeney, Ph.D. is assistant professor of science education and science education program coordinator in the Department of Teaching & Learning Principles at the University of Central Florida, Orlando, FL, USA. He was born in England to Montserratian parents, and has a keen interest in educational research and policies affecting the quality of public education in the Caribbean. His research areas of interest include *Science-Technology-Society issues in science teaching and learning, the professional preparation of elementary and secondary level science teachers*, and *the relationships between educational theory and instructional practice in science teaching*. Dr. Sweeney has served as an invited program reviewer for the U.S. Department of Education and the National Science Foundation, and also has served as a consultant to the Florida Department of Education. He currently serves on the Editorial Boards of the *Journal of Science Teacher Education* and the *Journal of Research in Science Teaching*.

Printed in the United States
24983LVS00001B/54

9 789766 320454